METROPOLITAN RAILWAYS

Railroads Past and Present
Series editor: George M. Smerk

Metropolitan Railways
RAPID TRANSIT IN AMERICA

William D. Middleton

INDIANA University Press

Bloomington & Indianapolis

This book is a publication of

INDIANA UNIVERSITY PRESS
601 North Morton Street
Bloomington, Indiana 47404-3797 USA

http://iupress.indiana.edu

Telephone orders   800-842-6796
Fax orders   812-855-7931
Orders by e-mail   iuporder@indiana.edu

The paper used in this publication meets the minimum requirements of American National Standard for Information Sciences—Permanence of Paper for Printed Library Materials, ANSI Z39.48-1984.

Manufactured in Canada

Library of Congress Cataloging-in-Publication Data

Middleton, William D., date
    Metropolitan railways : rapid transit in America / William D. Middleton.
        p.   cm. — (Railroads past and present)
Includes bibliographical references and index.
    ISBN 0-253-34179-5 (cloth : alk. paper)
    1. Local transit—North America—History. 2. Railroads, Local and light—North America—History. 3. Street-railroads—North America—History. 4. Subways—North America—History. I. Title. II. Series.
    HE4500.M53   2003
    388.4'2'0973—dc 21   2002006588

1   2   3   4   5   08   07   06   05   04   03

CONTENTS

PREFACE

M Y FIRST ENCOUNTER with the wonders of rapid transit came at a very young age, when an older cousin took me by "L" to visit Chicago's 1933 Century of Progress exhibition. While I have forgotten what we saw at the fair, the memory of that ride on the "L" is with me still, and it marked the beginning of what has been an enduring fascination with rapid transit.

It is no understatement to say that metropolitan railways—the all-embracing term I have chosen to represent the rapid transit subways, elevated railways, and light rail lines that now bind so many of our cities together—have shaped the urban centers they serve in profound ways. Few would question that New York City or Chicago would be unthinkable in their present form without the subway and elevated networks that form their circulatory systems. But even San Diego or Portland, Ore., places inhabited by only a small fraction of the numbers that live in those old-line rapid transit cities, would be much different, and far less livable or attractive, without the new rail systems that are now so significantly altering the patterns of their growth and enhancing their quality of life.

Quite apart from their unquestioned social importance, big city rapid transit railways compel one's interest simply for their great size, their extraordinary complexity, and the efficiency with which they transport such enormous numbers of passengers. The biggest of them all in North America—at New York and Mexico City—board more passengers in an average five-day week than Amtrak does in a year. More passengers pass through the turnstiles each year (43.6 million) at what is probably the single busiest subway station in North America—New York's 42nd Street–Times Square station—than all but a half dozen of the world's busiest airports. The largest of our metro systems dispatch trains by the thousands every day and operate them on headways as close as 90 seconds with a remarkable precision, reliability, and—above all—safety.

It is perhaps a particularly appropriate time to consider the story of these remarkable rapid transit railways. For after a long decline through several decades of neglect and misguided public priorities, metropolitan railways are now in the midst of an unparalleled period of growth and renewal that promises to make them even more a part of North American urban life in the twenty-first century than they had been in its nineteenth or twentieth.

Much of the historical and technical information upon which this book is based is drawn from the detailed contemporary coverage of the industry in the electric railway and railroad trade press; the exceptionally rich historical record developed in the publications of the several electric railway enthusiast organizations, most notably the Electric Railroaders'

Association and the Central Electric Railfans' Association; and a wide variety of books and other works on the subject, both technical and popular. These and other sources that have contributed to the story are summarized in the bibliography.

This book would have been all but impossible to accomplish without the willing advice and assistance of a great many individuals and organizations, and I am profoundly grateful to all of them.

Among the many individuals and institutions that have been particularly helpful with both reference material and illustration have been Mark Pascale, associate curator of prints and drawings at the Art Institute of Chicago; Randy L. Goss, photo archivist for the Delaware Public Archives; Richard C. Evans, at the Sprague Library of the Electric Railroaders' Assn.; the prints and photographs staff at the Library of Congress; Mary Corliss of the Film Stills Archive at the Museum of Modern Art; Sue-Ann Pascucci, the archives manager for the New York City Transit Museum; Tom Lisanti, manager of photographic services and permissions at the New York Public Library; Eleanor Gillers, rights and reproductions assistant at The New-York Historical Society; Albert S. Eggerton, volunteer in the transportation collections at the Smithsonian Institution; David B. Lawall, the now retired director of the University of Virginia Art Museum; the staffs of the Science and Engineering and Alderman libraries and the interlibrary loan staff at the University of Virginia Library; and Diane E. Kaplan, archivist for manuscripts and archives at the Yale University Library.

For the scope and diversity of the illustration in this volume I am also deeply indebted to the many individual photographers and collectors whose contributions are individually credited. Particularly helpful were Fred W. Schneider, III, who generously opened his extensive photographic collection, and Art Peterson and the late George Krambles, who kindly made available material from the unparalleled Krambles-Peterson Archive.

Many of the photographs and illustrations included in the book were printed by Scott Creasy of University of Virginia Health Sciences Center Media Services, Stan Kistler, and Fred Schneider, and I am grateful for the great skill and sensitivity they brought to the work.

Fred Schneider was particularly helpful, too, with many valued suggestions that had much to do with framing the original plan for the book. George M. Smerk, professor of transportation at Indiana University and the director of its Institute for Urban Transportation, offered much useful advice based upon his unparalleled knowledge of public transit. Still others who helped in important ways include Jeffrey G. Mora at the Federal Transit Administration, who provided much help with the story of that agency's Urban Rapid Rail Vehicle and Systems Program of the 1970s. Media relations staff for transit agencies all over North America have been exceedingly helpful in completing the transit agency profiles that appear in Appendix B. Mike Healy, the long-time media relations director for the Bay Area Rapid Transit District, was unfailingly helpful in providing information and illustration concerning the landmark BART project. Vaughn Vekony at the Reichman Frankie agency was ever helpful in responding to a variety of queries concerning Bombardier Transportation.

G. Mac Sebree skillfully undertook to prepare the maps that accompany each of the metropolitan railway profiles included in Appendix B. And once again, I am grateful to my wife, Dorothy, for providing her usual thorough review of the manuscript for any lapses in good grammatical and punctuation form. I, however, remain responsible for any that she may have overlooked.

William D. Middleton

METROPOLITAN RAILWAYS

There was no shortage of novel ideas for rapid transit in the late nineteenth century. One bizarre scheme was this steam-powered monorail invented by Civil War veteran Joe Vincent Meigs, who patented it in 1875. The train of cigar-shaped cars straddled a single supporting girder on the elevated structure. Meigs completed a demonstration line at East Cambridge, Mass., in 1886, and the system came close to adoption for elevated systems in both Boston and Chicago. Author's Collection.

CHAPTER 1

THE QUEST FOR RAPID TRANSIT

Street Railroads and Omnibuses have their uses; but we have reached the end of them. They are wedged for hours at night and morning with men, women, boys and girls sitting, standing, and hanging on; it would not be decent to carry live hogs thus, and hardly dead ones; they are unchangeably too slow; and their capacity is exhausted. To put on more cars or construct more roads is only to monopolize our streets and virtually drive all carriages out of them.

Gentlemen of the Legislature! Give us both the Underground and the Aerial Railway!

—*New York Tribune*, February 2, 1866

THE UNITED STATES in the post–Revolutionary War period was a fundamentally different society than it was soon to become. When the census-takers made the first of their decennial rounds in 1790, the United States was an overwhelmingly rural nation. There were then fewer than 4 million Americans, and scarcely 1 in 20 of them lived in cities. Philadelphia, then the nation's largest city, had a population of fewer than 55,000.

Within only a few decades this had begun to change. The cities were growing rapidly as the commerce and industry of the new nation developed. By 1830 more than a million people lived in American cities. Possessed of a great natural harbor and linked to the U.S. interior by the new Erie Canal, New York had become the center of American commerce. With a population that now numbered more than 200,000, New York had displaced Philadelphia as the nation's largest city.

For New York and other growing American cities, urban transportation had become an increasingly urgent need. The first urban public transportation had appeared at New York in 1827, when Abraham Brower inaugurated a regular stagecoach service up and down Broadway. Only a few years later John Mason incorporated America's first street railway, the New York & Harlem, which began transporting passengers along New York's Bowery in horse-drawn cars on November 14, 1832. These horse- or mule-powered street railways

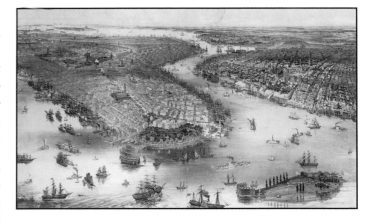

The rapidly growing cities of New York, on Manhattan Island, and Brooklyn, across the East River, are shown in this birds' eye view from New York Harbor dating to about 1851. Library of Congress (Neg. LC-USZ62-099118).

1

Broadway, New York's busiest thoroughfare, was so clogged with traffic by the mid-nineteenth century that it was said to sometimes take 20 to 30 minutes for a pedestrian to cross the street. Around 1852 a Broadway hatter named Genin proposed this footbridge as a solution to the problem, shown in an illustration from *Gleason's Pictorial Drawing Room Companion.* The structure was actually put up in 1866 at the instigation of Genin and other merchants, but was soon taken down. Library of Congress (Neg. LC-USZ62-348).

provided a popular answer to the growing need for urban transportation. Over the next several decades additional lines were constructed at New York, and new systems began operating at other cities. By the end of the 1850s, street railways were also operating at New Orleans, Brooklyn, Boston, Philadelphia, Pittsburgh, Baltimore, Cincinnati, and Chicago.

For most of these cities the street railways served the need for urban transportation well, and their growth was phenomenal. As early as 1855, New York's horse car lines were transporting more than 18 million passengers a year, and in another 30 years their annual traffic approached 188 million. By 1881 there were some 415 street railway companies in the United States, operating 18,000 cars pulled by more than 100,000 horses and mules over 3000 miles of track. By this time street railways had become an enormous industry, with annual revenues in the vicinity of $1.25 billion.

Long before the end of the nineteenth century, however, even this enormous street railway industry would prove inadequate to meet the public transportation needs of the largest American cities. Far from being a product of the automotive age as so many now regard it, street traffic congestion was a fact of urban life many decades earlier. Nowhere was this more evident than in New York City, which had begun to feel the effects of severe congestion as early as 1850. By this time the city's population had grown to more than half a million, and the city was heavily developed as far north as 42nd Street, nearly 4 miles north of the Battery. The long, narrow shape of Manhattan Island compounded New York's congestion problems, and the city's limited north-south thoroughfares were jammed with drays, cabs, omnibuses, and horse cars. The heaviest traffic was on Broadway, the principal north-south thoroughfare. Some of the worst traffic jams in the city were at Broadway and Fulton, where it was said sometimes to take 20 to 30 minutes to cross the street. An 1850 traffic check revealed that omnibuses made up nearly 40 percent of Broadway traffic, and a rush-hour count found them moving on average headways of only 13 seconds. Travel by horse-drawn vehicle between downtown business areas and the uptown residential districts had already become so time-consuming that growing numbers of New Yorkers were fleeing across the Hudson and East rivers to the New Jersey suburbs and Brooklyn, which could be reached more quickly by ferry services.

The great cities of Europe were confronting similar problems. Urban public transportation in the form of horse-drawn omnibus services had appeared on the streets of Paris and London even earlier than they had in New York, and European cities were soon installing horse-drawn street railways as well. By 1850 London traffic congestion, if anything, was even worse than that in New York, and in 1854 Parliament authorized the construction of underground railways. The city's first subway trains began operating nine years later. Original plans to operate the underground with "fireless" locomotives proved impractical, and smoke, cinders, and steam from the locomotives made travel on this pioneer subway an unpleasant ordeal. By the 1870s Paris would be debating the relative merits of subways and elevated railways, but it would be another thirty years before the first segment of the city's Métropolitain subway would finally open.

"People are packed into them like sardines in a box, with perspiration for oil," complained a New York *Herald* editorial writer of the city's street railways in 1864. A decade later conditions hadn't improved by much, if we take this cartoon from the February 12, 1876, *Frank Leslie's Illustrated Newspaper* at face value. Author's Collection.

New York's problems worsened over the next two decades. By 1860 the city's population had passed 800,000 and annual traffic on the omnibuses and street railways exceeded 36 million passengers. Even this figure more than doubled over the next five years, but the omnibus and horse car services were becoming ever more inadequate for the demands of New York traffic, if an 1864 editorial in the New York *Herald* is taken as a fair evaluation of the service:

> Modern martyrdom may be succinctly defined as riding in a New York omnibus. The discomforts, inconveniences and annoyances of a trip in one of these vehicles are almost intolerable. From the beginning to the end of the journey a constant quarrel is progressing. The driver quarrels with the passengers and the passengers quarrel with the driver. There are quarrels about getting out and quarrels about getting in. There are quarrels about change and quarrels about the ticket swindle. . . . Ladies are disgusted, frightened and insulted. Children are alarmed, and lift up their voices and weep. . . . Thus the omnibus rolls along, a perfect Bedlam on wheels. . . . It is in vain that those who are obliged to ride seek for relief in a city railway car. The cars are quieter than the omnibuses, but much more crowded. People are packed into them like sardines in a box, with perspiration for oil. The seats being more than filled, the passengers are placed in rows down the middle, where they hang on by straps, like smoked hams in a corner grocery. To enter or exit is exceedingly difficult. Silks and broadcloth are ruined in the attempt. As in the omnibuses, pickpockets take advantage of the confusion to ply their vocation. . . . The foul, close, heated air is poisonous. A healthy person cannot ride a dozen blocks without a headache. . . . it must be evident to everybody that neither the cars nor the stages supply accommodation enough for the public, and that such accommodations as they do supply are not of the right sort. . . . something more is needed to supply the popular and increasing demand for city conveyances.

What clearly seemed to be needed was some new form of transportation that could accommodate New York's enormous traffic volume quickly, free from the restrictions imposed by the city's clogged streets. There soon proved to be no shortage of promoters who thought they had the solution to the problem.

One of the earliest proposals for a rapid transit scheme came from Alfred Ely Beach, the flamboyant and inventive proprietor and editor of *Scientific American*, who advanced the idea of a subway for New York in an editorial, "An Underground Railroad in Broadway," in the November 3, 1849, issue of his magazine:

> The plan is to tunnel Broadway through the whole length, with openings and stairways at every corner. This subterranean passage is to be laid down with a double track, with a road for foot passengers on either side—the whole to be brilliantly lighted with gas. The cars, which are to be drawn by horses, will stop ten seconds at every corner—thus performing the trip up and down, including stoppages, in about an hour.

The Broadway subway plan was ahead of its time, but it was soon followed by a variety of innovative ideas for rapid transit, many of them set forth in the pages of Beach's *Scientific American*. Most of these early proposals were for some form of elevated railway. One of the first was advanced in 1853 by James H. Swett, a Pittsburgh inventor, who proposed a bizarre sort of elevated railway supported by iron columns placed along the curb. Arms branching from the top of the column like a tuning fork left room for the passage of a passenger car that was to be suspended from

This 1853 proposal of inventor James H. Swett for a sort of suspended elevated railway stood out among the many proposals for Broadway rapid transit as one of the more impractical. Although the artist has given us plenty of smoke, *Scientific American* assured its readers that the locomotives would be fired with coke, emitting neither smoke nor sparks. The illustration is from the November 5, 1883, issue of *The New York Illustrated News*. Collection of The New-York Historical Society.

Another proposal for Broadway transit was this "elevated railroad terrace" scheme illustrated in *Gleason's Pictorial Drawing Room Companion* for April 1, 1854. The elegant cast iron structure appears to have been little more than an elevated roadway for horse cars. Library of Congress (Neg. LC-USZ62-32300).

a steam locomotive running on rails at the top of the structure. Passengers boarded the cars from platforms reached by stairways from the sidewalk. "No wood as fuel is to be or would be allowed in Broadway on any engine," commented *Scientific American;* "it might set fire, by a stray spark, to one of Stewart's bales of fine French muslins, and that would never answer." Instead, the locomotives would be fired with coke, emitting neither smoke nor sparks.

A year later J. B. Wickersham, a New York manufacturer of iron railings, presented a plan for an elevated railroad terrace along Broadway. A single row of columns placed just inside the curb would support an ornate iron elevated structure above the sidewalk that would carry both a horse car line on the outside and a pedestrian promenade inside next to the buildings. Access stairways to the terrace would be constructed inside the adjacent buildings. To reduce the noise of the horse cars, Wickersham proposed to lay the rails on India rubber sills. At some future date the development of propulsion by "atmospheric pressure" would replace horse power.

Neither of these, nor any of the many other fanciful schemes for elevated railways that were advanced over the next few years, received more than passing attention. A quite different proposal for Broadway rapid transit put forth by Michigan railroad man Hugh B. Willson, who returned from a visit to London in 1863 much impressed by that city's new Metropolitan Railway Company, a 4-mile subway operated with coal-burning steam locomotives. Willson promptly rounded up New York backers and incorporated his own Met-

Yet another early proposal for Broadway rapid transit was this 1870 "arcade railway" scheme, depicted here in a contemporary lithograph. Several decades were to elapse before electric traction became feasible, and steam locomotives were proposed as the line's motive power. Arcade Railway promoter Melville C. Smith managed to get a series of bills authorizing its construction through the New York legislature between 1870 and 1885, but all were vetoed by incumbent governors. Library of Congress.

ropolitan Railway Company to build a similar line in New York. Willson's chief engineer, A. P. Robinson, came up with plans for a double-track brick arch tunnel to be constructed under Broadway from the Battery to 34th Street and thence under Sixth Avenue to 59th Street. Motive power, as on the London system, was to be steam. A bill to grant the subway enterprise a charter failed to make it through the New York State legislature in 1864, more than likely as a result of the intense opposition of the city's existing street railway companies. A second try the following year got past the legislature only to be vetoed by Gov. Reuben Fenton. And that was as far as Mr. Willson's subway went.

A somewhat similar scheme put forth a few years later was the Arcade Railway proposed by H. C. Gardner and Melville P. Smith, which was to operate from the Battery to the north end of Manhattan Island. A principal line would extend along Broadway and Ninth Avenue to a junction with the Hudson River Railroad near Fort Washington, while a branch from the Broadway line via Park Row and the Bowery would follow Third Avenue to the Harlem River and a junction with the New York & Harlem Railroad. Designed by civil engineer S. B. B. Nowlan, the Arcade Railway was to be built by excavating the street to a depth of 25 feet from wall to wall of the buildings on either side. The lower 10 feet was to be occupied by sewers and tunnels through which refuse removal carts would operate, above which four tracks were to be provided on the sub-street or arcade, with trains operating at five miles an hour on the outer tracks for way passengers, while trains operating at 15 miles an hour on the inner tracks would stop only at stated points. Locomotives "emitting neither smoke nor sparks" would power the trains.

Rows of iron columns and concrete arches would support a new street and walks at the original level, with openings surrounded by iron railings on each side between the street and walks to allow light to reach the arcade level. Pedestrian walks were to be provided at the arcade level on either side of the tracks, providing access to new stores in building basements or sub-basements to be constructed by the Arcade Railway Company. "Property owners on the streets will be gainers by an addition to their rentable property," commented *Scientific American*, "and the sub-roadway will become a favorite means of transit in stormy weather and as a shelter from torrid suns."

The promoters managed to get a series of bills authorizing construction of the Arcade Railway through the New York legislature between 1870 and 1885, but all were vetoed by the incumbent governors.

Even as the Arcade Railway promoters were developing their plans for a subway and seeking approval to build it, the *Scientific American*'s Alfred Ely Beach went right ahead and built one. Beach, who had long championed the idea of a subway for New York, had become an advocate of the pneumatic system of transmitting packages. If a container carrying a package of letters could be blown through a tube, reasoned Beach, why not a package of human beings in a car? Under this concept, passenger cars would fit into an elevated or underground tube like bullets in a rifle barrel and would be driven above or under the streets at high speeds by air pressure from giant fans. Beach exhibited a working model of his pneumatic railroad at the American Institute Fair held at New York's Fourteenth Street

Armory in 1867. A wooden tube 6 feet in diameter suspended from the roof of the building ran from Fourteenth to Fifteenth streets. A car open at the top and fitted with a piston end was drawn in and forced back through the tube by suction and pressure from a propeller fan, 10 feet in diameter and turning at a rate of 200 revolutions per minute. Great crowds came to see the novel device, and the car was kept in constant operation, transporting hundreds of people.

Beach soon organized the Beach Pneumatic Transit Company and obtained legislative authority to build pneumatic tubes not greater than 54 inches in diameter to convey letters, parcels, and merchandise under Broadway from Warren to Cedar streets. A later charter amendment authorized the construction of one larger tube that would hold two smaller ones. Construction was soon underway for what turned out to be quite a different project. Beginning from the rented basement of clothier Devlin & Company on the corner of Broadway and Warren Street, a tunnel 9 feet 4 inches in outside diameter was drilled about 400 feet south under Broadway to a point just south of Warren Street.

Scientific American proprietor and editor Alfred Ely Beach demonstrated his scheme for a pneumatic elevated railway at the American Institute Fair at New York in 1867. The car transported hundreds of fair-goers through the six-foot diameter wooden tube by air pressure. The drawing is from the January 18, 1896, issue of *Scientific American*. Author's Collection.

A notable feature of the work was the pneumatic shield employed to drill the tunnel. Patented by Beach, it was an advanced version of shields developed earlier in the century by British tunnelers Marc Isambard Brunel, James Henry Greathead, and Peter W. Barlow for tunneling under the Thames at London. Beach's shield was a short cylindrical section of heavy timber backed by a wrought iron ring, against which hydraulic jacks forced the shield forward. Doors in the front of the shield controlled the entry of material as the tunnel was excavated. The shield was driven forward about 16 inches at a time by jacking it against the completed brick tunnel. After another 16 inches of brick tunnel was completed, the operation was repeated.

The tunnel itself was drilled in only 58 days, largely in secret, with the excavated material removed through the sub-basement and basement of 260 Broadway, at Murray Street, which had been rented for that purpose. The public became aware of the work only after a New York *Tribune* reporter, disguised as a workman, gained access to the tunnel and his newspaper published an account of the project. His secrecy lost, Beach threw open the tunnel for public inspection, charging a 25-cent admission fee that went to charity.

Instead of completing the tunnel for the pneumatic transmission of packages, as called for in his charter, Beach decided to use it to demonstrate his idea for a pneumatic subway. A little 18-seat car that traveled through the tube was a veritable jewel box on wheels, richly upholstered and brilliantly illuminated by a zircon lamp. The waiting station was described as a commodious, airy, and comfortable apartment. With a shrewd sense of showmanship, Beach had the walls decorated with frescoes and elegant paintings and installed a grand piano, fountain, and goldfish tanks. Zircon lamps illuminated the room.

The giant steam-driven fan that powered the subway—called the "Roots Patent Force Blast Blower"—sent the car racing through the tunnel at speeds up to 10 mph. At the far end of the tunnel, a trip wire rang a bell in the engine room, the operator reversed the giant fan, and the car was "inhaled" back to its starting point.

According to Beach's not-necessarily objective *Scientific American*, the subway was entirely free of the discomforts of surface car travel:

> It is not cold in winter. It will be delightfully cool in summer. The air will be constantly changed in it by the action of a blowing machine. The filthy, health-destroying, patience-killing, street dust of which up town residents get not only their fill, but more than their fill, —so that it runs over and collects on their hats and clothes; fills their hairs, beards and eyes, and floats in their dress like the vapor on a frosty morning, —will never be found in the tunnel.
>
> When the tunnel is opened to the public it will be no dirty hole in the ground the people will be invited to enter, but a handsome subterranean avenue, through which they may be rapidly transported to their homes up town.

By early 1870 all was in readiness, and on February 26 Beach invited city and state officials, members of the press and other dignitaries to an "Under Broadway Reception" at which the splendid new facilities were opened for inspection. "In the 'depot' or reception room," reported the *New York Times*, "a first-class subterranean lunch was served continuously from 2 o'clock to 6 o'clock, and it was continuously appreciated."

"A myth, or a humbug, it has hitherto been called by everybody who has been excluded from its interior"; said the *Times*, "but hereafter the incredulous public can have the opportunity of examining the undertaking and judging of its merits."

On March 1 the Beach Subway was opened to the public for an admission fee of 25 cents, which went to the Union House for the Orphans of Soldiers and Sailors. The subway became a sensational public success, and in its first year of operation the little car transported some 40,000 curious sightseers. But whatever success he enjoyed with the public, Beach ran up against the usual obstacles in trying to construct a pneumatic subway system that would have extended up Broadway from the Battery to Central Park, with a branch to connect with the New York & Harlem Railroad at Grand Central Depot. Unfortunately, Beach needed a state charter for the planned system, and William M. "Boss" Tweed, New York State senator, New York City alderman, and notorious Grand Sachem of Tammany Hall, had other ideas.

Boss Tweed was backing something called the Viaduct Railway Company, a rapid-transit proposal that called for construction of an elevated railway on a massive masonry structure that would have extended from Chambers Street to Houston or Bleeker streets, where one

A series of woodcuts from the February 19, 1870, *Frank Leslie's Illustrated Newspaper* shows the elegant pneumatic subway that became the talk of New York after Beach unveiled it to an incredulous public following nearly two years of secret construction carried out beneath Broadway in the dead of night. The "richly upholstered" car that was wafted back and forth through the 312-foot tunnel by a giant fan afforded comforts that exceeded anything the city's subway riders have seen since. Beach, with a shrewd sense of showmanship, lavished particular attention on the subway's waiting room. The walls were decorated with frescoes and elegant paintings, and Beach installed a grand piano, fountain, and goldfish tanks. As a final touch, the spacious room was illuminated with zircon lights. Library of Congress.

branch would have extended up the East Side between Third Avenue and the East River, while another would have extended north to the west of Sixth Avenue past Central Park and all the way to the Harlem River or Spuyten Duyvil Creek. The long list of prominent New Yorkers who joined Tweed in the 1871 incorporation of the company included financiers, lawyers, merchants, contractors, and a plethora of Tweed's Tammany Hall associates and friends. Inventor, manufacturer, and philanthropist Peter Cooper was an incorporator. Prominent publishers and editors who signed on included *New York Herald* and *Evening Sun* publisher James Gordon Bennett, Jr., *New Yorker Staats Zeitung* editor and publisher Oswald Ottendorfer, *The Sun* editor and former assistant secretary of war Charles Anderson Dana, and the *New York Herald*'s legendary crusading editor and future presidential candidate Horace Greeley.

State Senator Henry W. Genet, a Tammany man, introduced a bill authorizing the Viaduct Railway scheme in the state legislature in 1871. Both Genet's bill and another authorizing the Beach pneumatic subway passed and landed on the desk of Gov. John T. Hoffman, a Tammany Hall man. Hoffman signed the Viaduct bill and vetoed the Beach bill.

On December 7, 1867, inventor Charles T. Harvey rode a little four-wheel car to make the first trial run over his cable-powered elevated railway in New York's Greenwich Street. Harvey's financial backers were sufficiently impressed with the trial that they authorized Harvey to continue construction to Cortland Street. Library of Congress (Neg. LC-USZ62-44471).

Beach tried again, and once more in 1872 the Beach bill made it past the legislature only to fall victim to Hoffman's veto. By 1873 Tweed was in jail and Hoffman had discreetly refrained from running for reelection. This time the Beach transit bill sailed through the legislature and won an enthusiastic signature from Gov. John A. Dix. But by now Beach had expended his fortune in the effort to promote the pneumatic subway. No one seemed willing to risk the $10 million needed to construct it, and shortly afterward the state charter was withdrawn. So much for the Beach subway. It was probably just as well. However effectively the pneumatic scheme might work for transporting mail and department store transactions, it was an unlikely technology for the frequent starts and stops of heavy urban transit traffic.

Even as Alfred Beach was perfecting the details of his pneumatic subway, still other inventors had arrived on the rapid-transit scene. In 1866 inventor William Hemstreet was promoting something called the Broadway Overground Railroad. Under this scheme cable-powered cars would operate over an elegant patented structure of glass and iron, supported by an arcade of elliptic iron arches that would span and roof the street. By allowing rain and snow to run off through the iron pillars the structure would save street cleaning costs, and . . . "it would cost nothing for extra lighting, warming, or police—like the underground plan."

Little more was heard of the Overground Railroad plan, but another elevated railway project at about the same time actually made it into operation. This was a scheme for a cable-powered elevated railway developed by Charles T. Harvey, a canal engineer. In 1866 Harvey managed to obtain legislation that allowed him to build his rail line and promptly organized the ambitious West Side & Yonkers Patent Railway Company. This was to operate up Greenwich Street and Ninth Avenue to Kingsbridge and Yonkers, while another line on the East Side was to operate up Third Avenue to the Harlem River and New Rochelle. To be built under Harvey's patents, the line would operate over an elevated structure, propelled by endless cables powered from stationary steam engines.

Construction began in the summer of 1867 on an experimental half-mile section extending northward in Greenwich Street from Battery Place. Work was sufficiently advanced by

Dating to about 1868–69, this drawing shows one of the little cars that operated above Greenwich Street on the single track "one legged" structure of Harvey's cable-powered elevated. Richard Jay Solomon Collection.

December 7 that Harvey was able to demonstrate the system by operating a small car—little more than a four-wheel truck—over an initial quarter-mile section of the line. A number of the line's financial backers were present and were so well impressed that they authorized Harvey to continue construction of the line to Cortlandt Street. By the following June the half-mile line was ready for operation. The members of a Rapid Transit Commission appointed by the Governor of New York inspected the line and gave their approval for its operation. Governor Fenton himself traveled down from Albany for a ride on the line's newly delivered car and was soon followed by New York City Mayor John Hoffman and numerous others. The final report of the Rapid Transit Commission was made on July 1, 1868, and the West Side & Yonkers Patent Railway Company was soon authorized to proceed with construction as far north as Spuyten Duyvil at the upper end of Manhattan.

The Harvey elevated was a rather graceful structure. A single track 30 feet above the street was supported by a single row of iron columns, with two arms that flared outward at the top to support the two running rails. Passengers reached the line's stations by means of staircases from the sidewalks. The cable that powered the elevated from stationary steam engines was a three-quarter-inch wire rope manufactured by John Roebling, the celebrated suspension bridge engineer, at his Trenton, N.J., wire rope plant. The cable, which ran through a wooden tunnel-box between the rails, was carried by small four-wheel trucks, or travelers, which were attached to the cable at 150-foot intervals. Each of these travelers had a horn, or shank, which projected up through a slot in the tunnel-box to make contact with a grip on the car. A grip mechanism designed by Harvey employed a rotating arm controlled by a gripman on the car platform to engage or disengage the horn to start or stop the car. The cables were arranged in series at intervals of about 1500 feet along the line. At the end of each section the cable passed through one of the support columns to reach a subterranean tunnel laid under the columns to enter a vault where the driving engine was located. The company acquired three low-slung wooden cars about 30 feet long, each mounted on a pair of four-wheel trucks. These operated individually under the control of a gripman at a speed of about 12 mph.

Over the next two years the cable elevated operated on a limited basis while its promoters worked to extend the line to the north up Greenwich Street and Ninth Avenue to 30th Street, where it would be linked with the terminal of the Hudson River Railroad. The competing street railway companies and property owners, fearful of the intrusion of the elevated, filed suits to block construction of the road, and it was not until February 14, 1870, that the line began operating to a new station at 29th Street.

The new line had more than enough operating problems. The cable system broke down frequently, stranding a car and passengers above the street until a team of horses could tow the car to the nearest station. This happened so often that a team was kept at the ready. Residents along the line complained about the noise of the cars and the continual clatter that came from the moving cable. There were accidents, too. One of these, on May 16, 1870, occurred when the company decided to test the capacity of the line by towing a freight car loaded with ten tons of pig iron behind a passenger car. The freight car plunged into the street on a sharp curve at Houston Street, dragging the passenger car with it. Some 175 feet of track was torn up and the cable mechanism was damaged. Two passengers were slightly injured, while the road's track master, Frank McKenna, was more seriously injured and was carried to his residence. Scarcely a month later, on June 14, the cable mechanism failed and a gripman was unable to detach his car from the moving cable as he approached the 29th Street station. His car then smashed into a stopped car, driving it about a half a

An 1869 photograph showed Charles Harvey's West Side & Yonkers Patent Railway Company elevated where it curved out of Greenwich Street into Ninth Avenue. Visible in the near foreground is the overhead structure that housed the cable propulsion system, which soon proved to be the downfall of the line. Collection of The New-York Historical Society (Neg. No. 3253).

block down the line and breaking the cable. Some 30 passengers were shaken up and frightened, and had to be rescued from the stranded car by ladder.

The frequent problems experienced by the line did not go unnoticed by the New York press, which had become highly critical of the elevated scheme. More or less typical was an editorial entitled, "The Man-Trap Railroad in Greenwich Street," which appeared in the *New York Herald* on May 21, 1870, a few days after one of the accidents. Said the *Herald*, in part:

What have the authorities done in reference to the construction which collapsed with such peril to human life on Monday last? We trust that steps have been taken to cause its removal forthwith. . . . One of our most frequented thoroughfares has been taken possession of, and, under cover of law, a stock company have appropriated to themselves a large portion of the sidewalk, destroyed the privacy of every house on the street, erected a novel and dangerous construction, the operation of which has been the cause of innumerable accidents from runaway horses, . . . inventions, however ingenious, are of no value if they attempt to controvert mechanical laws, which, being synonymous with the laws of nature, are immutable; and certainly no one will deny that the most glaring and reckless disregard of the laws of gravity—of the effect of centrifugal force, of the adhesiveness of metal and the capacity of iron to resist tension—has been shown throughout in the construction of this aerial man trap. Let it, therefore, be done away with at once, and let the true engineering talent of the country be enlisted to perfect a system of transit and locomotion which will do credit to that profession and give the city of New York a clear solution to a long vexed problem.

The growing uproar about the elevated even brought a grand jury investigation of its safety. The line struggled along for a few more months and then was shut down. "The Elevated Railway in Ninth Avenue has ended its precarious existence," commented the *New York Times* in late August. "The amusement of running empty cars up and down the road, while it gratified the pride of the inventors and excited the interest of the general public, was apparently too expensive to the stockholders to be longer indulged in."

In November 1870 the now bankrupt company was sold off at a sheriff's auction to a representative of the bondholders for just $960. This was the end of the line for Mr. Harvey as a rapid transit magnate—he was forced out in the reorganization of the bankrupt company—and for his concept of a cable-powered rapid transit. But more was yet to be heard from Harvey's pioneer elevated railway.

New Yorkers didn't have to wait long before they had another innovative elevated railway proposal to consider. Combining elements of both Alfred Beach's pneumatic subway and the various elevated railway proposals of the previous two decades, this was an extraordinary rapid transit scheme patented in 1870 by Dr. Rufus H. Gilbert, then an assistant to the superintendent of the Central Railroad of New Jersey. Ornate Gothic iron arches at intervals of 50 to 100 feet, carried on rows of iron columns along the curb line on either side of the street, were to support a pair of "atmospheric tubes," 8 or 9 feet in di-

Elegant Gothic arches of cast iron were to support the "atmospheric tubes" of Dr. Rufus H. Gilbert's proposed pneumatic elevated railway, shown here in an illustration from the April 13, 1872, *Scientific American*. Pneumatic elevators were planned for each station to eliminate the strenuous climb to the elevated platform. The novel scheme was never built, but the Gilbert Elevated Railway later emerged as one of New York's first steam-powered elevated roads. Author's Collection.

ameter. Passengers would be carried in cars, rounded to fit the tubes and propelled by atmospheric power. As an additional benefit, the iron supporting arches were designed to carry two or more sets of atmospheric tubes for the transmission of mail and packages. Stations for the Gilbert Elevated Railway were planned at intervals of about one mile, and were to be equipped with pneumatic elevators to eliminate the strenuous climb up stairways to the elevated platforms.

By 1872 Gilbert had succeeded in obtaining a franchise to build his novel tubular elevated road along Sixth Avenue, but financing it was another matter. In the depressed conditions that followed the Panic of 1873 investors were nowhere to be found. The prospective cost of Gilbert's elaborate structure of cast iron arches and the unproven nature of his atmospheric power scheme likely helped to discourage prospective investors as well.

Although neither the Harvey nor the Gilbert elevated railway schemes were to survive in their original form, both projects would emerge as more conventional elevated railway systems, about which more later. But even though New York would be well on its way toward building a Manhattan-wide elevated railway system before the end of the 1870s, there was no shortage of new and innovative rapid transit schemes, both underground and elevated. Drawings and descriptions of the latest ingenious solution to the urban transportation problem remained a staple of such popular weeklies as *Scientific American*, *Frank Leslie's Illustrated Newspaper*, and *Harper's Weekly* well into the twentieth century.

In April 1872, for example, *Scientific American* provided its readers with drawings and a description of the "endless traveling or railway sidewalk" patented by Alfred Speer of Passaic, N.J., and proposed for installation on Broadway. The Speer scheme called for a continuously moving sidewalk running on rails mounted on an elevated structure on each side of the street. Made up of a train of platform cars, or a "sidewalk in sections," this moving sidewalk was to be a continuous platform moving up one side of the street and down the other at a speed of about 10 mph. Each of the platforms was to be fitted with benches, while awnings would protect passengers from the sun or rain. Two years later Speer's improved scheme for his endless railway was described and illustrated for readers of the March 21, 1874, issue of *Frank Leslie's Illustrated Newspaper*. In addition to the moving benches, Speer now proposed to include an enclosed parlor car every hundred feet, some to be designated ladies' drawing rooms under the charge of a female attendant, while others would be gentlemen's smoking rooms. Passengers boarding or disembarking from the 12-mph "endless railway" would use small transfer cars.

Inventor Alfred Speer proposed quite a different scheme for Broadway transit with his patented "endless traveling or railway sidewalk" that would move up Broadway on one side and down on the other at a speed of 10 mph. The illustration is from the April 20, 1872, issue of *Scientific American*. Author's Collection.

In October 1875, readers of *Leslie's* learned about the improved prismoidal, or "saddle-bag," railway for rapid transit developed by General LeRoy Stone. Exhibited at the Phoenixville, Pa., plant of the Phoenix Iron Company, the Stone system employed a prismoidal girder about 4 feet deep, 9 inches wide at the top, and 3½ feet wide at the bottom. A two-level car, powered by a steam engine, was carried on double flanged wheels running on a single rail mounted on the top of the girder. Horizontal wheels running along the bottom of the girder on either side held the car in position. Outside platforms provided access to outward-facing passenger accommodations on either side, while staircases led to the upper level. A somewhat similar scheme advanced at about the same time for a proposed elevated railway at London would have similarly placed passengers back to back, facing outwards, with one side for first class and one for second class passengers.

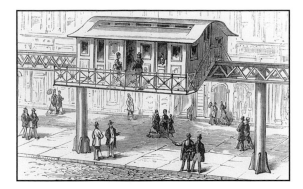

In September 1888 *Scientific American* unveiled Thompson's Gravity System for Rapid Transit. Devised and patented by L. A. Thompson of Philadelphia, who had built a number of amusement park switchback coasting railways using a similar technology in the U.S. and Europe, the concept was not unlike a roller coaster. No motive power was required on each train or along the line. Instead, a cable propulsion system powered by a stationary engine extended a short distance to each side of every station. As a train left a station an automatic grip mechanism engaged the cable, which pulled the train up to the top of an undulation or "hump" in the track. There, the cable was automatically released and the train coasted down a slight grade to the next station. As it approached the station, another undulation slowed the train, and an automatic grip mechanism engaged the cable, which brought it into the station.

"There being no traveling engines or motors of any kind," commented *Scientific American*, "the construction of roadway need cost scarcely half the amount that would be required if engines were employed. All hissing steam, droppings of dirt, hot water, oil and coal are avoided. The roadway, being light and airy, does not darken the streets, and the cars running noiselessly is a feature of no small moment."

The Clarke Elevated and Surface Railroad System described in a May 1890 issue of *Scientific American* rather neatly combined the needs of an elevated railway and surface streetcars in a single structure. Devised by New York consulting engineer T. C. Clarke, the system employed single columns at a spacing of about 80 feet in the center of the street flared outward to each side at the top to support two elevated tracks, at the same time supporting the overhead trolley wire for streetcar tracks on either side of the columns.

General LeRoy Stone's improved prismoidal or "saddle bag" railway, which operated astraddle a prismoidal girder, was depicted for readers of the October 23, 1875, *Frank Leslie's Illustrated Newspaper*. Double-flanged wheels running on top of the girder would have supported the car, while horizontal wheels on each side of the girder held it in position. Author's Collection.

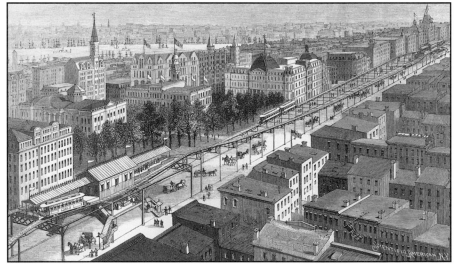

The propulsion system for Philadelphia inventor L. A. Thompson's patented gravity system for rapid transit was not unlike that for a roller coaster. As a Thompson system car left a station it would engage a cable system that would pull it to the summit of a "hump," from which it would then coast downhill toward the next station. As the car approached the next station it would be slowed by another undulation in the track, and would then engage another cable system, which would pull it up into the station. "All hissing steam, droppings of dirt, hot water, oil and coal are avoided," commented *Scientific American*, which ran this illustration in its September 8, 1888, issue. Author's Collection.

The proliferation of columns, always an objection-able feature of elevated railways, would have been sub-stantially reduced by the Day system of elevated railway construction, which employed a combination of stiffen-ing trusses and suspension cables to enable the use of spans as much as a block in length. The trusses and sus-pension cables would have been supported from towers spanning the cross streets at each block.

One of the most enduring ideas in transportation has been the monorail, which in a variety of forms has been offered as the solution to urban transportation ever since the late nineteenth century. Among early monorail pro-posals was a system developed by Joe Vincent Meigs, a Tennessee-born Union artillery battery commander in the Civil War, who patented his scheme in 1875. The Meigs system involved two pairs of closely spaced rails, mounted one above the other on girders supported by a single line of iron columns. A steam locomotive and cars were supported on the lower set of rails by wheels mounted at a 45-degree angle. Steam-driven horizontal wheels on the locomotive gripped the upper rails by hy-draulic pressure, with flanges lipped under the lower edge of the rails to make derailment virtually impossible. Similar horizontal wheels balanced the cars.

In 1886 Meigs constructed a 1114-foot demonstration line at East Cambridge, Mass., over which he operated a Meigs system train made up of a curious sausage-shaped locomotive and two cars. The scheme attracted much attention, and in 1888 Meigs was granted a char-

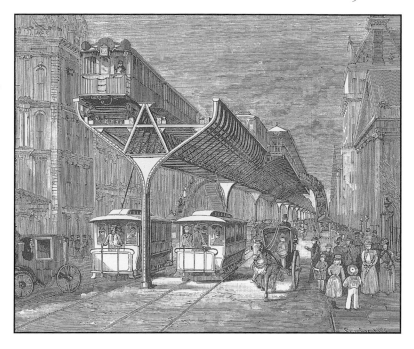

New York consulting engineer T. C. Clarke came up with this neat combination elevated and surface railroad system. The elevated cars would move at high speed, making few stops and carrying passengers quickly over long distances, while the surface cars would move more slowly, stopping often and transporting local passengers. "Long distance passengers can ride on the surface cars to the nearest elevated station and then take an express train," commented *Scientific American*, which ran this illustration in its May 10, 1890, issue. Author's Collection.

Inventor Joe Vincent Meigs attracted wide attention to his patented monorail scheme with an 1114-foot demonstration line completed at East Cambridge, Mass., in 1886. The occasion for this commemorative photograph was a May 1887 visit to the demonstration line by the Philadelphia City Council. Meigs himself is the sixth man from the right in the second row, while seated at the center of the front row with his walking stick leaning against his leg and silk top hat on his knee is former Union General and Massachusetts Governor Benjamin F. Butler, who had joined Meigs as president of his company. Meigs Collection, Manuscripts and Archives, Yale University Library.

ter to build a line from Cambridge to Boston. Nothing came of it, for Meigs was apparently unable to attract the necessary financing. Meigs got a second chance in 1894, when he was granted a charter for the Boston Elevated Railway, but once again a Meigs system project stalled for lack of financing. At least one other company, Chicago's Lake Street Elevated Railroad, planned to employ the Meigs system. Before construction began, however, the company decided that it was impractical for Chicago conditions and proceeded to build a conventional elevated railroad. The Meigs system soon vanished from view.

A more bizarre early monorail proposal was the Boynton Bicycle Railway system developed by Eben M. Boynton. This employed a steam locomotive with a single double-flanged driving wheel that rode on a single running rail. The locomotive and cars were balanced by small wheels running against a wooden upper guiding beam supported by frames arching over the roadway. The 15 foot 6 inch high locomotive had a two-story cab, with the fireman on the lower level and the engineer on the upper level, while two-story passenger cars 4 feet wide, 14 feet high, and 40 feet long

An even more bizarre monorail proposal that actually reached the demonstration stage was the Boynton Bicycle Railway, which operated on a single running rail, balanced by an overhead guiding beam supported by frames over the roadway. This Boynton steam locomotive, illustrated in the September 7, 1889, issue of *Scientific American*, employed a single double flanged driving wheel. The locomotive fireman performed his duties in the lower level of the two-story cab, while the engineman rode on the upper level. The locomotive was tested on Long Island that year. Author's Collection.

would carry 108 passengers each. A Boynton locomotive was built at Portland, Me., in 1889 and brought to Gravesend, New York, on Long Island, for testing.

"The prospectus of the company," reported *Scientific American*, "promises nothing less than a revolution in the railway business of the country as a result of the introduction of the bicycle railway system, but a few practical proofs of its merits will probably be necessary before this happens."

Although nothing came of Boynton's steam-powered bicycle railroad, the inventor was back in the news in 1894 with the Boynton Bicycle Electric Railway, for which claims of 75 mph to 100 mph speeds were made. Although a prospectus promised "a four track road to all the paying points on Long Island," a 2-mile test track between Bellport and Patchogue was all that was ever built. This illustration, from the February 17, 1894, *Scientific American*, showed the line's only car, the *Rocket*. Author's Collection.

Germany's Wuppertal Schwebebahn, or suspended railway, of 1901 was a remarkable anomaly—a successful monorail—that has encouraged new generations of monorail system inventors to this day. This early photograph shows a portion of the line that was constructed above the Wupper River. Author's Collection.

Nothing much more was heard of Boynton's steam-powered bicycle railroad, but in 1894 the inventor was back in the news with the Boynton Bicycle Electric Railway, which was to operate at speeds of 75 to 100 mph or more. The system employed a narrow car, with sharpened ends, that operated on a single rail installed on an elevated structure. Similar to Boynton's original scheme, the car was carried on a double-flanged wheel at each end, while a set of four guide wheels above each wheel bore against an overhead wooden guide beam, which also carried the power rail for an electric propulsion system. The system, reported *Scientific American*, "has the equilibrium of the bicycle, and like the latter disposes at once of the violent transverse wrenching strains which affect four-wheeled vehicles of the everyday type." A single car, the *Rocket*, was built and operated for about two years over a 2-mile test track at Patchogue, N.Y., but nothing more ever came of this scheme either.

The idea of monorail rapid transit achieved new popularity in 1901 with the successful opening of the Wuppertal Schwebebahn, a 9.3-mile suspended monorail, in Germany. Constructed above the Wupper River and city streets, the system operated with cars suspended from trucks that ran on rails mounted on overhead girders, which were supported at intervals by sloping latticed box girders spanning the river or inverted portal U-frames in streets. For close to a century, however, the Schwebebahn would prove to be the only monorail installation to achieve commercial success. It would not be because of any lack of ideas.

This monorail scheme exhibited at the 1907 Jamestown Exposition at Norfolk, Va., by Howard Hansel Tunis had many similarities to the Boynton Bicycle Railroad of a decade earlier. Electrically powered trucks with double flanged wheels carried the car over the single running rail, while the overhead structure doubled as a power supply source and guidance rail. The illustration is from the February 15, 1908, *Scientific American*. Author's Collection.

Yet another of a procession of monorail schemes put forward by imaginative inventors was this straddle beam monorail of 1911 developed by William H. Boyes. If it did nothing else, Boyes' racy vehicle forecast the age of streamlining that was to come a few decades later. Library of Congress (Neg. LC-USZ62-060230).

What might be termed a subterranean version of the Speers "traveling or railway sidewalk" of 1872 was this "continuous variable-speed system of rapid transit" devised by New York engineers B. R. Adkins and W. Y. Lewis in 1907. An endless procession of cars would be driven by a continuous screw mechanism alongside the track. Variations in pitch would allow the cars to run slowly through stations, allowing passengers to board and alight safely, and then accelerate to higher speeds while running between stations. *Scientific American* illustrated the new system in its April 6, 1907, issue. Author's Collection.

In 1907, for example, a system somewhat similar to the Boynton Bicycle Railway was demonstrated at the Jamestown Exposition by Howard Hansel Tunis. The Tunis scheme employed two electrically powered trucks, each with two double-flanged wheels, operating on a single running rail. Two small guiding trucks, mounted on the roof, engaged overhead guidance rails, which also served to supply power to the electric traction motors. Although a four-track high-speed system between New York and Newark was said to be under "serious consideration," the Tunis monorail, like almost all monorail schemes, was soon forgotten.

In 1909, British inventor Louis Brennan demonstrated a gyroscopically stabilized single rail monorail design at London, while a German inventor, Richard Scherl, exhibited a similar scheme at the Zoological Gardens at Berlin. In 1910, New York financier August P. Belmont, who headed the city's IRT subway, built a single rail monorail, the Pelham Park & City Island Railway, between City Island and the nearby New Haven station at Bartow, in the Bronx. Trains were stabilized by two D.C. power rails suspended from an overhead "grape arbor" structure. Although it was said to be capable of 50 mph operation, speeds were restricted after the "arbor" collapsed and a car derailed with 100 passengers, and the line was soon replaced by a conventional rail line.

In 1921, the Russian government began construction at Leningrad for a 20-mile monorail that employed a gyroscopically stabilized design. Some 7 miles of line had been completed when the project ran out of money two years later. British inventor George Bennie demonstrated still another monorail scheme in 1929. Operated over a short section of track near Glasgow, Scotland, the Bennie Railplane was a streamlined diesel-electric car suspended from a single rail and driven by propellers at either end.

Biographical Profiles

ALFRED ELY BEACH (1826–1896), a native of Springfield, Mass., joined with schoolmate Orson D. Munn at an early age to form a publishing firm and acquire *Scientific American* magazine, later becoming its editor. Beach made the magazine a showcase for the latest inventions and developments in science and technology of every kind, and for many years the magazine aided inventors in securing patents for their work. Beach was a gifted inventor in his own right, holding patents for diverse inventions as an early typewriter design, the cable railway devices that were adopted for Charles T. Harvey's pioneer elevated railway, and a pneumatic tube system for transmitting letters and packages that he adapted for his extraordinary Broadway subway of 1870. The most significant of all Beach's inventions, however, was the improved pneumatic tunneling shield he developed to drill the Broadway subway. Much larger shields based upon the Beach patents were used to drill the pioneer railroad tunnel under the St. Clair River between Sarnia, Ont., and Port Huron, Mich., during 1889–1891, and for the many railroad and subway tunnels under the Hudson and East rivers at New York. Beach continued to oversee publication of the *Scientific American* and its support to inventors until shortly before his death from pneumonia on New Year's Day, 1896.

Alfred Ely Beach.
Author's Collection.

CHARLES THOMPSON HARVEY (1829–1912), who was born in Thompsonville, Conn., first made his mark as chief engineer for the construction of the Sault Ste. Marie Canal between Lake Huron and Lake Superior that was, at the time, the largest public works project in America. Harvey's resourcefulness and skill saw the difficult work through to completion, and he went on to other engineering work in railroad construction and mining before returning to the east, where he took up the problem of rapid transit for New York. In 1866 Harvey gained the authorization of the New York legisla-

Charles Thompson Harvey.
Collection of The New-York Historical Society
(Neg. No. 43580).

ture for what would be America's first elevated railway. The cable-powered elevated experienced a number of operating problems and strong opposition from residents along its path, and was shut down a few years after it opened. By the time it reopened in 1871 with steam locomotive power, Harvey had been forced out of the company. The "father of the elevated railway," as he was sometimes called, maintained his interest in urban transit for the remainder of his long life. On the day he died at New York at the age of 83 he was scheduled to go before the Public Service Commission to submit patent devices for new elevated lines to be constructed in the city.

RUFUS HENRY GILBERT (1832–1885) was a native of Guilford, N.Y., who studied at New York's College of Physicians and Surgeons to become a surgeon of some renown. During a period of study in Europe he became concerned about the health problems of the poor living in the densely populated tenement districts of large cities, attributing them to the lack of sunlight and air. Gilbert became convinced that cheap and rapid transportation that would allow urban residents to live in a cleaner atmosphere would be an effective means of improving public health. After service as a surgeon during the Civil War, becoming medical director and superintendent of Army hospitals by war's end, Gilbert gave up medicine to become assistant superintendent of the Central Railroad of New Jersey, at the same time developing his ideas for rapid transit. He obtained patents for his pneumatic elevated railway system in 1870, and two years later obtained passage in the New York legislature of an act incorporating the Gilbert

Dr. Rufus Henry Gilbert.
Library of Congress (Neg. LC-B813-3720).

Elevated Railway Company. Gilbert was less successful in gaining financing for the company, and when he finally did, his financing agreement gave the New York Loan and Improvement Company substantial control of his company. Soon after the road opened for service in 1878, Gilbert was forced out of the company entirely. Claiming that his former associates had defrauded him, he threatened to bring suit against them. Troubled by failing health for several years, he was only 53 when he died at New York.

THE EAST RIVER BRIDGE—STREET BRIDGE AT FRANKLIN SQUARE.

Against a backdrop of New York's engineering marvel of the nineteenth century, John and Washington Roebling's East River Bridge to Brooklyn, a New York Elevated Railroad train steamed into the Franklin Square station on its way down the East Side to South Ferry. This illustration for the August 5, 1882, issue of *Scientific American* required a bit of artistic license, for it would be another year before the great bridge was complete and open to traffic. Author's Collection.

CHAPTER 2

THE ERA OF
THE ELEVATED

The elevated roads have been of the greatest service to New York. . . . there
can be no doubt that the problem of rapid transit has been effectually and
quickly solved. Travelers are independent now of the weather. The trains run
on time and with ease in the heaviest snow storms, blockades are impossible,
and time is saved and comfort secured to the passenger. In good weather and
with a clear track the horsecars took from three-quarters of an hour to fifty
minutes from 59th street to the City Hall. The elevated trains make the same
distance now in twenty-eight minutes, including stoppages.

—James D. McCabe, *New York by Gaslight*, 1882

Although Charles Harvey's cable-powered elevated proved a failure and
Rufus Gilbert's proposed atmospheric tube elevated system never even reached
the construction stage, the two projects did lay the foundation for the development of an
elevated railway system for New York.

Soon after Harvey was forced out of his bankrupt company, the property and franchise
were taken over by new owners and reorganized as the New York Elevated Railroad Company. Backed by wealthy businessmen, the new company had a capital of $10 million, and
soon came up with plans for a 160-mile system of elevated lines that would include both

Soon after Charles Harvey's pioneer cable-powered elevated reopened as the steam-powered New York Elevated, four-wheel steam
dummy No. 13, *Yonkers*, powered a train over the company's "one-
legged" El structure. The Brooks Locomotive Works at Dunkirk,
N.Y., built the little four-wheel locomotive in 1876, while the drop-
center "shad belly" cars came from the Jackson & Sharp Company
at Wilmington, Del. Author's Collection.

East Side and West Side routes, crosstown lines, and extensions north of the Harlem River to Yonkers, Westchester, New Rochelle, and Tarrytown. Harvey's cable system was removed and the company ordered a diminutive steam locomotive from the Albany Street Iron Works to power the trains. Named the *Pioneer*, this was a little four-wheel steam "dummy," with the boiler and machinery enclosed within a box-like body, to avoid frightening horses it was said. Operation began with the new locomotive and three cars on April 20, 1871, with a 10-cent fare collected that day from a total of 237 passengers.

Steam-powered service proved successful. New stations were added, and by July 30, 1873, the line was extended to West 34th Street and Ninth Avenue. At the beginning of 1874 the company was operating four steam dummies and ten 48-seat passenger cars, with a fastest running time of 18 minutes over the 4-mile line. In a practice that would not last long in New York City, passengers on the trains were limited to the number that could be seated. In 1872 the line had carried 242,190 passengers; the following year traffic had tripled to 723,253. New York's first elevated railroad continued to grow over the next several years. The elevated structure was strengthened to handle heavier equipment, and service was extended north to 42nd Street late in 1875, and to 61st Street in January 1876, by which time it was running 40 through trains every day. Trains began operating to South Ferry station at the lower end of Manhattan in April 1877.

Success did not come easily to the new company. At about the same time operation resumed with steam power, the Viaduct Railway plan backed by Tammany Hall's "Boss" Tweed was launched with the formation of the New York Railway Company, with such distinguished New Yorkers as John Jacob Astor, Horace Greeley, Peter Cooper, August Belmont, Charles Tiffany, and James Gordon Bennett, Jr. among the incorporators. A Tammany-backed bill that would have authorized the demolition of the Harvey Elevated by New York's Commissioner of Public Works, who happened to be none other than Boss Tweed, was voted down in the New York legislature. That proved to be the end of the Viaduct Railway, and Tweed himself was soon forced out of power and on his way to jail.

Meanwhile, Rufus Gilbert's elevated railway had finally come to life. For several years following granting of the franchise in 1872, Gilbert had tried unsuccessfully to obtain financing for the project. This changed in 1875 when the New York legislature passed the

This woodcut from the January 4, 1879, issue of *The Graphic*, shows a New York Elevated train on the somewhat sturdier version of the one-legged elevated structure along Third Avenue. The train is powered by one of the patented Forney tank engines that had begun to enter service on the El the previous summer. Library of Congress.

Husted Act, which authorized the Mayor of New York to appoint a Board of Rapid Transit Commissioners that would determine the city's need for rapid transit, select the route or routes, and, if expedient, organize a company to build the lines. Appointed by Mayor William H. Wickham, the five-member commission was organized and began work on July 8, 1875.

Believing they could raise the necessary capital if they could build a simple elevated railroad instead of the costly and impractical pneumatic propulsion scheme required by its charter, the Gilbert company persuaded the commission to approve the change. By September the commission had also established routes for both the New York Elevated and the Gilbert Elevated. The New York Elevated was authorized to extend its line up Ninth Avenue to Harlem and down to South Ferry, and to build up Third Avenue. The Gilbert road was authorized comparable routes on Second and Sixth avenues. The two companies had also agreed upon arrangements to build joint facilities at locations where their routes coincided.

With the support of the Rapid Transit Commission, financing proved much easier to obtain, and construction of the Gilbert road got underway at the corner of Sixth Avenue and 42nd Street on April 19, 1876. That fall construction of both the Gilbert and New

The Gilbert Elevated Railroad emerged as an early competitor for the New York Elevated. This drawing from the February 1938 *Railroad Magazine* shows the moving platform that was used to erect the Gilbert line in Sixth Avenue during 1877–78. Author's Collection.

York elevated lines was halted by injunction for close to a year while property owners and horse car companies attempted to persuade the courts that the Husted Bill was unconstitutional and the actions of the commission illegal. The courts finally found in favor of the elevated companies and construction resumed in November 1877. The first segment of the Gilbert line was opened to the public on June 5, 1878, operating from Rector Street to Central Park via Church Street, West Broadway, and Sixth Avenue. The fare was 10 cents, although the public was invited to ride free on opening day.

What should have been a moment of triumph for Rufus Gilbert proved to be anything but that. In his eagerness to arrange financing for the company, Gilbert had agreed to terms that made it possible for his new financial partners to wrest control from him. Shortly after the line opened, Gilbert was forced out altogether and the name of the company changed to the Metropolitan Elevated Railroad Company.

Both roads continued to extend their lines at a brisk pace through the end of the decade. By August 1878 the New York Elevated had completed the first section of its new Third Avenue line that extended from South Ferry and Chatham Square through lower Manhattan to Third Avenue and thence north to 42nd Street, where a branch extended west to Grand Central Depot. Construction continued north in Sixth Avenue, opening in consecutive stages all the way to 129th Street by the end of the year. By this time the company was carrying more than 84,000 daily passengers over its two lines. The Metropolitan continued building northward as well, reaching 53rd Street and Eighth Avenue early in 1879, while in June the two roads jointly completed an extension in Columbus (Ninth) Avenue all the way to 104th Street.

The elevated structures and stations built by the two roads were marvels of nineteenth-century engineering and architecture. The New York Elevated structure typically used what was

Financiers Cyrus Field and Russell Sage, who were among the line's principal backers, inspected construction of the Gilbert Elevated at Church and Cortlandt Streets in 1878. The illustration is from the April 27, 1878, issue of *Frank Leslie's Illustrated Newspaper*. New York Transit Museum Archives, Brooklyn (Neg. X4-193).

Perhaps the most exhilarating elevated railway trip anywhere was the ride around this celebrated serpentine curve at 110th Street and Eighth Avenue on the Manhattan Elevated's Ninth Avenue line. The spindly structure soared 63 feet above street level and became known as "Suicide Curve" after it became popular for death leaps. This view dates to 1894. J. S. Johnston, Library of Congress.

called a "one legged plan," with the iron girders supporting the roadway placed directly above a row of single iron columns. At most locations each track was carried on an independent structure, with the columns usually placed along the curb line. At some locations the columns were placed within the street. The Metropolitan, on the other hand, typically supported the roadway girders from transverse girders that spanned between pairs of iron columns placed at the curb line or in the street. By placing the tracks at the side of the roadway, the New York Elevated structure avoided blocking light to the street. The Metropolitan's approach, while its placement of the tracks directly over the street tended to block off light and air, at least had the advantage of placing the noisy trains a little further from the second story windows of the buildings facing the street.

The elevated railroad stations were ornate structures typical of their era. Writer James D. McCabe, in his 1882 *New York by Gaslight*, described the stations of the Metropolitan Elevated:

> The stations along the route are of iron and are painted a light and dainty green. They are fitted up in elegant style, and are provided with every convenience for passengers and the employees of the road. They were designed by the celebrated landscape architect J. F. Cropsey, and are tasteful cottages, provided with ticket offices, waiting rooms for gentlemen and ladies, and toilet conveniences for each. The platforms extend beyond the station houses at each end, and are covered with a light and graceful iron pavilion roof. The stations are reached from the street by light iron stairways enclosed at the side and roofed over. The up stations are on the east

Stations on New York's new elevated railways were wonders of Victorian ornamentation. Those on the Gilbert road were designed by the noted architect J. F. Cropsey. Writer James D. McCabe called them "tasteful cottages." This illustration from McCabe's *New York by Gaslight* of 1886 shows the line's station at Sixth Avenue and 23rd Street. Author's Collection.

side of the streets, and the down stations on the west side. Passengers purchase their tickets at the office on entering the station, and drop them in a patent box in charge of an attendant upon passing out on the platform.

Both roads began operation with small steam "dummy" locomotives that were designed to operate in either direction and enclosed in windowed car bodies that gave them the appearance of passenger cars so as not to frighten horses. The New York Elevated locomotives were given distinctive names, most of them New York area place names. They were painted a glossy black, with gold lettering on a wine-red background, surrounded by fancy striping and ornamentation. The Metropolitan Elevated's engines were a little larger, finished in a pea green, with fancy lining and decorative work. Both roads soon dispensed with the shrouded dummy design in favor

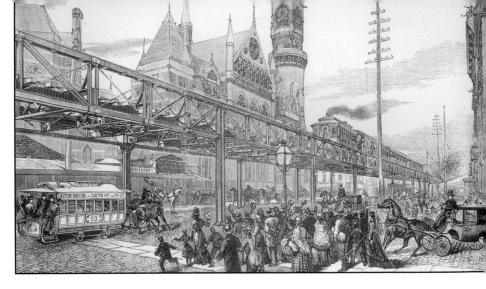

This illustration from a French magazine shows the Gilbert Elevated's new Sixth Avenue line at Chatham Square soon after it opened in June 1878. The train is powered by one of the company's steam dummy locomotives that were outfitted with Pullman-built car bodies meant to disguise them as passenger cars. Library of Congress (Neg. LC-USZ62-31040).

of more conventional locomotives, and both later adopted double-ended tank locomotives[1] of the design developed by Mathias N. Forney for the demanding operating conditions of the elevated railways.

Both roads employed conventional wooden cars, similar to steam railroad equipment, although somewhat smaller. The New York Elevated tried a few cars with a novel low center of gravity "shad belly" arrangement, but these were soon rebuilt into more conventional cars. Passengers boarded and alighted from open platforms at each end, and both roads employed elevated station platforms at car floor level to speed entrance and exit. New York Elevated cars were finished in claret red, with ornate gold lining and decorative work. "The exteriors are painted a rich carmine, highly decorated after the Queen Anne School and impress one favorably," reported the September 7, 1878, issue of *Leslie's Weekly*. The Metropolitan's cars were finished in apple green, with pea green and gold trim. In common with the standards of the time, interiors were finished with elaborate paneling and inlaid work, but the accommodations were usually on the austere side, with plain longitudinal benches, illuminated by oil lamps and heated by coal stoves.

Metropolitan Elevated conductors, brakemen, and station attendants were handsomely outfitted in uniforms of blue flannel or cloth, with ornamental braiding on the shoulders, brass buttons on coat and vest, and a cap encircled with two gold cords and marked with the title, "conductor," "brakeman," etc., in silver letters. New York Elevated staff were similarly uniformed, and were said to be more efficient, since the company made it its business to hire experienced railroad men.

Well before the end of the 1870s, New York's elevated railroads had attracted the attention of the city's Wall Street financiers. In the spring of 1877 Cyrus W. Field, a wealthy capitalist and the promoter of the first Transatlantic cable, acquired a controlling interest in the New York Elevated Railroad and assumed its presidency. Under his leadership the elevated road expanded from 6 to 31 miles in less than two year's time.

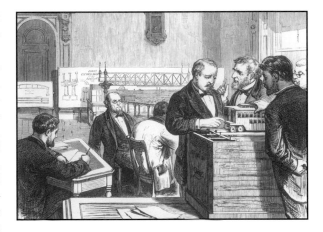

Aiming to resolve the many problems of bringing rapid transit to New York City, the state legislature established a new Rapid Transit Commission in 1875 that would determine what additional rapid transit roads were needed, select routes and develop plans, and take the necessary steps toward the organization of a company to build the road. A drawing from the August 7, 1875, *Frank Leslie's Illustrated Newspaper* shows the Commission in the New Court House soon after their appointment by New York Mayor William H. Wickham. "The Commissioners are now industriously at work," reported *Leslie's*, "and are hopeful of giving to the public a perfect system of rapid transit." Author's Collection.

---

1. These were 0-4-4 locomotives, without separate tenders, that carried a water tank and coal space on an extended frame behind the cab.

A Manhattan Elevated Forney locomotive and crew waited for their next assignment at the terminal of the Third Avenue line in this undated photograph. Engineman Robert Evans was at the throttle of No. 100, an 1879 product of the Baldwin works. New York Transit Museum Archives, Brooklyn (Neg. X8-179).

The sweeping reverse curve at Coenties Slip, on the lower East Side, was always a popular location for photographs of the elevated. A Forney locomotive pulled a five-car train through the curve in 1894 on its way to the El terminal at South Ferry. J. S. Johnston, Library of Congress (Neg. LC-USZ62-074595).

An elevated railway journey could be a pleasant excursion, looking down upon the frantic urban streetscape from among the treetops. This was the view from a coach window of a Ninth Avenue El train on a curve near Battery Place. Duke-Middleton Collection.

Along the Bowery, Manhattan Elevated trains ran on one-legged elevated structures placed along the curb line on each side of the street, an arrangement that left the street open to the sunlight but that all but brought the trains into second story living rooms. In this splendid glass plate view by the Detroit Publishing Company, a South Ferry-bound train on the Bowery nears Grand Street. Library of Congress (Neg. LC-D4-12678).

The Rapid Transit Commission appointed in 1875, although it had put elevated railroad expansion in the hands of the two existing companies, also went ahead as it was authorized to do under the 1875 legislation to form the new Manhattan Railway Company. This was done, as the commissioners stated in its communication to Mayor Wickham, "to render assurance doubly sure that our labors will result in rapid transit actually." The Manhattan company was established with a capitalization of $2 million and was granted franchises for routes virtually identical to those of the other two companies, with the idea that it would build the lines if the other two companies failed to do so. The entire capital stock was quickly subscribed for but for several years the company remained a paper organization while the other two roads expanded their routes.

The Manhattan Railway Company came to life in an unexpected way in 1879. Apparently with the backing of the other two companies, it leased the two lines for 999 years in return for $6.5 million in its own stock to each and an agreement to guarantee interest on their bonds and to pay a 10 percent dividend on their stock. In effect, the Manhattan company had become a holding company with its sole asset the leases on the two elevated companies.

There followed two years of convoluted maneuverings among the three companies, attacks on the Manhattan company by the daily press, legal actions, and Wall Street chicanery, at the end of which financier Russell Sage and Jay Gould, the notorious railroad and Western Union baron, emerged with a controlling interest and Gould the presidency of the Manhattan Railway Company. Cyrus Field remained financially involved in the elevated roads until 1887 when, in an unsuccessful attempt to corner Manhattan stock with borrowed money, he lost heavily and was bought out by Gould, who then reigned as the financial master of New York rapid transit.

Not everyone thought that rapid transit was such a good investment. Although the New York Central's Commodore Vanderbilt had incorporated the New York City Rapid Transit Company in 1872 to build an underground line from City Hall to connect with his railroads, he never did proceed with the project, and was said to have remarked of one subway project, "I shall be underground a damned sight sooner than this thing."

William H. Vanderbilt, the commodore's eldest son and successor, was apparently no more sanguine about rapid transit. Asked to invest in one of New York's early elevated railway projects, he is said to have replied, "Nobody will go upstairs to take a train."

Despite the intense level of traffic the safety record of the elevated railroads was remarkably good, but there were occasional accidents. This was a March 25, 1879, head-on collision at 42nd Street on the New York Elevated's East Side line, seen in a drawing from the April 12, 1879, *Frank Leslie's Illustrated Newspaper*. The result of a switchman's error, the collision fortunately involved no deaths or injuries. Library of Congress (Neg. LC-USZ62-33932).

While legal and stock market struggles were to rage on for several years, the Manhattan company took control of the two leased elevated companies on September 1, 1879, and continued the rapid expansion of New York's elevated system. At the time of the Manhattan takeover, the two companies had completed more than 81 miles of elevated structure. Before the end of the year the Sixth and Ninth Avenue lines had been opened from 104th Street all the way to 155th Street, including a spectacular serpentine curve at 110th Street and Eighth Avenue that stood 63 feet above the street and became known as "Suicide Curve" after it became popular for death leaps. By late summer of 1880 the Manhattan elevated system had reached its full extent with the opening of the Second Avenue line all the way to the Harlem River at 127th Street and a 34th Street branch to the Long Island Rail Road's East River ferry terminal, while major sections of the early Ninth Avenue elevated structure had been replaced. By 1880 the elevated roads were operating close to 2000 daily trains and transporting almost 61 million annual passengers.

While the Manhattan system was essentially complete by 1880, the New York City elevated network continued to expand over the next two decades. Elevated trains began operating across the new Brooklyn Bridge in September 1883, carrying as many as 225,000 daily passengers across the East River between Brooklyn and Manhattan. Unlike the Manhattan elevated roads, the bridge line was powered by a cable system, with steam locomotives to switch the cars at the terminals at each end of the bridge and to push them on to the cable section. Cable propulsion proved much more satisfactory than it had for Charles Harvey's pioneer elevated line, and the cable system remained in operation until it was replaced by electric power in 1908.

Brooklyn had transportation problems of its own, and the city's first elevated railroad, the Brooklyn Elevated Railroad Company, was chartered in 1874 to operate from Brooklyn to Queens, but it would be another decade before the company could finance construction of an initial 5-mile section on Lexington Avenue, which opened in 1885. Three years later a second elevated company, the Union Elevated Railroad, completed a line between Gates and Driggs avenues, connecting with the Lexington line, as well as lines in Myrtle and Fifth avenues. A third company, the Kings County Elevated, also opened its first line, in Fulton Street, in 1888. The Brooklyn Elevated took over the Union Elevated in 1890, and by 1906 all of the Brooklyn elevated lines, as well as several steam lines that operated to the Atlantic Ocean beaches, had been consolidated into the new Brooklyn Rapid Transit Company (BRT).

The success of the New York elevated roads inspired this 1875 musical effort. Smithsonian Institution.

The elevated system next advanced north across the Harlem River into the Annexed District north of the river that would later become the Borough of Bronx. In May 1886 the Suburban Rapid Transit Company, a new company organized in 1880, began operating from a connection with the Second Avenue line across a new Harlem River drawbridge as far north as 143rd Street, and had extended service all the way to 170th Street by September 1887. The Suburban came into the Manhattan Railway system by lease in June 1891, by which time the lines under Manhattan operation were transporting 547,000 daily passengers. Service to the Bronx was extended further north to 177th Street a month later, and the line would finally reach its northernmost terminal at Pelham Road in July 1901.

Unlikely as it seems, Kansas City was the first city outside the New York metropolitan area to boast its own elevated railroad. This was the steam powered Inter-State Elevated, which in 1886 began operating a 2-mile section of elevated across the West Bottoms between Kansas City, Mo., and Kansas City, Kans., connecting with surface lines at either end. The line was bankrupt by 1892 and was subsequently electrified and absorbed by the Kansas City Street Railway Company, which continued to operate streetcars over the elevated structure until 1950.

Sioux City, Iowa, an even less likely venue for an elevated railway, was close behind Kansas City with its very own El. Apparently organized to help promote a real estate development, the Sioux City Rapid Transit Company built an elevated line across several railroads, a swamp, and the city's stockyards to reach the new Morningside development. Trains began running over the El behind steam power in 1891. The line was electrified a year or two later and torn down around 1901, making it the first elevated railroad to end operation.

Chicago was the next North American city to take up elevated railroad construction, and the city would ultimately develop an "L"[2] system that would closely

Editorial cartoonist W. A. Rogers commented on the dominance of the elevated railway companies in this cartoon for *Harper's Weekly*. New York Transit Museum Archives, Brooklyn (Neg. X8-446).

---

2. In Chicago, the Elevated railway is almost always referred to as the "L," while in New York it's usually the "El."

Brooklyn opened its first elevated railroad along Lexington Avenue on May 13, 1885. The crowd of top-hatted gentlemen and well-dressed ladies that greeted the first train was depicted by artist W. P. Snyder for readers of the May 23, 1885, issue of *Harper's Weekly*. Collection of The New-York Historical Society.

Much like those at New York, Chicago's elevated stations were gems of fussy Victorian era architecture. This was the station at Dearborn and Van Buren on the newly completed downtown elevated loop that linked Chicago's "L" lines together. Krambles-Peterson Archive.

The Baldwin Locomotive Works garnered extensive publicity with this special train that transported 20 brand new Vauclain compound Forney locomotives for the Chicago & South Side "L" all the way from Philadelphia to Chicago in 1892. The locomotive that pulled the train, Vauclain compound 4-6-0 No. 82, had already been extensively tested on a number of roads, and was on its way to further tests on three midwestern roads. The South Side Forneys would prove to be some of the very last ones built for any elevated road. Author's Collection.

The South Side line, popularly known as the "Alley L," was the first to open in Chicago, in May 1892. Forney No. 41, seen here with a train on 63rd near South Park Avenue, was a product of the Baldwin Locomotive Works. Krambles-Peterson Archive.

rival that of New York. Chicago's elevated railway development was carried out by four independent companies, which built lines radiating south, southwest, west, northwest, and north from the central business district, while a fifth company built the celebrated downtown Chicago "Loop" that tied them all together into an integrated rapid transit system.

The first two of the Chicago lines to begin operation were steam-powered elevateds, much like those of New York. The first to get underway was the Chicago & South Side Rapid Transit Railroad Company, which obtained a franchise from the City of Chicago in 1888 that authorized it to build south from downtown Chicago to the city limits at 39th Street. Anticipating strong opposition from property owners to the construction of an elevated railway in the street in front of their property, the company decided instead to acquire property adjacent to city-owned alleys, soon becoming known as the Alley "L" or the Alley Road. Construction began early in 1890, and within the year plans were already being made for an extension south to 63rd Street and then east to Jackson Park, which had been selected as the site for Chicago's 1893 World's Columbian Exposition, which would commemorate the four hundredth anniversary of Columbus's discovery of America.

The South Side "L" benefited much from New York's experience in elevated railway construction and operation. Indeed, the company's chief engineer, R. I. Sloan, had come to the company from the same position with the Manhattan Railway. When it came time to begin operation, eight crews from the Manhattan were brought from New York to train the South Side enginemen. Construction details of the elevated structure and stations were similar to those of the New York system, and the South Side company chose for its motive power the same Forney type 0-4-4T tank engine that had proved so successful at New York, and 20 Vauclain four-cylinder compound Forneys were ordered from the Baldwin Locomotive Works. The company's initial fleet of 180 passenger coaches, built by the Gilbert Car Manufacturing Company of Troy, N.Y., and the Jackson & Sharp Company of Wilmington, Del., were typical double truck, open platform cars of wooden construction.

All was in readiness between the downtown Chicago terminal at Congress Street and 39th Street by May 1892. A six-car train carried 300 guests of the company over the line on May 27. A lunch was served at 39th Street, and stops were made at each station to inspect the facilities. The following day two special trains carried some 500 guests of the company over the line. After a week of scheduled operation without any passengers to break-in engine crews and trainmen, the line was opened to the public on June 6, 1892. "There was no brass band, no oratory, no enthusiasm," reported the next day's Chicago *Tribune*, "but the opening was a decided success just the same."

Service was gradually extended southward as additional elevated structure and stations were completed. By the end of the year work had been completed as far south as 63rd Street, and service was extended to the 61st Street station in January 1893. The remainder of the line east to Jackson Park was completed by late spring and service to Jackson Park began on May 12, just two weeks after the World's Columbian Exposition had opened to the public. The enormous crowds that flocked to the Exposition helped the new line off to a good start, with the daily passenger count reaching an average of 116,000 during June 1893.

Close behind the South Side "L" was the Lake Street Elevated Railway Company. Also organized in 1888, the company planned to build west from downtown Chicago along Lake Street to the Village of Oak Park. The Chicago city council and mayor approved the necessary franchise by the end of the year, and the first construction work began late in 1889. Although the company originally had planned to use the patented Meigs monorail system for the line, this was given up and the line built as a conventional elevated railroad much like the South Side line. Twenty Forney type locomotives were acquired from the Rhode Island Locomotive Works at Providence in 1893, with another ten to follow in 1894. The Gilbert company at Troy, N.Y., and the hometown Pullman Palace Car Company supplied a total of 125 open platform passenger coaches.

More than a thousand guests were present on November 4, 1893 for a dedication of the new Lake Street "L" at its downtown terminal at Madison and Market streets, followed by

Chicago's Lake Street line was the last of the steam-operated elevateds to begin operation. Locomotive No. 10, the *Clarence A*, is seen here at Oakley Avenue with a single coach on what was probably a pre-opening inspection trip in the summer of 1893. The Rhode Island Locomotive Works built the little Forney type locomotive in 1893. Krambles-Peterson Archive.

a tour of the line with five five-car inspection trains, with a lunch stop on the Canal Street station platforms. Regular service began between the downtown terminal and California Avenue on Monday, November 6, but it would be another several years before service would reach all the way west to Oak Park.

The Lake Street line would prove to be the last new steam-powered elevated railway to open in North America. However well the little Forneys performed, steam power was far from an ideal motive power for a densely operated urban transit service. Residents and businesses along the elevated routes objected violently to the steady rain of smoke, cinders, and steam from the locomotives and the noise, while hot coals and sparks dropped into the streets below to the discomfiture of pedestrians. Moreover, steam power was manifestly uneconomical and inherently limited in its performance characteristics for this class of service. Something better was needed.

Although Charles Harvey's experiment with cable power had been unsuccessful, the later 1883 cable-powered elevated installation for the New York & Brooklyn Bridge line had proved satisfactory. This was a much simpler installation limited to a straight run of little more than a mile. There was one other attempt at a cable-powered elevated railroad. This was a mile-and-a-half elevated structure completed in 1884 by the North Hudson Railroad Company to link the Christopher Street ferry at Hoboken, N.J., with Jersey City Heights at the top of a cliff to the west. This installation used a cable system to power the streetcars operated over the

Rapid transit was established across the Brooklyn Bridge with the cable-powered New York & Brooklyn Bridge line. This drawing from *Scientific American* shows one of the cable-powered cars, the cable power plant, and one of the little steam locomotives that switched cars at the New York and Brooklyn terminals. Library of Congress.

New terminals for the Brooklyn Bridge line were built at both the Brooklyn and New York ends of the bridge in 1895. Artist G. W. Peters illustrated the new Brooklyn terminal for the June 15, 1895, issue of *Harper's Weekly.* Author's Collection.

With the East River and the Brooklyn skyline obscured by a heavy snowfall that has already covered roadways and rooftops, a long train of cable-powered cars descends from the Brooklyn Bridge into the New York terminal. Library of Congress. (Neg. LC-D4-016664).

The North Hudson Railroad built this rather spectacular inclined cable railway structure in 1885 to link the Christopher Street ferry at Hoboken, N.J., with Jersey City Heights. The line was eventually converted to electric operation. The illustration is from the February 20, 1886, issue of *Scientific American*. Author's Collection.

structure. A mile-long extension of the elevated south to the Hudson County Court House, begun in 1890, was also planned for cable operation; but before the work was complete, the company had elected to convert the entire elevated to electric operation.

There had been several attempts, too, to develop compressed air locomotives for elevated railway service. At least two different designs were tried on the New York elevated lines in 1881 and again in 1897, but neither was successful enough to encourage further trials.

As far back as the mid-1880s, interest had begun to develop in the possibilities of electric power for the elevateds. A long period of experimentation with electricity for street railway operation was beginning to show real promise. German electrician and inventor Dr. Ernst Werner von Siemens had built a small electric locomotive powered from a generator that successfully pulled passenger cars around a track at the 1879 Berlin Industrial Exhibition. Thomas Edison operated a small electric locomotive at his Menlo Park (N.J.) laboratories in 1880, while Stephen D. Field, a son of Cyrus Field, built and tested a small electric locomotive at Stockbridge, Mass., at about the same time.

In 1885 British-born inventor Leo Daft, who had already built several successful exhibition lines, was permitted to test a 9-ton, four-wheel electric locomotive, the *Benjamin Franklin*, on the Manhattan Railway's Ninth Avenue line. A third rail was laid in the center of the track over a 2-mile stretch between 14th and 53rd streets. A 300-amp, 185-volt motor rated at 75 h.p. powered the locomotive's two driving wheels through a novel friction drive. During several months of testing, the locomotive reached a top speed of 30 mph on an August 26, 1885, test run with a four-car train. Nothing much came of the tests, but the *Benjamin Franklin*, rebuilt with cranks and side rods that powered all four wheels, was back on the Ninth Avenue elevated for more tests between 14th and 50th streets during an eight-

In 1885 inventor Leo Daft tested his experimental nine-ton electric loco-motive, the *Benjamin Franklin*, on the Manhattan Elevated's Ninth Av-enue line. Nothing much came of these tests, but the rebuilt locomotive was back in 1888 for more tests with heavy four-car trains. This illustration appeared in the December 8, 1888, *Scientific American*, which com-mented, "It appears to be only a question of time when our city elevated trains will be hauled as rapidly by electricity as with steam." It turned out to be more than a decade more, however, before the Manhattan made the change to electric power. Author's Collection.

month period in 1888. This time Daft's motor attained speeds as high as 28 mph with heavy, four-car trains, and in one test, an eight-car train was pulled up the line's maximum grade of nearly 2 percent at 7 mph. This was nowhere near the performance that was pos-sible with a Forney steam engine, however, and no more was heard of the Daft electric locomotive.

Close behind Daft was Frank J. Sprague, one of the most important of the inventors who developed elec-tric traction for street railways into a commercially fea-sible technology during the 1880s. Sprague outlined a detailed plan for the electric operation of the Manhat-tan Railway in a paper presented to the Society of Arts in Boston in December 1885; and he devoted much of the next year to a series of experiments on the 34th Street branch of the Manhattan company with one of the line's elevated cars. Probably the most important outcome of these tests was Sprague's development of a method of electric motor mounting for a power truck that permitted the motor to be geared directly to the axle. In this arrangement, sometimes called a "wheel-barrow" mounting, one side of the motor was hung from the truck frame on a spring mounting, while the other was supported directly by the axle. Bearings in the axle side of the motor permitted the motor to rotate slightly about the axle, thus maintaining perfect align-ment between the gearing on the motor shaft and the axle, no matter how irregular the track or the motion of the axle. This solved one of the most vexing problems facing elec-tric railway inventors, and Sprague's wheelbarrow mounting was almost universally adopted for electric railway use.

Among witnesses to one of Sprague's early tests were Jay Gould and members of the Cyrus Field family—the principal owners of the elevated. During the operation of the car one day, Gould stood near the controller and an open lead safety fuse. "Desiring to make an impressive demonstration of how readily the car could be controlled and braked in the short distance available for movement," Sprague later recalled, "I handled the controller rather abruptly, whereupon the fuse blew with a violent flash and Mr. Gould attempted to jump off the car. My explanation that this young volcano was only a safety device was not convincing and he did not return."

Despite the highly successful results of Sprague's tests, the Manhattan showed no im-mediate interest in electrification; and the inventor soon turned his attention to street rail-way electrification, completing the first fully successful electric streetcar installation at Richmond (Va.) during 1887–88.

The Manhattan continued to support electrical experimentation, however, and in 1887 Stephen Field tested an experimental electric locomotive on the elevated's 34th Street branch. This was a small, wooden-bodied steeple cab locomotive mounted on one un-powered truck and a four-wheel power truck that employed a counterbalanced crank at one end of the armature shaft of the traction motor to drive the wheels through a side rod drive. The locomotive was said to prove capable of pulling a single car at a speed of only 8 mph, which was hardly likely to arouse the Manhattan's interest.

Despite the Manhattan's support of all this electric traction experimentation, or perhaps because of it, the company would not be found among the early elevated railroad converts to electric operation. Instead, leadership in the application of the new technology went to Chicago.

The first full-scale elevated railway to operate with electric power was a remarkable line developed to transport visitors to the 1893 World's Columbian Exposition. The exposition would occupy a 633-acre site in Jackson Park, with some 200 major buildings. Exposition President H. N. Higinbotham estimated that 30 million people would attend the exposition, with an average daily attendance of 200,000, while transportation planners estimated that the peak number of visitors arriving at the site might exceed 100,000 an hour. To help accommodate the crush of visitors, exposition officials planned a 3½ mile Columbian Intramural Railway that would serve a total of ten stations within the fair grounds. In keeping with an unofficial theme of the exposition, the use of the new technology of electric power, the line would be electrically operated. Bids were solicited early in 1892, and a contract to construct and operate the line was awarded to the Western Dummy Railway Company of Chicago, which was backed by the Thomson-Houston Electric Company that would be one of the key constituent companies in the 1893 formation of the General Electric Company.

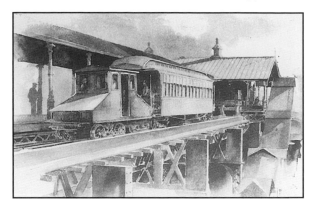

Given the temporary nature of the installation, the elevated structure was made up of timber bents carrying the I-beam stringers that supported the track. There was a loop at each terminal of the line, which encircled the site on the north, west, and south sides. A station at the Exposition's railway terminal was also linked to the Chicago & South Side "L" terminal. A battery of oil-burning Babcock & Wilcox boilers powered five steam engines in a central power plant that drove generators with a total capacity of 2700 kw. A gallery in the plant allowed exposition visitors to observe the machinery. Power was supplied to trains through double third rails mounted on wooden blocks between the running rails.

Electrical inventor Stephen Field was another who tried to interest the Manhattan Elevated in electric motive power. Field's little wooden-bodied steeple cab motor was tried on the El's 34th Street branch in 1887. It proved capable of pulling only a single car at 8 mph, hardly enough to interest the Manhattan in electric traction. Author's Collection.

The Columbian Intramural Railway on the grounds of the 1893 World's Columbian Exposition at Chicago was the first significant electrically powered rapid transit railroad anywhere and proved to be a triumph for the new General Electric Company. Here, we see one of the motor cars with a train of three trailers. The Jackson & Sharp Company of Wilmington, Del., built the cars, while GE supplied the electrical equipment. General Electric, Duke-Middleton Collection.

An aerial view of the Exposition grounds facing to the north shows the North Loop of the 3½-mile Intramural Railway, with Lake Michigan in the background. The circular building to the left of the train is part of the Fisheries exhibit, while beyond the train are some of the foreign exhibits. Smithsonian Institution (Neg. No. 2001-3252).

The Jackson & Sharp Company of Wilmington, Del., supplied 72 double truck cars. These were operated in four-car trains, with every fourth car a power car fitted with four 50 h.p. Thomson-Houston motors. The 46-foot open-sided cars seated 84 passengers each in six-passenger cross benches. The system was designed to operate at 1½ minute headways, or 40 trains an hour, with an aggregate carrying capacity of 15,000 passengers per hour.

The Intramural Railway was a huge success for the brand new General Electric Company, demonstrating convincingly the suitability of electric traction for the heavy demands of urban elevated railway systems. During the 184 days of the Exposition, from May 1 to October 31, the railway carried a total of 5,083,895 passengers, with a daily average of 70,000 to 80,000.

With the example of the Intramural Railway before it, Chicago's third planned elevated railway soon scrapped its plans to operate with steam power. Incorporated early in 1892, the Metropolitan West Side Elevated Railway Company obtained a franchise to build a line west from downtown Chicago to a point on the west side, where it would branch southwest to Douglas Park, west to Garfield Park, and northwest to Humboldt Park and Logan Square. A contract to acquire right-of-way, construct the line, and supply rolling stock was awarded in April 1892, and work was soon in progress. Based upon the success of the Intramural Railway, the line's directors in May 1894 changed the contract to allow the substitution of electric operation. The contractor promptly cancelled an order with the Baldwin Locomotive Works for 60 steam locomotives, and placed an order with the Barney & Smith Car Company of Dayton, Ohio, for 55 electric motor cars. An order for 100 trail cars remained in force with the Pullman Palace Car Company.

A substantial part of the railroad was ready for operation by April 1895, when testing and employee training began. An April 17 inspection trip took company officials and guests over the main line and the Garfield Park and Northwest branches, with a refreshment stop at Center Avenue and a tour of the company's power plant on the way back. Regular service on the Northwest branch began in May, followed by the Garfield Park line in June, and the Humboldt Park branch in July. The Douglas Park branch opened the following year. Both a high level of reliability and much-reduced operating costs demonstrated the wisdom of the Metropolitan's shift to electric operation. Late in 1895 it was reported that the Metropolitan's operating cost per train mile had been cut to 22½ cents a mile, less than half the 48 cents per train mile reported for the steam-operated South Side line.

The Lake Street "L" soon followed the example of the Metropolitan. The company decided to convert to electric operation in January 1895, and contracted with the local Wells & French car building firm to convert 37 of its passenger coaches to motor cars. General Electric supplied electrical equipment for the cars, and their original trucks were replaced with ones supplied by the McGuire Manufacturing Company. The conversion was substantially complete by April 1896, when the power was turned on and motorman training begun. The steam locomotives made their last runs on the evening of June 13, and electric operation commenced early the following morning.

From the very beginning of Chicago "L" service, the absence of a suitable downtown terminal represented a severe handicap. Construction into the heart of the downtown area was expensive, and was generally opposed by property owners. Instead, each line created its own terminal, usually on the periphery. Consequently, a trip that involved the use of two "L" lines required both two fares and a long walk between terminals. Many simply traveled on the streetcar system. As early as 1892 there were proposals for some kind of consolidated terminal, and a few years later there was even a proposal for a system of elevated moving sidewalks.

A solution to the problem came late in 1894 with the incorporation of the Union Elevated Railroad, which proposed to build an elevated loop through the central business district that would link all of the "L" lines. Backing the project was Charles Tyson Yerkes, the most powerful man in Chicago transit. Yerkes had come to Chicago in 1882, and within only a few years controlled all of the major North Side and West Side streetcar lines. Under his control the lines were consolidated, major lines were converted to cable operation, and electrification was begun. Yerkes moved into the elevated railways in 1893, when he became a principal backer for the newly incorporated Northwestern Elevated Railroad Company, and in mid-July 1894 he acquired a controlling interest in the Lake Street line. A central loop linking all of the elevated properties was clearly in the best interest of his properties. Agreements governing trackage rights on the future loop were soon worked out with the other companies, and the consent of affected property owners and the necessary franchises obtained for a rectangular loop that would enclose the central business district on Van Buren, Wabash, and Lake streets, and Fifth Avenue. This was all in place by mid-1896 and construction began immediately. One already complete seg-

Even though separate companies operated the Chicago "L" lines, the completion of the Union Elevated Railroad loop through the downtown area in 1897 tied them all together in a way that created a unified system. The Loop was still new and the street traffic horse-drawn when a three-car "L" train was recorded on the Wabash Avenue leg of the Loop around the turn of the century. Library of Congress.

Dating to shortly after the turn of the century, this view shows Tower 12 at the southeast corner of the Loop, at Van Buren Street and Wabash Avenue. At the left, a South Side train is leaving the Loop en route to Jackson Park, while in the right background a Northwestern Elevated train waits to make the turn to follow Van Buren as it continues a circuit of the Loop. Donald Duke Collection.

ment of the planned Loop in Lake Street had been placed in service as early as 1895, and an inspection train made a complete circuit of the Loop in September 1897.

Regular operation on the Loop began on October 3, 1897, and all three downtown "L's" were using it by mid-month. Traffic on all three of the lines using the Loop grew substantially. The Metropolitan, for example, saw a 50 percent increase, from a daily average of 40,000 to 60,000 passengers. Within a few years, each of the two tracks on the Loop was handling upwards of 60 to 65 trains an hour. Completion of the Loop had given Chicago a remarkably well integrated elevated railway system; and it quickly became an enduring symbol and distinguishing characteristic of the city.

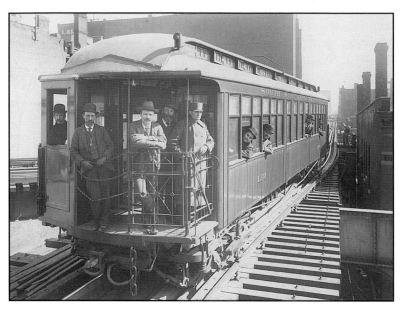

Aside from the application of electricity itself to urban rapid transit, Frank J. Sprague's development of the multiple-unit control system ranks as one of the most important rapid transit technological advances. Sprague contracted with Chicago's South Side line in 1897 to install the still untried system on its entire fleet of 120 cars, provided it could be satisfactorily demonstrated first on 20 test cars. Here, we see a bowler-wearing Frank Sprague in the end door of M.U. test car No. 139 during an 1898 test run. The tests were successful, and rapid transit history was made. Fred W. Schneider, III, Collection.

Both the Lake Street and Metropolitan electrifications retained the locomotive-drawn train concept employed by the Intramural Railway, with a single heavy motorized passenger car pulling a train of several trailer cars. This method was patently superior to steam operation, but it still retained the drawbacks inherent in locomotive operation. Train size was limited to the hauling capacity of the motor cars, and the modest acceleration characteristics imposed by the limited power and adhesion available from a single motorized car in turn limited the overall schedule speeds possible in stop-and-go elevated service.

At this point the opportunity arose for a reentry into active electric traction development by trolley car pioneer Frank J. Sprague, and for a major advance in electric railway technology.

Soon after Sprague's successful completion of the street railway system at Richmond (Va.), his electrical firm was absorbed into the Edison General Electric Company, and Sprague soon resigned to take up the development of the electric elevator. In one of his first major elevator installations—for New York's Postal Telegraph Building in 1893–94—Sprague had evolved a system of control whereby a single master switch in the basement could be used to regulate the movement of any elevator in the building, or the simultaneous movement of all of them.

Pondering the problem of elevated railroad train operation, Sprague conceived the idea of applying the same control principle to train operation. Why, he reasoned, couldn't a train be made up of any number of electric cars, with provision made for working all of their controllers at the same time through a train line from a master switch on any car, this giving a train of any length the performance characteristics of a single car? Details for the necessary equipment were speedily developed, and Sprague's "multiple-unit system," as he called it, was shortly to prove one of the most fundamental advances in the history of electric traction.

There remained the problem of exhibiting the practicality of the new Sprague control system. Two efforts to gain the privilege of demonstrating the system on the Manhattan Railway elevated system, at Sprague's own risk and expense, were rebuffed. But in 1897 came unexpected opportunity. The South Side line, Chicago's only remaining steam-operated elevated, had decided that it, too, would electrify, and the road retained Sprague as a consulting engineer. An inspection of the property convinced Sprague that the line would be an ideal showcase for his multiple-unit, or M.U., system, and his report recommending its adoption in place of the contemplated locomotive cars was accompanied by an offer personally to undertake the installation.

The four-track line of the Metropolitan West Side "L" crossed the Chicago River on these two parallel rolling lift draw spans designed by civil engineer William Scherzer and completed in 1894. A West Side train inbound to the Loop crossed the span in 1907. Library of Congress (Neg. LC-D4-070152).

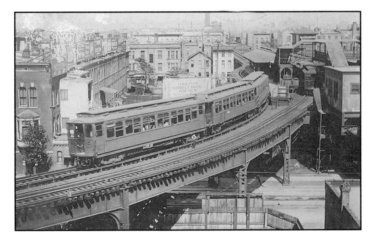

Early in the twentieth century a Metropolitan West Side "L" train headed north toward the Logan Square line from the junction at the Marshfield station. Durable wooden cars like these transported Chicago commuters for a half-century and more. Krambles-Peterson Archive.

The Northwestern Elevated was the last of Chicago's elevated railways to begin operation. Splendid in its newness, a three-car Northwestern train paused for passengers at the Chicago Avenue station on its southbound journey to the Loop. It was June 2, 1900, just three days after the line had opened for service. Krambles-Peterson Archive.

Sprague won a contract to provide the entire equipment for 120 South Side cars, but only under conditions that were onerous in the extreme. Under terms of the contract, Sprague had but two months to prepare a group of six cars for testing. Should the tests prove unsatisfactory or the time limit not be met, the contract was subject to cancellation. Rigid requirements were established for delivery of the remainder of the cars, and a further stipulation was imposed for the testing of 20 cars under service conditions for a period of not less than 10 days once the powerhouse and power installation were complete. If this final test proved unsuccessful, the elevated company had the right to cancel the contract and to require waiver of all claims. Moreover, Sprague must post a $100,000 performance bond.

The contract was executed while Sprague was in London in connection with an elevator proposal, and most of his initial instructions for preparation of the trial equipment were transmitted by cable. When Sprague returned to New York on June 24, only 21 days remained before a July 15 deadline for test operation of the six-car train. On July 16 two cars were put into operation on the General Electric test track at Schenectady, N.Y., and on July 26 Sprague's 10-year-old son Desmond successfully operated the entire six-car train in the presence of South Side Elevated officials and engineers.

By November 1897 a test train of five cars was running in Chicago. By the following April 20 the stipulated 20 cars were in operation, although no less than 17 of them (one in flames) were taken out of service before the end of the day because of defective rheostats. Sprague took what satisfaction he could from the occasion in seeing the remaining three-car train push a stalled steam train around a curve. The defects were soon remedied, and within three months the entire 120 cars were operating satisfactorily. By the end of July 1898, steam operation on the South Side Elevated had been discontinued; and by the end of the year, the elevated railway's monthly net earnings had more than trebled. Electric multiple-unit control was a success.

The performance of the Sprague multiple-unit control system on the South Side Elevated quickly prompted similar installations elsewhere. Over the next decade both the Metropolitan and Lake Street lines converted to M.U. operation. When Chicago's newest elevated, the Northwestern Elevated Railroad, opened the first segment of its line to the North Side from the Loop in May 1900, it was operated with M.U. electric equipment.

Brooklyn began the conversion of its elevated system to electric operation in 1898, but there was still some resistance to electrification of the great Manhattan Railway elevated system. An August 1900 editorial in *Locomotive Engineering* urged caution on the Manhattan company, pointing out that the recently electrified Brooklyn system had experienced more accidents and delays in one year than had the steam-powered Manhattan system in 10. Fires were said to be frequent on the electric trains because of burning fuses and overheated motors.

Hot motors set a Coney Island train afire on January 2. Passengers saved themselves only by beating out the flames with their overcoats. Only three weeks later overheated traction motors set the motor car of a five-car train ablaze in the station at Atlantic and Flatbush avenues. Firemen called to the scene turned their hoses on the blazing car. "The moment the streams struck the third rail on the elevated structure, the circuit with the surface rails was completed," reported the *New York World*, "and the firemen got a shock that sent them sprawling and their hose lines twisting and squirming like great snakes, spouting water, drenching people, flooding the streets." Power to the third rail was finally cut off, and the firemen climbed up to the elevated structure to put out the blaze, but by this time the burning car was consumed.

Nevertheless, by now the advantages of electric operation were all too clear, and the Manhattan finally decided to proceed. On November 21, 1900, a test train equipped with Sprague multiple-unit control and made up of two motor and four trailer cars was

Electrification of the elevated railways brought new hazards from such mishaps as burning fuses and overheated motors. This was the outcome when overheated motors set the motor car of a Brooklyn train ablaze in the station at Atlantic and Flatbush avenues in 1900. Luckily the train's passengers escaped to the station platform, commented the *New York World*, "but the mid-air blaze gave to them and many thousand others one of those delightful experiences that diversify life in Brooklyn Borough." Author's Collection.

operated on the Second Avenue line between 65th and 92nd streets. The results were convincing, and by the following May the Manhattan had awarded a contract to General Electric for the necessary car equipment and power supply installation, while the Westinghouse Electric & Manufacturing Company landed a contract for the generators and other electrical equipment for an enormous new power generating station that would supply what was the largest electrification project yet undertaken anywhere.

Electric operation began on the Second Avenue line on January 9, 1902, with the operation of a special six-car train that carried two hundred guests, including such luminaries as George and Edwin Gould and John D. Rockefeller, over the entire Second Avenue division of the Manhattan. Third Avenue service had been converted to electric operation by the end of March and the suburban Bronx line was converted in July, while electric operation had been extended over the entire Sixth Avenue line by November 2. The last segment of the Manhattan El to begin electric operation was the Ninth Avenue

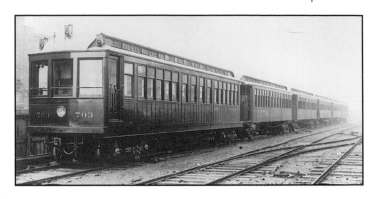

Electric multiple-unit operation got its first test on the Manhattan Railway when this six-car train was operated on the 34th Street El on November 21, 1900. The test train is seen in the 65th Street yard on the Second Avenue line. Lead motor car No. 703 was a steam coach built by Pullman in 1880, motorized and rebuilt with a steel frame and an enclosed motorman's cab. Sprague Library, Electric Railroaders' Association.

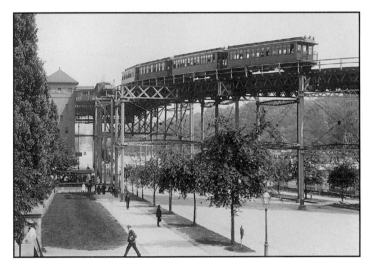

Electrification of the Ninth Avenue El was completed as far north as 155th Street by the end of 1902. A four-car M.U. train rounded the celebrated "Suicide Curve" at 110th Street in this 1904 view. Visible at the left is the 110th Street station and elevator tower that were added in 1903. A. Loeffler, Library of Congress.

This view of M.U. trains on the one-legged El structures along the Bowery dates to 1904, just two years after electrification of the Third Avenue elevated was completed. Four tracks of trolley traffic and horse-drawn traffic filled the wide street below. A. Loeffler, Library of Congress.

A Brooklyn Rapid Transit train paused at the Atlantic Avenue station on the Fifth Avenue Line around 1908. Behind the elevated structure is the Long Island Rail Road's Brooklyn terminal; to the left is the Atlantic Avenue station for the IRT's Brooklyn extension, which opened in 1908. The El train employed the BRT's distinctive convertible cars that were fitted with removable sides for summertime open air riding. Library of Congress (Neg. No. LC-D4-072144).

line, between South Ferry and 53rd Street, in February 1903. The very last steam operated passenger train on the Manhattan system operated over the Sixth Avenue line on April 4, 1903. Electrification of the world's greatest elevated railway system was complete, and it had cost the Manhattan Railway $18 million.

Electrification of the Manhattan had included the conversion of some 500 existing passenger coaches to electric motor cars, as well as the purchase of a hundred new cars; the installation of a 600-volt D.C. third rail system over the entire railroad; and the construction of the new power plant on the East River between 74th and 75th streets that was said to be the largest in the world. This enormous plant was rated at a capacity of 100,000 h.p., and was equipped with 64 500 h.p. Babcock & Wilcox boilers. Eight Allis-Chalmers compound condensing steam engines of 8000 rated and 12,500 maximum horsepower each drove eight Westinghouse generators, each weighing 445½ tons, said to be the largest yet built in America.

Meanwhile, new elevated railway projects were underway in two other American cities. As early as 1879 proposals for elevated railways at Boston had been put before the Massachusetts Legislature. Other proposals followed, and in 1891 the Mayor of Boston and the Governor of Massachusetts jointly appointed a rapid transit commission that was charged with finding a solution to the city's growing transit needs. Their report, issued the following year, proposed a streetcar subway under or near Tremont Street, and elevated lines that would have extended from Charlestown to South Boston, and from Roxbury to Cambridge. The two lines were to be connected at Causeway and Elliot streets in downtown Boston. Bostonians were apparently not too keen to have steam-powered elevateds like those in New York and Chicago, and the commission urged the use of the Meigs monorail system that had been demonstrated at East Cambridge several years earlier.

The principal outcome of the commission's work was an 1894 bill that created the Boston Transit Commission to build the subway, and the Boston Elevated Railway to build an elevated railroad through the congested part of the city that included three main lines reaching Charlestown, Milton, Somerville, Forest Hills, Cambridge, and Jamaica Plain, with branches to Brookline, Everett, Chelsea, South Boston, Brighton, and "other suburban places." The Boston Elevated franchise, granted to Joe V. Meigs and others, authorized

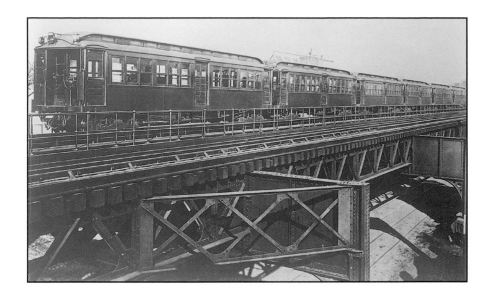

The earliest cars for Boston's Main Line elevated were 150 of these 46-foot Type One wooden cars built over a two-year period from 1899 to 1901 by the Wason, Osgood Bradley, and St. Louis car companies. This six-car train was photographed on the elevated structure some time after the cars had been modified with enclosed platforms and air-operated doors during 1905–06. Robert A. Selle Collection.

A Main Line elevated train rumbled across the Charles River on the Charlestown High Bridge on February 2, 1902. Kevin T. Farrell Collection, from Fred W. Schneider, III.

Designed to facilitate transfer between El trains and surface trolleys, Boston's Main Line elevated terminals were notable early examples of intermodal transportation facilities. This was the line's southern terminal at Dudley Street shortly after it opened on June 10, 1901. Elevated trains looped through the terminal's upper level, which was flanked by two elevated loops for surface cars terminating at the station. Additional platforms for through surface cars were installed at ground level. Library of Congress (Neg. LC-D4-017030).

the building of the elevated road "according to plans or systems shown in patents granted to Joe V. Meigs, or according to such other plans or systems, except the system now in use in New York known as the Manhattan system, as the board of railroads commissioners may approve."

The commission's first effort was the development of America's first subway, a line under Tremont Street for the streetcars that clogged downtown Boston's narrow, congested streets. Work began in March 1895 and the first segment of the subway opened in 1897. Meanwhile, principal stockholders of the West End Street Railway Company, Boston's streetcar operator, had acquired the Meigs franchise and initiated studies of using the new subway in connection with an elevated system. The Legislature was asked to amend the 1894 Act to delete that portion which authorized the Meigs system and prohibited the use of the "Manhattan system." Perhaps the availability of electric power for elevated operation had helped to quiet the opposition to a "New York style" road. In any event, by the time the Tremont Street subway opened in 1897, final routes for the Boston Elevated had been established.

Based in part upon lines proposed in the 1892 report, a planned 4.9-mile Main Line elevated would extend from Sullivan Square in Charlestown to Dudley Street in Roxbury. Main Line trains would operate through central Boston in the Tremont Street streetcar subway, where they would run on separate tracks. The segments between Sullivan Square and North Station, where the line would be linked with the subway, and from a link with the subway at Pleasant Street to Dudley Street, would operate on elevated structures. The plan also included an Atlantic Avenue elevated line that would provide a second route through the downtown area, serving the waterfront area and South Station.

Construction began early in 1899. The Boston Elevated took a very deliberate approach to the procurement of electrical equipment for its car fleet. Three car bodies built by the Wason Car Company were separately equipped with General Electric, Westinghouse, and Sprague multiple-unit equipment, while two Westinghouse-equipped cars were borrowed from Brooklyn's King County elevated. At the conclusion of tests, a total of 97 cars were ordered from Wason, the St. Louis Car Company, and the Osgood Bradley Car Company at Worcester, Mass., all to be equipped with Sprague multiple-unit control, and either Westinghouse or GE motors.

Construction techniques for Philadelphia's Market Street line were typical of elevated railway construction. Two boom cranes mounted on a traveler worked from the completed structure to erect the columns and girders ahead of them. The work was progressing eastward from 39th and Market streets at the time of this fall 1905 photograph. Harold E. Cox Collection.

The Main Line elevated opened on June 10, 1901, serving a total of 12 stations. The two terminals, at Sullivan Square and Dudley, were early examples of what have come to be known as "intermodal" facilities. At the Dudley Street terminal elevated trains looped through an upper level of the terminal, which was flanked by two elevated loops for streetcar lines terminating at the station. Platforms for surface cars operating through the terminal were provided on the lower level. The Sullivan Square terminal was similar except for the absence of a loop for turning the streetcars, which instead terminated at one of 10 upper level tracks. The Atlantic Avenue elevated opened on August 22, with trains operating between the same Sullivan Square and Dudley Street terminals used by the Main Line service.

The Main Line service in particular proved immensely popular, and within months the company was modifying its fare collection and transfer facilities to better accommodate the crowds. Before the end of the year, platforms had been lengthened to permit the lengthening of trains from three to four cars.

Philadelphia, too, had been considering a variety of rapid transit plans. One line, the Quaker City Elevated, had actually started construction in the early 1890s, but was halted almost as soon as the first supporting column was erected in the street. In 1901 a man named John Mack had incorporated companies to build both a network of surface lines and five elevated railways. Union Traction, the existing street railway company,

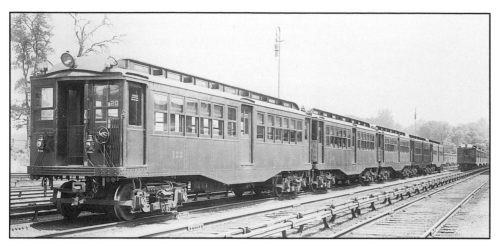

Between 1906 and 1913 the J. G. Brill Company and the Pressed Steel Car Company built 250 of these steel cars for Philadelphia's Market Street elevated. Known as the "Easy Access Car," they had three air-operated doors on each side to speed loading and unloading. This train of Pressed Steel Car units was photographed in the line's 69th Street yards in June 1911. LeRoy O. King, Jr. Collection.

set to work to head off the threat, with the result being formation of a new company—the Philadelphia Rapid Transit Company—which absorbed both the existing Union Traction Company and the various properties set up by Mack. The new PRT quickly set out to build the city's first rapid transit line in the heavily traveled east-west Market Street corridor. The City Council authorized construction of an elevated line in Market Street, but required that it be placed underground east of the Schuylkill River. Work began in April 1903 on the subway east of the Schuylkill River, while a new bridge over the river was begun a few months later. Work began on the elevated structure in August 1905, with the structure erected in two sections, one extending east from 69th Street in Upper Darby to 45th Street, while the second worked east from 45th to the Schuylkill River. At the east end of the line, an elevated structure was erected in Delaware Avenue to reach the terminals of the Delaware River ferries that carried commuters between Camden and Philadelphia. At

The Market Street line's original cars transported Philadelphia commuters for almost a half-century before they were finally replaced by a newer generation of modern cars. A five-car train of the durable steel cars was westbound on the El in May 1951, against a backdrop of the downtown Philadelphia skyline. Robert Foley, from Richard Allman.

Demonstrating the all-weather capability of rail transit, a long train of the Market Street elevated's original Easy Access cars raced into the line's 46th Street station in the midst of a fierce snowstorm in 1947. Jacques L. Singer, Karl P. Then Collection, from Richard L. Allman.

A four-car train eastbound to Frankford had just emerged from the eastern portal of the Market Street subway in May 1956. In the background is
the Ben Franklin Bridge across the Delaware River. At one time, a branch
from the Market Street line at this point took passengers to the Delaware
River ferries. The bridge eventually displaced the ferries, and the branch
ceased operating in 1939. Fred W. Schneider, III.

the western end of the line at 69th Street a major terminal was built to link the elevated trains with suburban and interurban electric railway lines.

The Pressed Steel Car Company of Pittsburgh built
40 steel multiple-unit cars for the line in 1906. Operation of the elevated/subway line began between 69th
Street and 15th Street in downtown Philadelphia in
March 1907 and had been extended over the full route
to the Delaware River ferries by October 1908. By 1910
the line was carrying 29 million passengers annually,
and the rolling stock fleet had been expanded by 60 additional cars. North America's newest elevated railway
system was off to a good start.

By 1908, however, the subway had clearly become
the preferred alternative for urban rapid transit, and
Philadelphia's Market Street line would represent the
last entirely new elevated railway system in North
America. Improvements and some expansion to the existing systems continued for several decades. At New
York the Manhattan Railway was leased in 1903 to the
new Interborough Rapid Transit Company, which was
building the city's new subway system. In Brooklyn,
elevated and subway lines were consolidated under the
Brooklyn Rapid Transit Company, later the Brooklyn-Manhattan Transit Corporation
(BMT), and finally integrated with the remainder of the New York City system in 1940.

Over a period of several decades there would be a number of extensions or modifications to the elevated system as it was integrated with the city's expanding subway network.
During 1913–1916 some $44 million was expended in additions and improvements to add
express tracks and stations to provide additional capacity for the Second, Third, and Ninth
avenues elevated lines. The elevated lines would carry some 374 million passengers in 1921,
one of their busiest years ever, and the capacity was badly needed. The last expansion of
the elevated system came in 1920, when a Webster Avenue extension was completed in the
Bronx, allowing Third Avenue express service all the way to 238th Street. Gradually, however, subways replaced principal sections of the elevated. Some lines were closed, while
other segments were incorporated into the subway network. Major segments of the Sixth
and Second avenue lines had been closed by 1942, following the 1940 unification of New
York's rapid transit systems. Closure of the remaining segment of the Third Avenue line
south of 149th Street on May 12, 1955, brought an end to elevated railway service on Manhattan Island. The Third Avenue El proved to be sorely missed, for the Second Avenue
subway that was promised to take its place remains unbuilt to this day.

The elevated railway fared much better in Chicago, where ambitious plans for new subways
went unfulfilled for many decades. Construction of the four elevated companies continued well
into the new century as planned lines were completed, and later additions continued until as
late as 1924. The four companies were brought together into the consolidated Chicago Elevated
Railroads in 1911, with Chicago utilities magnate Samuel Insull as its chairman and Insull lieu-
tenant Britton I. Budd as president. A full merger of the companies as the Chicago Rapid Transit
Company followed in 1924, with Insull and Budd in the same positions.

At Boston, the Main Line and Atlantic Avenue lines remained the city's only elevated lines,
although Main Line extensions were completed south to Forest Hills in 1916 and north to
Everett in 1919. At Philadelphia the success of the Market Street elevated/subway led to
ambitious plans for new elevated and subway lines. Most never materialized, but one that
did was a Frankford Avenue elevated line that would extend from a connection with the
Market Street line into Northeast Philadelphia. Construction began before World War II but
was interrupted by the war, and the work was not complete and the line opened until 1922.

Despite the advent of the subways, portions of New York's original elevated railways continued to operate until as late as 1955. A southbound local on the IRT's Ninth Avenue El rumbled above Manhattan's Battery Park in 1935. The Ninth Avenue line was abandoned in 1940. Francis J. Goldsmith, Jr., Fred W. Schneider, III, Collection.

Northbound from City Hall to 129th Street over the Second Avenue El, a four-car train approached the Chatham Square station on June 9, 1940. Just two days later the line was shut down north of 60th Street, and the remainder was gone only two years later. James P. Shuman.

It was the very last day for the last of Manhattan's Els as a northbound Third Avenue train pulled away from the platforms at Houston Street on May 12, 1955. Only scattered remnants of the once extensive elevated railways remained as part of New York's subway system. Today, almost a half-century after the Third Avenue line was closed, the Second Avenue subway that was to take its place is yet to be built. Herbert H. Harwood, Jr.

There was little about the elevated roads to endear them to those who lived or worked along the lines. Until they were electrified, the smoke, cinders, and steam of elevated trains soiled clothing, home, and office everywhere they ran. The noise and the violation of privacy that came with trains thundering past second and third floor windows every few minutes must have been close to intolerable. The massive elevated structures blocked light and air from the streets, and the rows of iron columns impeded traffic. Property values were depressed.

Typical of the invective heaped on the elevateds is this passage from a June 15, 1878, issue of *Scientific American*, whose editor, Alfred Ely Beach, may well still have been aggrieved over the defeat of his 1870 pneumatic subway plan:

(Facing page, top)   The Lake and Wells streets Tower 18 on the Chicago "L," at the junction of the North Side and Lake Street divisions with the downtown Loop, has been called the "world's busiest railroad crossing." At one time the tower commonly passed 200 rush-hour trains, made up of 900 to 1000 cars, in a single hour. When a memorable snowstorm in March 1930 disrupted surface traffic, 21,270 elevated cars passed the tower in a 24-hour period. Chicago's elevated lines had been consolidated under common management when these three trains passed the tower in 1919. Fred W. Schneider, III, Collection.

(Facing page, middle)   This was a busy moment at the Indiana Avenue station on the South Side "L" in June 1952. In the center background an inbound train to the Loop approaches the platforms, while at left a single-car Kenwood Branch shuttle waits for passengers. In the foreground, just below the camera, an outbound train waits at the platform. Krambles-Peterson Archive.

(Facing page, bottom)   Contrasting sharply with more usual scenes of the busy Chicago elevated system was the Westchester Branch in the far western suburbs that was built to support a real estate boom that never seemed to come. A single-car train rattled over the lonely branch in May 1947. The Chicago Transit Authority substituted bus service and tore up the line in 1951. Soon afterward the once open fields were filled with homes and apartments as Chicago finally began to spread out to the west. Robert G. Lewis.

When the elevated railways, now in the progress of construction in this city, are completed, four great iron bridges, with numerous branches, will run lengthwise Manhattan Island. Perhaps in the future, after people become habituated to trains thundering over them, to thoroughfares blocked with great iron columns, to the impartial distribution of ashes, oil and sparks upon the heads of pedestrians and on awnings (a couple of the latter were set on fire this way the other day), to the diffusion of dirt into upper windows, to the increased danger of life from runaway horses and the breaking of vehicles against the iron columns, to the darkening of lower stories and shading of the streets so that the same are kept damp long after wet weather has ceased, and to the numerous other accidents and annoyances inherent to this mode of transit, more such bridges will be erected, and we shall have two storied streets. Doubtless steps will be made in second stories on the lofty railway lines, with bridge connections, after the manner which a large fancy-goods dealer on Sixth avenue is already taking measures to put in practice. The business population of some thoroughfares will be troglodytes—dwellers in dark and shaded caverns—and the other portion will be aerial. There will thus be a differentiation, so to speak, the probable results of which students of evolution might profitably, perhaps, speculate over.

Travel on the elevated, too, could be less than pleasant, particularly during the daily two-hour rush periods or "commission hours" when the ten-cent fare was reduced to five cents. This is the way writer James D. McCabe described it in his 1882 *New York by Gaslight*:

During the five-cent hours the trains on all the lines are crowded, the seats, aisles, and even the platforms being filled to their fullest capacity. The station platforms are black with a struggling crowd, each individual of which is striving with all his powers to be the first on the train when it arrives. At such times the jam is dangerous. The seats are usually occupied before the train leaves the end of the line, and the throngs who wait at the way stations rush on board only to find standing room, and sometimes hardly that. Passengers leaving the trains at such stations have literally to fight their way out of the cars, and the stop is so brief that they are often carried one or two stations beyond their destination before they can reach the platform of the car. The conductors crowd as many into a car as can be packed into it during these hours, and the air soon becomes foul, and the danger of contracting contagious or infectious diseases, from being jammed in too closely with all sorts of people, is very great. Trains often start while passengers are in the act of getting on board, and men are frequently dragged some distance before they can be rescued from their perilous positions. The dense throngs on the narrow platforms of the station afford a rich harvest for pickpockets, and a free field for bullies and ruffians. When the platforms are so heavily crowded there is actual danger of being pushed over into the street, or under the wheels of the approaching trains.

Despite the extraordinary intensity of train operations that characterized the busy elevated railways, they enjoyed a remarkably good safety record. In 1901 Chief Engineer George A. Kimball of the Boston Elevated Railway compared 1893–96 accident data for his own company's West End Street Railway with that for New York's Manhattan Railway elevated system, finding that the accident rate for the streetcar system was almost 44 times that for the elevated. In 1916, *Electric Railway Journal* reported that Chicago's elevated system had carried 1.2 billion passengers over the previous eight years without a single fatality.

Everyman's greatest fear in riding the elevated seems to have been that the train might plunge off the structure into the street below. As we have already noted, the builders of New York's first elevated even procured low center of gravity "shad belly" cars to help alleviate such fears. Such accidents were extremely rare, but occasionally they did happen. One early example happened on Chicago's newly electrified Lake Street "L" on June 20, 1896, when a westbound train derailed just west of Rockwell Street, apparently because of ex-

(Top) Judging from this cartoon in a July 1878 issue of *Puck*, the coming of the elevated railway was not happily received everywhere. The opening of the Sixth Avenue line was the occasion for the weekly's displeasure. The lady tied on the iron horse was clearly a reference to the popular play *Mazeppa*, based loosely on the story of a 17th-century Cossack hetman of that name, then running at the Broadway Theater, with actress Fannie Louise Buckingham and her trained steed James Melville in the two roles. Collection of The New-York Historical Society.

(Middle) Employees of the elevated were less than courteous if this depiction by a nineteenth century cartoonist is to be accepted. Then, as now, crowded cars were an inescapable feature of the daily rush hour. New York Public Library.

(Bottom) Another view of the rigors of travel on the New York elevated railways was depicted in this *Puck* cartoon of the period. "So long as one finds conductors, and a public, on the elevated railroad," commented the German caption, "then accidents are inevitable." Author's Collection.

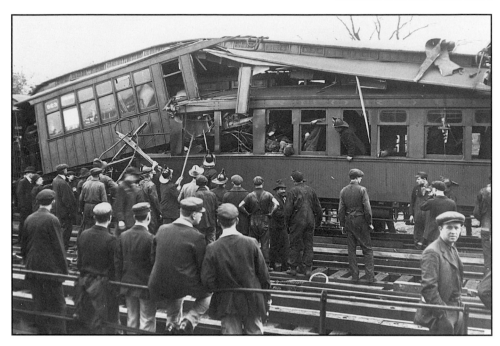

Considering the density of their traffic, accidents on the elevated railways were remarkably rare. This savage telescoping took place when a Bronx Park local collided with an empty train at the 175th Street station on the IRT's Third Avenue El in 1919. Three people were killed. Delaware Public Archives.

cessive speed in a curve. The lead motor car plunged off the 30-foot-high elevated structure, landing on its roof in the street below, while one of the train's two trailer cars hung precariously off the elevated structure. Almost miraculously, there were no fatalities.

A similar accident on the New York El on September 11, 1905, had far more serious consequences when a fast-moving southbound train derailed in a sharp curve at Ninth Avenue and 53rd Street. The first car of the three-car train stayed on the rails, but the second car, packed with an estimated 75 to 100 passengers, overturned and fell into the street below. The roof of the overturned car was ruptured as it overturned, and some of its passengers fell to the ground beneath the falling car. The third car was thrown part way off the elevated structure and struck a dwelling at the corner of Ninth Avenue and 53rd Street. Most of its passengers escaped by crawling into the house through a second story window. The trucks of derailed cars had fouled the third rail, and the resulting electrical explosion and fire added to the chaos of the scene. All told, 14 passengers lost their lives and 50 or more were seriously injured. The train's motorman escaped uninjured and fled the scene.

In a much more recent accident of this type on February 4, 1977, two trains collided at the Wabash-Lake curve on the Chicago Loop, sending two cars toppling off the structure into the street below, killing 11 and injuring 183 passengers.

Despite their many shortcomings, it was also possible to find much to appreciate in these remarkable elevated railways. New Yorkers and Chicagoans took great pride in their wonderful overhead trains that made traveling around their great cities so much easier. The fussy Victorian details and decorative work of the elevated stations brought a touch of elegance into everyday lives. Above all, the El could be a pleasure to ride. The subway rider rode in perpetual darkness, while the surface car passenger traveled in the midst of the clamor and uproar of crowded city streets. The elevated passenger rode above it all, amidst fresh air and sunlight, rewarded by endlessly changing views of the great city skyline. New York writer McCabe recommended the El as the best way to see the city:

The following trip, which may be made within three hours, will show the visitor more of the great city than can be seen in two days by any other means: Take the Third avenue line at the City Hall and ride to 130th street—the Harlem river. It is but a step from the station to the landing of the East river steamers. Embark on one of these and ride to the end of the route, at Peck Slip, near the Fulton Ferry, on the East river. The sail down the river is superb. A short walk along South street, from Peck Slip, brings the traveler to the terminus of the West Side Elevated Road at the South Ferry. Take the Ninth avenue line here and ride to 155th street. Return by the Sixth avenue line, and ride to the terminus at Rector street. This leaves out the Second avenue line, but the Third avenue road commands very much the same view, and nothing of importance is lost.

Wherever they ran, the elevated railways represented a highly visible element of the urban landscape, and several generations of artists found inspiration in them. The visual appeal of the steam-powered elevateds, for example, was vividly captured by W. Louis Sonntag, Jr. in his brilliant watercolor, "The Bowery at Night," of 1895. Charles Dana Gibson's fashionable "Gibson Girls" sometimes traveled on the elevated in his sharply drawn pen and ink illustrations for popular magazines. John Sloan, who spent much of his working life as an artist in New York, was long fascinated with the form of the elevated railway, turning to the El as a principal theme in at least a half dozen of his paintings and many more of his etchings. "Ashcan school" artist Edward Hopper captured scenes of life on the elevated in several of his etchings. Artists from a later generation, too, found inspiration in the now aging elevated railways. In such Precisionist works as his 1920 canvas, "Church Street El," elevated tracks and trains were often a key element of Charles Sheeler's dramatically lighted paintings that viewed New York from the bird's-eye viewpoint of tall buildings. New York's Third Avenue elevated turned up as a recurring theme in the paintings and etchings of Reginald Marsh.

The grand vistas of the city seen from the elevated were captured in a splendid etching of 1921 by Edward Hopper, "House Tops." Print Collection, Miriam and Ira D. Wallach Division of Art, Prints and Photographs, The New York Public Library, Astor, Lenox and Tilden Foundations.

Travel on the New York elevated as depicted by Charles Dana Gibson, the incomparable delineator of American womanhood and the creator of the "Gibson Girl." This Gibson drawing, "Fellow Passengers," ran in the December 19, 1903, *Colliers.* Author's Collection.

Artist Reginald Marsh was another who found subject matter for his work in New York's elevated railways. This Marsh etching of 1929 depicted passengers on the Second Avenue elevated line. Library of Congress (LC-USZ62-40355).

In the 1940s, Farm Security Administration–Office of War Information photographers Marjory Collins and John Vachon composed memorable views of the New York and Chicago elevateds.

Sometimes, too, the elevated trains drew supporting film roles. In perhaps the most memorable of all elevated railway film appearances, in the 1933 RKO Radio *King Kong*, the crazed, giant gorilla tore up tracks and smashed a Third Avenue elevated car filled with terror-stricken passengers on his way to the film's famous Empire State Building denouement. Oddly enough, in the classic Henry Fonda jury room drama of 1957, *12 Angry Men*, what a witness saw—or didn't see—through the windows of a passing elevated train was a central element of the story, but the elevated train was never seen. The Academy Award winning *The French Connection* of 1971 featured a dramatic auto-train chase scene on and under a Brooklyn elevated structure. While New York seemed to be the favored venue of filmmakers for subway or elevated scenes, the Chicago elevated finally landed on the wide screen in Warner Brothers' 1993 *The Fugitive*, in which Harrison Ford duked it out with the villain in a shootout onboard a speeding "L" train.

Artist Joseph Pennell spent more than two decades recording the wonders of New York—"The city that inspires me, that I love," he said of it—in a series of memorable etchings. This one depicted the strong structural shapes of the El against a backdrop of towering Manhattan buildings. JOSEPH PENNELL (American, 1857–1926). *The Elevated*, 1921. Etching, W789, 9⅞″ x 7″. Gift of Persis D. Judd and Children, Picker Art Gallery, Colgate University, Hamilton, NY. Acc. No. 1977.60. Photo Credit: Warren Wheeler.

Biographical Profile

Frank J. Sprague.
Virginia State Library
(Neg. 45.3411).

FRANK JULIAN SPRAGUE (1857–1934) was a prolific electrical inventor and first in the pantheon of inventors who developed commercially feasible electric traction in the late nineteenth century. Sprague was born in Milford, Conn., and brought up by an aunt at North Adams, Mass. In 1874 he won appointment to the U.S. Naval Academy, where he developed an intense interest in electricity. Sprague continued his electrical experimentation following his graduation, producing a number of inventions and installing various electrical systems on several ships. In 1882 he was ordered to the British Electrical Exhibition at the Crystal Palace in London, where he was made secretary of the jury testing dynamos and gas engines and produced a voluminous report on the test results—published in full by the Government. While at London, Sprague often rode on the city's pioneer steam-powered underground railway, and began to think seriously of the application of electric power to railway operation, conceiving the idea of using the tracks and an overhead conductor for power supply.

Sprague left the Navy in 1883 to join Thomas Edison as an assistant. Finding Edison uninterested in electric traction, he left a year later to form the Sprague Electric Railway & Motor Company, and to take up the development of his electric railway ideas. He was soon involved in tests with electric power on the Manhattan Railway and with battery-powered streetcars in several cities. In 1887 Sprague landed contracts for the electrification of street railways at St. Joseph, Mo., and Richmond, Va. The St. Joseph installation was a modest one, but the Richmond contract called for what was by far the most important street railway electrification yet attempted anywhere. Sprague's successful completion of the work over the next year made his reputation and launched the electric street railway as a major industry.

Sprague next took up electric operation of elevators, where his work on control systems led to the idea of multiple-unit operation of electric trains that he perfected for Chicago's South Side "L" in 1898. In 1902 he was a member of the Electric Traction Commission that guided electrification the New York Central's lines into the new Grand Central Terminal at New York, then the greatest railroad electrification project yet undertaken anywhere in the world. Sprague remained a prolific inventor throughout his long life. He developed, among other things, an automatic train control system in 1906, depth charges and fuses for the Navy during World War I, and a dual elevator system in 1927. At the time of his death the New York *Herald-Tribune* ranked Sprague with Thomas Edison and Alexander Graham Bell as a "remarkable trio of American inventors who made notable the closing quarter of the last century. Perhaps no three men in all human history have done more to change the daily lives of human kind."

Artist Howard V. Brown captured the drama of New York subway construction for readers of *Scientific American*. The illustration appeared in the July 10, 1915, issue, soon after the Dual Contracts plan of 1913 had set in motion a period of unprecedented subway construction for the city. Author's Collection.

CHAPTER 3

RAPID TRANSIT
GOES UNDERGROUND

We have met here to-day for the purpose of turning over a new page in the
history of New York; for the purpose of marking the advent of a new epoch in
her development. If this new underground railroad that we are about to open
proves as popular and as successful as I confidently expect it to be, it will
only be the first of many more that must ultimately result in giving us an
almost perfect system of interborough communication. When that day arrives
borough boundaries will be remembered only for administrative purposes,
and New Yorkers, forgetting from what part of the city they come, and only
conscious of the fact that they are the sons of the mightiest metropolis the
world has ever seen, will be actuated by a common hope and united in a
common destiny.

—Mayor George B. McClellan
at the opening of the IRT, October 27, 1904

E VEN AS NEW YORK'S elevated railway system grew, there were some New Yorkers
who never gave up the idea that an underground system would provide a far
superior form of rapid transit. The idea went back at least as far as 1849, when Alfred Ely
Beach proposed a Broadway subway in an editorial in his *Scientific American.* In addition
to Beach's pneumatic subway project, which reached the demonstration stage in 1870,
there were no less than half a dozen companies incorporated to build subways at New York,
and many times that number of proposed projects, before the end of the nineteenth century. In almost every case, lack of sufficient capital made it impossible to proceed.

Too, there was always the question of motive power for an underground railroad. Until nearly the end of the century the steam engine was the only workable choice available.
The world's first urban subway, the 4-mile Metropolitan Railway at London, had been
operating ever since 1863 with steam locomotives fitted with equipment to condense the
exhaust steam. The Metropolitan worked satisfactorily, but the steam engine, with all the
smoke, gases, steam, and heat that it produced, was hardly a desirable choice for operation
in a confined space. There were proposals, such as Beach's, for pneumatic operation.
Others espoused some sort of cable propulsion system. DeWitt Clinton Haskin, whose
Hudson Tunnel Railroad Company had begun a tunnel under the Hudson River in 1874,
proposed—somewhat vaguely—that trains would be drawn through his tunnel by specially
designed engines "consuming their own steam and smoke," or run by compressed air.

The City & South London Railway, the world's first electrically powered subway, opened at London in December 1890. This drawing from the November 29, 1890, issue of *Scientific American*, shows the interior of the City & South London's tube-like cars, and a view of a train entering a station. Author's Collection.

By the mid-1890s, however, the development of electric traction finally offered a feasible alternative. The world's first electrically powered subway, the 3.5-mile City & South London Railway at London (England), had been operating successfully with electric locomotives since December 1890, while the development of electric traction equipment for heavy elevated railway service at Chicago over the next several years had clearly established the effectiveness of electric operation for heavy urban rapid transit applications. At last there was a clearly suitable form of motive power for subway operation.

At New York, there was renewed interest in subways as a preferred solution to the city's still-growing need for rapid transit. A new rapid transit act of 1891 had replaced the 1875 act, although the same commissioners were in office. Provided they determined there was a need for construction of a rapid transit railroad, the new Rapid Transit Commission was required to adopt a route and a general plan of construction, to obtain the consent for its construction from local authorities and property holders, to adopt detailed plans for its construction and operation, and to sell the right to construct and operate the railroad to a corporation formed for that purpose. To assist it in this daunting task the commission appointed William E. Worthen as its chief engineer, and a 32-year-old civil engineer, William Barclay Parsons, as deputy chief engineer, thus—in Parsons—bringing into New York subway development the formidable engineering talent that would lay the foundation for the world's greatest subway system.

Within the year, the commission had concluded that a new rapid transit railroad was indeed needed, and that construction of underground roads would be the only adequate solution. Careful study by the engineers had established a route for the new subway extending from the Battery under Broadway to 59th Street, and thence north on the West Side to the city line. At 14th Street the line would turn and follow Fourth and Madison avenues to the Grand Central Depot, and then follow Madison Avenue north to the Harlem River. The lines would have anywhere from two to four tracks. Both double-deck tunnels, each with two tracks, and single-level tunnels were considered for the four-track segments, with the latter chosen as the preferred scheme.

Before the end of 1892 all of the necessary approvals had been obtained from both municipal authorities and property owners, and bids were sought for the franchise to build and operate the subway system. The results were disappointing in the extreme. The costs would be extraordinarily high, and there was simply too much uncertainty about the prospective revenues. No investors were prepared to undertake such a vast project. The only response received was from William N. Amory, who offered a bid of $1000. Amory failed to make a required deposit of $1 million, and his proposal was rejected. With no satisfactory bidder for a subway franchise in sight, the commission decided instead to seek some expansion of the elevated system.

Through much of 1893 the commission attempted to develop agreements with the Manhattan Railway for franchises that would permit extensions of the existing elevated routes and the addition of new routes. No satisfactory agreement could be reached, and the commission had begun the task of laying out independent new elevated routes, which

As New York's Rapid Transit Commission struggled to find the best possible rapid transit solution for the growing city, this cartoon, titled "A Scheme for Rapid Transit Respectfully Submitted to the Commission," was offered—perhaps not altogether seriously—by *Harper's Weekly* in its June 11, 1892, issue. Author's Collection.

it could franchise separately, when an 1894 act of the New York legislature replaced it with a new rapid transit commission. Although the 1891 commission had been unsuccessful in attracting private investors, the detailed work of its engineers in determining the physical conditions that would be encountered would prove invaluable to the city's next effort to build a subway.

While New York struggled unsuccessfully through much of the 1890s to begin a subway system, Boston went ahead and built North America's first subway. By the beginning of the decade, the narrow, crowded streets of downtown Boston had become jammed with streetcar traffic. So severe was the congestion that at times there was an unbroken line of streetcars stretching from Scollay Square to Boylston Street. It was said that the cars were so closely spaced that a man could walk the entire distance on the roofs of streetcars. By 1894, 150,000 passengers a day were being carried on the car lines in Tremont Street. A streetcar subway under or near Tremont Street had been among the recommendations of a rapid transit commission appointed in 1891, and its construction was the first task taken up by the new Boston Transit Commission formed in 1894.

The route selected for the 1.8-mile subway extended under Tremont Street from Pleasant Street to Scollay and Adams squares, and thence via Haymarket Square to a surface terminal opposite the North Union Station, with a branch alongside Boston Common under Boylston Street from Tremont to the Public Garden. The subway was built with "cut-and-cover" construction, with a temporary roadway surface erected over the excavation until the work was complete and a permanent surface restored. Some sections of the subway were built with arch sections, with a concrete base and side walls and a brick arch, while others, where the subway was close to the surface, were constructed by a system of steel columns and girders, with short brick arches spanning between the roof beams.

The construction of Boston's new cut-and-cover streetcar subway under Tremont Street was depicted in this illustration from the August 31, 1895, issue of *Scientific American*, which showed the intense street railway congestion the subway was designed to solve. In the background can be seen Boston's landmark Park Street Church. Author's Collection.

A speculative view of one of the completed stations in the Tremont Street subway was depicted in another illustration from the August 31, 1895, *Scientific American*. Author's Collection.

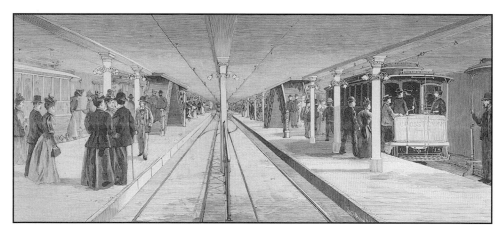

Excavation for the subway and its Park Street station were well along when this view was made along the east side of Boston Common, facing north toward the Park Street Church. The Society for the Preservation of New England Antiquities (Neg. BTC 548).

As planning progressed for New York's great new subway, the popular weeklies offered their readers speculative illustration of what the new system might look like. This drawing by W. Louis Sontag from the February 6, 1897, *Harper's Weekly*, depicts the line's proposed Manhattan Valley Viaduct in a view to the south along the Boulevard from 129th Street. Author's Collection.

The commission wasted no time. Construction bids were opened on March 20, 1895, and the first work started only eight days later when John Crocker, chairman of the Transit Commission, turned the first shovel of earth. Massachusetts Governor Frederick T. Greenhalge was on hand for the occasion, although newspaper accounts said that he just happened to be walking by. Once started, the work proceeded rapidly, but not without a few problems. Opponents of the project filed suit, claiming—unsuccessfully--that the construction violated the Fourteenth Amendment. The need for removal of trees in Boston Common was a contentious issue, and the builders were obliged to carefully remove and replant a number of large trees. The old Central Burying Ground along the Common on Boylston Street was disturbed by the work, and the bones of some 910 persons were removed and reinterred elsewhere in the burial ground. On March 4, 1897, there was a massive explosion of illuminating gas leaking into the excavation at the corner of Tremont and Boylston streets. Ten people were killed and many others injured, and two streetcars were destroyed.

By August 30, 1897, the West End Street Railway was able to begin training runs in the subway, and an initial section between the Public Garden and the Park Street station opened to the public on September 1, 1897. The new subway was an immediate success, with the number of first day riders estimated to be anywhere from 60,000 to 250,000. It was another year, however, before the entire subway was open for regular service. Boston's pioneer streetcar subway became a full-fledged rapid transit subway in 1901, when Main Line elevated trains began using the subway, usurping two outer tracks that had originally been intended for streetcar operation.

Meanwhile, New York City tried once again to begin subway construction. On May 22, 1894, New York Governor Roswell P. Flower had signed the act that created a new rapid transit commission for New York City. While many of the provisions of the previous act were retained, an important new provision raised the question of public funding for subway construction. The new commission, having either adopted the old plans or made new ones, and having obtained the necessary consents, was required to submit to the voters at the next general election "the question whether such railway or railways shall be constructed by the city and at the public expense." The city was authorized to issue bonds for the project up to a limit of $50 million.

The new commission was organized early in June. Alexander E. Orr, a prominent merchant and financier, government reform activist, and newly elected president of the New York Chamber of Commerce, was elected president of the commission, while William Parsons was appointed chief engineer. The question of city ownership and public financing won the approval of voters on the general election ballot in the fall of 1894 by a wide margin. The commission then began a detailed review of the plans developed by the earlier commission. Some changes were made, with the final route selected beginning at a loop at the Battery and passing under Broadway to 59th Street, thence under the Boulevard to 124th Street, with a viaduct between 124th and 134th streets, and under the Boulevard again to 185th Street. There would also be a loop at City Hall and a connection to the Brooklyn Bridge. A second route would diverge from this line at 14th Street and run under Fourth and Park avenues to 98th Street, and then across the Harlem River by viaduct to 146th Street in the Bronx. The West Side line would have four tracks from Broadway and Park Place to 135th Street, while the East Side line would be four-tracked between Union Square and Grand Central Station. The system would have two tracks everywhere else.

No previous rapid transit project for Manhattan had been easily or quickly realized, and this one would be no different. While the commission was able to obtain the necessary approval of local authorities for the work, it was unsuccessful in seeking the consent of property owners. Under the Rapid Transit Act this made necessary the alternate consent of the New York Supreme Court. The court first refused to consider the matter at all, and finally took the matter up only when its order refusing to hear the case was reversed by the Court of Appeals. In March 1896 a commission appointed by the Supreme Court to review the project recommended that the subway should be built, but still the Court refused to act. The judges apparently had a number of concerns, among them that the planned system would not provide adequate rapid transit on a city-wide basis, and that the city could ill afford the huge expenditure, but principally there seemed to be a belief that the line should not be built under Broadway, particularly if it did not extend from one end of the city to the other.

Next, an action was brought in the Supreme Court to prevent the city from proceeding with the subway on the grounds that the 1894 act was unconstitutional. This was decided in favor of the city, while the Rapid Transit Commission revised its plans to overcome the Court's objections.

In the end, the commission came up with still another route for the subway. As it was finally worked out, the subway would extend from Broadway and Park Row to Center Street, Elm Street, and Lafayette Place, and then follow Fourth and Park avenues to Grand Central Station at 42nd Street. The subway then turned west to follow 42nd Street to Broadway, where it turned north in Broadway to 59th Street and then continued in the Boulevard to 124th Street. The line was to be built on a viaduct between 124th and 134th streets, and would then continue in subway under the Boulevard and Eleventh Avenue to 190th Street and then under private property and several streets to a terminal near the New York Central's Kingsbridge station. The plans provided for a loop at City Hall, and tracks and connections to the Post Office and Grand Central Station.

In order to meet the cost conditions imposed by the Court, the commission had abandoned any plans for an East Side subway from Grand Central to the Harlem River. Instead, a second planned line was to branch from the first at 103rd Street to tunnel under Central Park to the intersection of Lenox Avenue and 110th Street, where it would turn north to follow Lenox Avenue to 140th Street, and then under the Harlem River to 149th Street and River Avenue. The subway would then follow 149th Street to Westchester Avenue, where it would continue on viaduct along Westchester, Southern Boulevard, and Boston Road to a terminal at Bronx Park.

The subway was to be double track between Park Row and City Hall, with four tracks all the way from City Hall to 103rd Street. Both routes would be double track north of 103rd. Except where required by special conditions, all tracks were to be on the same level. All of this could be built for an estimated $35 million, well within the bonding level authorized by the Rapid Transit Act, and it substantially satisfied the Supreme Court's other concerns by providing a system that extended the full length of the city, while avoiding the use of Broadway in its most congested area below 34th Street.

The commission's plan was back before the Supreme Court by mid-1897, a commission appointed by the Court recommended approval, and the Court agreed. But there were still more problems to come. "No sooner was one obstacle surmounted than another, perhaps more formidable, was presented," commented the Chamber of Commerce of the State of New York in a 1905 account of the city's effort to develop rapid transit.

The Supreme Court insisted upon liability bond conditions for the builder and operator of the road that seemed prohibitive. The Metropolitan Railway Company, the elevated railroad operator, proposed that it be given new franchises for surface lines and additional elevated lines that would enable it to meet the city's rapid transit needs. Under the Greater New York Charter, which annexed Kings, Richmond, and part of Queens counties to Manhattan and the Bronx on January 1, 1898, the city was obliged to assume the indebtedness of the annexed territory, casting in doubt its ability to incur the debt for the subway. There were grave doubts that anyone would be willing to assume the monumental task of building and operating the subway. The Manhattan Railway declined, as did the Metropolitan Street Railway interests. Both the New York Central and the New Haven railroads were approached, but neither was willing to consider the task. Somewhat earlier Chauncey M. Depew, president of the New York Central & Hudson River and a noted after-dinner speaker and wit, had commented, "Americans do not like to go under ground until they are dead."

Despite all of the uncertainties, the commission proceeded with the work of preparing a contract for the construction and operation of the road. This was complete by the end of March 1898, and there the project stalled for more than a year. But gradually the problems were worked out. When offered new franchises under terms acceptable to the Rapid Transit Commission, the Manhattan Railway declined. The city's debt limit problem was resolved through increases in property valuations, and a more suitable bonding limit was established. Finally, after some modifications required by the city's corporation counsel, the contract was approved by the city on October 11, 1899.

It was a complex and demanding contract. The city, on its part, was obliged to provide the right-of-way required for the subway and terminals, and to pay up to $35 million for its construction, with additional payments of up to $1.75 million for terminal construction and $1 million for property acquisition for stations. The successful contractor would be required to construct and fully equip the subway on the routes and in conformance with the general plans of the Rapid Transit Commission, put the road into operation, and then operate and maintain it under a 50-year lease from the city, with annual lease payments equal to the city's annual interest on its construction bonds, plus as much as one percent of the total value of the city's bonds. The minimum average speed of trains was specified, stops included (local trains not less than 14 mph and express trains not less than 30 mph), 24-hour operation was required, and the contractor was obliged to provide clean stations, with sanitary toilet facilities, and good drinking water. Stations and cars were to be heated and lighted so that passengers could comfortably read, and so on, all for a fare of no more than five cents. It was a very demanding contract.

At long last New York was ready to begin construction of what would become the world's greatest subway system, and bids were invited in November 1899. To assure that a subway could be built without exceeding the city's $35 million debt limitation, contractors were asked to bid on four sections of the subway, with the Rapid Transit Commission reserving the right to award contracts for separate sections, beginning with the first, at intervals of not more than a year.

There were just two bids to be opened when the commissioners gathered at their office at noon on January 15, 1900. New York contractor John B. McDonald bid a total of $35 million for all four sections, while a second New York contractor, Andrew Onderdonk, bid a total of $39.3 million for the four sections. The commission quickly determined that the award should go to McDonald. The Irish-born contractor seemed the right man for the job. McDonald had more than 30 years of construction experience, much of it in major railroad projects. Perhaps the most notable—and relevant—of these was the construction of the Baltimore & Ohio's belt railroad at Baltimore, which included a long tunnel under Howard Street in the city center.

Just as all seemed in readiness to execute a contract and begin work, disappointment loomed once again. McDonald, it seems, had not yet made arrangements to secure the substantial capital that would be required to carry out the contract, and he was obliged to post a $1 million bond, with a later requirement for a $5 million construction bond. For New York's financial market there was too much uncertainty about the eventual earning power of a subway, and McDonald was unable to obtain the financing he needed. Indicative of the skepticism about the costly subway project is a remark attributed to financier Russell Sage: "The most foolish thing ever heard of. New York people will never go into a hole in the ground to ride." Sage, however, was a major stockholder in the Manhattan Elevated, which may have had something to do with his view of a potential competitor.

In any event, it was time for another towering figure to enter the long story of New York subway development.

Just days before the expiration of the time limit for executing a contract, McDonald turned to financier August P. Belmont for assistance. Belmont was just the man to rescue the subway project. Long a proponent of improved rapid transit for the city, Belmont had headed one of the city's earlier rapid transit commissions a decade previous, and he was a

New York financier August P. Belmont stepped in at just the right moment to organize the financing that brought New York's first subway to reality. Library of Congress.

respected and influential figure in New York's financial community and the American representative of the house of Rothschild. Following graduation from Harvard in 1874 he had entered the August Belmont & Company banking house founded by the senior August Belmont, becoming the head of the firm on his father's death in 1890.

Belmont promptly developed and took to the commission a plan for the incorporation of a new company that would back the contractor by providing the required security, furnishing the required capital, and overseeing the entire undertaking. The commission approved the plan and obtained the consent of the Supreme Court to changes in the surety requirements. Belmont's new Rapid Transit Subway Construction Company was quickly organized. Joining Belmont as incorporators of the firm were Charles T. Barney, Walter G. Oakman, William A. Read, and McDonald. The new company quickly completed arrangements for the required bonds, and on February 26, 1900, the subway contract was awarded to McDonald.

Belmont himself took a leading role in the new company as its president and executive head, organizing the company, assembling the staff of engineers needed to direct the construction, supervising the award of subcontracts, and—most importantly—completing the financial arrangements. E. P. Bryan, vice president and general manager of the Terminal Railroad Association at St. Louis was hired to plan the operation of the completed system as the building and equipment of the road progressed.

Within weeks all was in readiness, and on "Tunnel Day," March 24, 1900, a huge crowd gathered opposite City Hall at City Hall Park for the ceremonial start of the work. Two bands played, New York Mayor Robert A. Van Wyck and Rapid Transit Commission Presi-

A ceremonial groundbreaking at Bleeker and Greene streets on March 24, 1900, marked the start to Interborough Rapid Transit subway construction. Chief engineer William Barclay Parsons wielded a pick as other officials waited their turn. New York Transit Museum Archives, Brooklyn.

dent Orr made speeches, and then the mayor turned a ceremonial first shovel of dirt with a sterling silver shovel made by Tiffany's, playfully emptying it into his silk hat. There were still more speeches and a commemorative bronze tablet was installed in the sidewalk in front of City Hall. The great work finally was underway.

General plans for the work had already been completed under the direction of Chief Engineer Parsons. In order to permit both express and local service, the most heavily traveled section of the subway between lower and mid-town Manhattan was planned for four tracks. Wherever possible, a shallow "cut-and-cover" tunnel as close to the street surface as possible was used, with a flat roof to avoid the loss of headroom required by an arch. At other locations deep tunnels were excavated. In order to avoid interference with the Fourth Avenue streetcar tunnel of the Metropolitan Railway north of 33rd Street, the four-track subway was planned as two separate two-track tunnels, one on each side and below the streetcar tunnel. Elevated viaducts were planned to carry the West Side line across the Manhattan Valley between 122nd and 135th streets on the upper West Side, and north of Fort George on the West Side and north of Third Avenue on the East Side. Altogether, the planned line included 10.46 miles of cut-and-cover construction, 4.55 miles of tunneling, and 5.8 miles of viaduct.

The typical construction for the shallow cut-and-cover sections employed a concrete base slab overlaid with waterproofing material and a second slab that supported the track and column foundations. Rows of steel columns every five feet at each side of the tunnel and between tracks supported transverse roof beams. Concrete arches between the "I" beam side columns and roof beams formed the sides and roof of the rectangular tunnel. An outside layer of concrete or brick protected waterproofing material on the sides and roof. At some locations a reinforced concrete roof slab was substituted for steel beam roof construction.

Semicircular concrete arches were typically used at locations where the line was tunneled, some of these being wide enough to accommodate three tracks. For the East Side

Almost everywhere, Manhattan's hard rock lay in the path of the IRT subway builders. Seen here is excavation for the subway in Broadway, between 119th and 120th streets, on December 21, 1900. New York Transit Museum Archives, Brooklyn (Neg. X8-654).

line's underwater crossing of the Harlem River, the engineers planned twin tubes 16 feet in diameter and made of bolted cast iron segments.

Construction of the elevated sections of the road was similar to earlier elevated railway structures, except for a sturdier design that was required to carry the subway's planned 50-ton motor cars. A novel feature of the massive, 2174-foot-long viaduct that carried the West Side line across the Manhattan Valley was the graceful, 168½ foot two-hinged steel arch that carried both tracks and station platforms over Manhattan Street.

Actual construction work began just two days after the ceremonial ground breaking with a start to some required sewer relocation in Bleecker Street. Little work was done in that first year on the section of line below 59th Street because of modifications being made to the plans, but work was underway on the remainder of the system well before the end of 1900.

Everywhere the engineers and builders faced extraordinarily difficult construction problems. Water and gas mains, sewers, steam lines, pneumatic tubes, and electrical conduits buried under the city streets had to be replaced, relocated, or temporarily supported during construction. Sewers were a particularly difficult problem, requiring the construction of more than 12 miles of new sewer for an almost complete reconstruction of the system along the subway route. Between the General Post Office at Park Row and 28th Street a system of pneumatic mail tubes had to be carefully supported to avoid disrupting postal service.

Shafts of sunlight filtered through the planking of the temporary roadway above as the subway tunnel was cut and blasted out of Manhattan's hard rock in 42nd Street west of Fifth Avenue on April 14, 1902. New York Transit Museum Archives, Brooklyn (Neg. X8-492 (B)).

Loose and unstable rock required the tunnelers to erect supporting timbers for the tunnel arch as they drilled a deep subway tunnel along Broadway at 151st Street. The photograph dates to May 19, 1903. New York Transit Museum Archives, Brooklyn (Neg. X8-686).

Almost all of the 10 miles of cut-and-cover subway construction required measures to keep the affected streets at least partially open to traffic. Typically, this was done by building the subway tunnel in sections. For the five-track section along busy 42nd Street, for example, the contractors first excavated a 30-foot wide trench on the south side of the street and constructed the tunnel for two tracks. At 50-foot intervals, transverse tunnels were driven toward the north side of the street, just above the level of the future tunnel roof. These transverse tunnels were then connected by a tunnel driven parallel to the line of the subway, and just outside the line of the fourth track. Earth and rock in all of these tunnels was then excavated to their final depth. A concrete foundation was placed and steel columns erected in the parallel tunnel, ready to carry the tunnel roof. The earth between the transverse tunnels was then excavated to the level of the subway roof, with poling boards and struts supporting the material above. Following this, the tunnel roof was constructed and the earth and rock below excavated to the full depth of the tunnel.

Careful provision had to be made to protect or underpin the foundations of the tall buildings along the narrow streets of lower Manhattan. At Park Row, where one track of the City Hall loop passed through the pressroom of the old *New York Times* building, the required excavation had to be carried well below the bottom of the building foundations. Steel channel sections driven around the foundations and thoroughly braced prevented any disturbance. Extra heavy girders and foundations were required at 42nd Street and Park Avenue, where the subway passed under the Hotel Belmont. At 42nd Street and Broadway, where the pressroom of the new *Times* building was beneath the subway, the first basement alongside it, and the first floor above it, the columns supporting the building extended right through the Times Square subway station. At Columbus Circle still other special supporting measures were required where the subway passed under one side of the foundations of the 700-ton, 75-foot-high Columbus Monument.

The presence of streetcar tracks in many of the streets followed by the subway added to the construction problems. New York's street railways used an underground conduit system for power collection that was supported by cast iron yokes beneath the street, and this required careful protection during excavation or blasting. At Union Square, where the rock to be blasted came right up to the surface, the tracks were temporarily relocated out

Shield tunneling was required as the subway was drilled down under the East River to Brooklyn. This view at Battery Park on December 6, 1903, shows an erector arm used to install segmental sections of the cast iron tunnel lining. New York Transit Museum Archives, Brooklyn (Neg. X8-742).

This view of IRT construction in 42nd Street at Grand Central Station on June 1, 1903, conveys some idea of the traffic disruption created by cut-and-cover tunneling. Enough of the street has been covered over to permit two lanes of traffic, while most of the remainder has been left open to permit removal of excavated materials and delivery of construction materials. New York Transit Museum Archives, Brooklyn

This great steel arch bridge spanned 168½ feet to carry the IRT's Manhattan Valley Viaduct across Manhattan Street. Station platforms on the bridge were reached by means of escalators. New York Transit Museum Archives, Brooklyn.

of the way. In one long stretch along Broadway between 60th and 104th streets, the street-car tracks and conduit system were carried on temporary timber bridges while the subway was excavated beneath them. At a number of locations supporting columns for elevated railway structures had to be underpinned. At 64th Street and Broadway the El supporting columns were removed entirely and the structure supported by temporary wooden scaffolding until the subway was complete.

Almost everywhere on Manhattan the tunnel excavation required extensive rock excavation. Where deep tunnels were required, they were usually excavated by a top or bottom heading method, working from vertical shafts driven down at intervals. The headings were drilled with percussion drills, usually by a night shift. Blasting was done early in the morning, and a day gang then removed the spoil, which was hauled out to the portals or shafts in mule carts.

Some novel methods were adopted for constructing the tunnel that carried the East Side line under the Harlem River, where the War Department required a 20-foot minimum depth, and allowed no more than half the width of the river be blocked for construction.

A Detroit Publishing Company photographer recorded this typical view of IRT station construction. This was the Brooklyn Bridge station, which had four tracks, with local platforms on the outside, and express platforms on each side between local and express tracks. Library of Congress (Neg. LC-D4-017294).

The 641-foot underwater crossing was made up of two sectional cast-iron tubes, 16 feet in diameter, which were enveloped and lined with concrete. The west section of the crossing was built first. A trench was dredged along the line of the tunnel in the soft bottom material, working platforms of piling and timber erected on each side, and a trussed supporting framework sunk into place over the line of the tunnel, supported by piling. A well-caulked, heavy timber roof was then floated into place and sunk to form the top of a huge timber caisson. Sheet piling driven at the sides and ends completed the structure. Working under air pressure, sandhogs then completed the required excavation and the cast-iron and concrete tubes were put in place.

These ornate kiosks of cast iron and wire glass quickly became a highly visible icon of the Interborough Rapid Transit. This one was at an entrance to the uptown line in City Hall Park. New York Transit Museum Archives, Brooklyn (Neg. X8-367).

The east end of the tunnel was built using a somewhat different procedure, in which sections of the top halves of the cast-iron tunnel shells were erected, their ends closed with steel diaphragms, and covered with concrete to act as the top of a caisson. Timber sheet piling was then driven to complete the caisson, the excavation was carried out under air pressure, and the lower half of the permanent tubes put in place.

New York's great subway was not completed without serious mishap. One of the worst construction accidents occurred on January 27, 1902, when a storage shed containing nearly 600 pounds of dynamite for subway blasting caught fire and exploded. Six were killed and some 125 people injured by the lunch hour explosion at Park Avenue and 41st Street, which severely damaged the nearby Grand Union and Murray Hill hotels, killing a guest and two employees at the latter. The façade of the Manhattan Eye and Ear Hospital was ruined, the 42nd Street front of Grand Central Station seriously damaged, and buildings were damaged and windows broken within a half-mile radius of the blast.

Less than six months later Chief Engineer Parsons narrowly escaped death in a June 17 rock fall in the tunnel not far from the site of the January explosion. Together with Assistant Chief Engineer George S. Rice and Major Ira A. Shaler, the subcontractor for the section of line, Parsons was inspecting a section of tunnel at 39th Street and Park Avenue that had not yet been timbered. Shaler had just stepped out from under a timber brace for a closer look at a section of rotten rock when a thousand-pound boulder fell from the tunnel roof. Parsons and Rice escaped without injury, but Shaler's neck was broken and he died 11 days later.

By the time of his death, the unfortunate Shaler had been dubbed the "hoodoo" contractor. He had already been ruined financially, it was said, by the suits filed against him as a result of the January explosion, and had been indicted for manslaughter by a grand jury. A major fire at the 71st Regiment Armory and Park Avenue Hotel late in February, while not connected to the subway work, had seriously impeded the work, with further financial loss to the contractor. On March 4 stratified and rotten rock in a section of tunnel along Park Avenue between 37th and 38th streets had collapsed under four houses, with damages estimated at $100,000.

Another rock fall the following year proved to be the single worst construction accident of the entire subway project. This one occurred on the upper West Side, where the long double-track tunnel from 157th Street to Fort George was being blasted through schist of a particularly dangerous and unstable nature. The site of the accident at 195th Street and St. Nicholas Avenue, where the tunnel was about 110 feet below the surface, was one of the deepest points on the entire subway. Late on the evening of October 24, 1903, about 10 minutes after three blasts had been set off, a work gang of 22 men moved in to begin clearing the blasted rock from the tunnel. Just as they reached the blast site a mass of rock estimated at 300 tons fell from the roof of the tunnel. Fourteen men were caught in the collapse; 10 were killed and the other four seriously injured.

Hardly had the contract been awarded for New York's first subway than the Rapid Transit Commission took up consideration of an extension from Manhattan into Brooklyn. All necessary approvals of the route and general plan for the extension had been secured by January 1902, and bids were received the following July. The Brooklyn Rapid Transit Company offered to do the work for $7 million for subway construction and another million for terminals. The Rapid Transit Subway Construction Company submitted two bids, both offering to build the terminals for $1 million, and one offering to complete the extension for only $2 million, while the second offered to build the Brooklyn extension, plus an extension of the original system from 42nd Street south in Broadway to Union Square, for $3 million. The lowest bid, without the Union Square extension, was accepted, and construction began on November 8, 1902.

The 3-mile extension began at a junction with the original subway near Broadway and Park Row and extended south to the Battery, at the southern tip of Manhattan. The line then tunneled under the East River to Brooklyn, continuing under Joralemon and Fulton streets and Flatbush Avenue to a connection with the Long Island Rail Road terminal at Atlantic Avenue. Cut-and-cover construction of the subway on Manhattan and in Brooklyn was similar to the original subway. The East River crossing employed two 6544-foot cast-iron tubes 15½ feet in diameter and lined with concrete. These were drilled through hard rock under compressed air pressure from the Manhattan side to the middle of the river, while four hydraulic shields were used to drive the tunnels through sand and silt on the Brooklyn side.

Express stations were located on the four-track section of the subway between City Hall and 96th Street at intervals of about 1½ miles, while local stations were provided at intervals of about a quarter mile. Typically, the express stations had two island platforms located between the express and local tracks, one for uptown and one for downtown traffic, while local station platforms were located outside the tracks, alongside the local tracks. Station floors were of concrete; the walls were finished with a base of buff Norman brick below a glass or glazed tile surface and a faience or terra cotta cornice. Ceilings were either arched between the supporting beams and girders, or flat surfaces, separated by wide ornamental mouldings into panels, which were decorated with narrow mouldings and rosettes.

Different decorative treatments and colors were used at each station. Terra cotta plaques displayed the number of intersecting streets or the initial letter of the street name. Sixteen of them had special decorations worked into the design. At Astor Place a beaver bas-relief suggested the fur trading origins of the Astor family fortune. Grand Central Station had a mosaic steam locomotive, while Fulton Street had a bas-relief of Robert Fulton's steamship *Clermont*. A mosaic design at the Columbus Circle station depicted the navigator's caravel *Santa Maria*, while one at the 116th Street station incorporated the seal of Columbia University. At the City Hall station, which was located on a single-track loop at the south end of the line, the arch of the tunnel section was continued through the station with an ornate arched ceiling of terra cotta tile vaults. Among the most distinctive features of the subway was the elegant design of the cast iron and wire glass kiosks that enclosed the entrances to underground stations.

In the spring of 1902, when subway construction was well in hand, August Belmont organized a second company, the Interborough Rapid Transit Company, which would take on responsibility for the equipment and operation of the road. Belmont himself became president and active executive head of the new IRT. Other key officials included E. P. Bryan as vice president and Frank Hedley as general superintendent, and a large engineering staff headed by S. L. F. Deyo was assembled to deal with the requirements of electrical equipment, mechanical installations, cars, and the signal system.

The power supply to the subway came from an enormous generating plant adjacent to the Hudson River in the block bounded by 58th and 59th streets and Eleventh and Twelfth avenues. Five generating sections, with room for two more, were each outfitted with 12 coal-fired boilers, two engines, and all necessary supporting equipment, driving a 5,000-kilowatt alternating current generator. Capable of producing 100,000 horsepower, it was said to be the largest electrical plant ever built. High-voltage alternating current was supplied to eight

Easily the most elegant of the IRT stations was at City Hall, where the subway curved through the station on a loop track. Handsome tiled arches spanned over the track and platforms, while the walls were finished in Norman brick. New York Transit Museum Archives, Brooklyn (Neg. X8-481).

The City Hall ticket booth was of varnished oak, with bronze window grills and fittings. Library of Congress (Neg. LC-D4-017292).

This enormous IRT power plant occupied an entire city block between 58th and 59th streets and Eleventh and Twelfth avenues. Capable of producing 100,000 horsepower, it was said to be the largest electrical plant ever built. Sprague Library, Electric Railroaders' Association.

substations, where rotary converters produced the 625-volt D.C. distributed to the third-rail power supply. An elaborate installation of electro-pneumatic automatic block signals and interlocking was installed on all of the main operating lines of the subway, with automatic train stop "trippers" at all block signals and many interlocking signals that automatically applied brakes if a red signal was overrun.

Cars for the road were designed for multiple-unit operation in trains of both motor and trailer cars. Although the IRT would have preferred an all-steel car, the car building industry was not yet ready to take on such an order, and the company's first 500 cars were a composite wood and steel design. Interior accommodations were comparable to elevated railway equipment of the time, with a combination of longitudinal and transverse seating upholstered in durable rattan and roller shades on each window. Interiors were finished in paneled wood, with glossy white ceilings. The exterior finish was Tuscan Red with burnt orange trim.

The IRT's contract with the city permitted it to provide "additional conveniences" for passengers willing to pay an extra charge on not more than one car per train. In addition to testing various design features for the production cars, two sample cars—the *August Belmont* and the *John B. McDonald*—assembled by the Wason Manufacturing Company at Springfield, Mass., in 1902 were fitted with different styles of seats, ornate lighting fixtures, ceilings, and ventilation arrangements for a possible "first class" service. In the end, the company decided against an extra fare service, and the two cars were assigned to other uses.

Even with 500 composite cars on the way, the Interborough continued its search for an all-steel car. The Pennsylvania Railroad's shops at Altoona, Pa., completed a prototype steel car in 1902, and some 200 production cars were soon under construction at the Pressed Steel Car Company. This equipment proved highly successful, and all subsequent IRT car orders would be for all-steel equipment.

New York's grand new subway was ready for business on October 27, 1904, and the city marked the occasion with both solemn ceremony and raucous celebration. Long before noon that day a huge crowd had gathered in the park opposite the flag-bedecked City Hall. At 1 p.m. the mayor, board of aldermen, rapid transit commission, and numerous other dignitaries and guests gathered in the aldermanic chambers for celebratory speeches. *The World*, an ardent and long-time subway advocate, had arranged for a noisy salute to mark the start of the first official train. At 2 p.m., the planned departure time, factory and power plant whistles blew, salutes were fired, church bells chimed; and all the way from the Battery to Harlem, steamships, ferries, and tugs in the Hudson and East rivers sounded their whistles. It turned out to be a bit premature, for it was another half hour before the speeches wound up. Finally, the silk-hatted procession descended to City Hall station to board the first train as the crowd cheered. At exactly 2:35:30 p.m., Mayor George B. McClellan himself started the first train out of City Hall station with a silver controller handle presented by August Belmont, enjoying the experience so much that he stayed at the post until the train reached Broadway and 103rd Street.

Some 15,000 invited guests rode the official first trains that afternoon, and then at 7 p.m. the stations were thrown open to the paying public. Huge crowds had gathered at every station waiting to board the trains. An unusually large crowd at the 145th street terminal of the line grew so unruly that police were called out from seven stations to maintain order. "Hats were broken and coats torn off and the excitement was great," reported the *New York Herald*. By midnight, the next day's *Times* estimated, 150,000 people had traveled on

October 27, 1904, opening day for the IRT subway, was a day of exuberant celebration in New York. This was the crowd gathered at festively decorated City Hall for the opening ceremonies. New York Transit Museum Archives, Brooklyn (Neg. X8-827).

TO-DAY

Using a silver controller handle provided by August Belmont, New York's Mayor George B. McClellan piloted the official first train out of City Hall station. This drawing of the occasion is from the October 28, 1904, *New York Herald*. Author's Collection.

An exuberant Father Knickerbocker celebrated the opening of the city's first subway in this editorial cartoon from the October 27, 1904, *New York World*. Author's Collection.

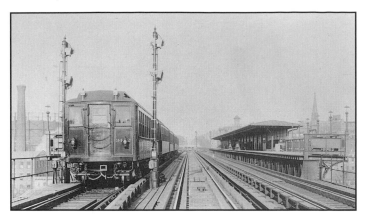

Headed by one of the IRT's pioneering all-steel cars designed by engineer George Gibbs, a southbound train paused at the Manhattan Street station on the Manhattan Valley Viaduct on the upper west side. Francis J. Goldsmith, Jr., Collection, from Fred W. Schneider, III.

the new subway. The first man to give up his seat to a woman on the New York subway, according to the *Times*, was F. B. Shipley of Philadelphia, a guest on the official train. The woman was good looking, but Mr. Shipley said that made no difference—in Philadelphia everybody was polite. An unidentified guest on the first train became the first person to ask for a transfer as the train passed through the Spring Street station. And that evening Henry Barrett of West 46th Street became the first pickpocket victim on the subway, having been relieved of his $500 diamond horseshoe pin at the 28th Street station just three minutes after the subway opened to the general public.

The new IRT got off to a good start. Despite the size of the crowds there were no major problems. On Friday, October 28, the subway's first full day of operation, some 350,000 passengers rode the trains, and the following Sunday 500,000 turned up at the turnstiles to try out their new rapid transit.

New York's new subway really was an occasion for celebration, for there was nothing like it anywhere. The IRT was larger and grander than the London underground, the Paris Métropolitain, or Boston's streetcar subway. It was a technological triumph as well, providing a system of unprecedented performance and capacity, and its builders had pioneered subway design and construction practices in a congested, complex urban environment that—in large measure—are still followed today.

Composer H. J. Lincoln celebrated the IRT opening with his *Subway or Rapid Transit Intermezzo March and Two Step*. New York Transit Museum Archives, Brooklyn (Neg. X8C-9).

Most importantly, the subway—even more than the elevated railways—gave New York City the mobility to grow into the open areas of upper Manhattan, Harlem, the Bronx, and Queens. Mayor McClellan had indeed been right that afternoon. "Without rapid transit Greater New York would be little more than a geographical expression," he said. "It is no exaggeration to say that without interborough communication Greater New York would never have come into being."

A well-dressed crowd boarded an IRT train in a drawing by Charles Bauer titled "Step Lively." Library of Congress.

Before the subway opened, there had been gloomy predictions that the general public would be afraid to ride the subterranean trains. Taking note of rumors that "the fluttering sensation of the eye experienced when a passenger looks out of the car windows at the rows of pillars flitting past caused pain," the *New York Tribune* reassured its readers that there was no truth to the report that riding in the subway caused a new disease of the eye. Any doubts about public acceptance of subway travel, whatever the reasons, were quickly dispelled by the success of the IRT line, which before the end of its first year of operation was carrying over 400,000 passengers a day.

Even before its initial segment opened, the IRT in January 1903 had acquired a 999-year lease on the Manhattan Railway elevated system, making the company the sole Manhattan rapid transit operator. Except for the IRT's one extension under the East River to Brooklyn,

The new IRT subway was one of New York's early twentieth century showplaces, and both the elite and the masses made use of it. For a 1909 periodical, artist G. W. Peters drew this view of theatergoers waiting for a train at Grand Central Station. New York Public Library.

Drilling the first tunnel under the Hudson River proved an arduous undertaking. One of the many setbacks was a flooding of the tunnel on August 20, 1882. This illustration from the September 2, 1882, issue of *Scientific American*, depicts the escape of the tunnel workers. An earlier flooding in 1880 had cost 20 lives. It would be another 26 years before Hudson & Manhattan trains would begin operating through the completed tunnel. Author's Collection.

New York lawyer William Gibbs McAdoo took over the dormant Hudson River tunnel project in 1901 and soon brought it to a successful conclusion. Author's Collection.

the Brooklyn Rapid Transit Company, which operated all Brooklyn elevated and surface lines, enjoyed a similar dominance of Brooklyn rapid transit.

The initial IRT and its Brooklyn extension were only the beginning for a New York subway system that has grown almost continuously ever since. Even before the IRT was complete, another long-dormant New York underground rapid transit project had come back to life. Thirty years earlier DeWitt Clinton Haskin, a Californian who had made his fortune in western railroad construction and mining, had become interested in the use of compressed air caissons for underwater construction after James B. Eads had used the technique to build the piers for his famous steel arch crossing of the Mississippi River at St. Louis. Haskin proposed to use the same technique for underwater tunneling, patenting his "Improvement in the Art of Tunneling" in 1874. The Haskin scheme would use the pressure of compressed air to keep water out while a tunnel was driven under water, eliminating the need for a tunneling shield. Air pressure would hold the roof and walls of the tunnel in place as the tunnel advanced until the permanent tunnel lining could be placed.

Even before he had obtained his patent, Haskin had joined with New York financier Trenor W. Park to incorporate the Hudson River Tunnel Railroad, which was to tunnel from Jersey City to the foot of Morton Street on Manhattan and then across Manhattan to a connection with a proposed underground railway under Broadway. Originally planned for use by all of the railroads terminating on the New Jersey shore of the Hudson, the tunnel was expected to transport 400 passenger and freight trains every 24 hours.

The company struggled for the next 20 years to complete the tunnel. Work began in 1874 and was halted almost immediately by an injunction obtained by the Delaware, Lackawanna & Western, which operated ferry service across the river. Tunneling finally started anew in 1879, only to be brought to a halt again less than a year later when a compressed air blowout flooded the tunnel, drowning 20 tunnel workers. Work was resumed in January 1881 and continued through 1887, with several halts while new funding was sought. New mortgage bonds were floated in England early in 1889 and the British tunneling firm S. Pearson and Son was brought in to resume the work using a Greathead tunneling shield. Work continued until August 1891, when the company again ran out of money with almost 4100 feet of the northernmost of two tubes complete. The shield was left where it was under the river, and the bondholders took over the tunnel and wondered what to do.

A decade later the idea of a tunnel to New Jersey was revived once again, this time by a well-connected New York lawyer who thought there ought to be a more convenient way than the ferries to travel back and forth across the Hudson. William Gibbs McAdoo became aware of the abandoned tunnel project in 1901, and within months incorporated the New York & New Jersey Railroad Company to complete the project, raised the necessary capital, and acquired the abandoned tunnel from the bondholders. Charles M. Jacobs, a British-born tunneling expert who had headed the work a decade previous and who was then the chief engineer for the Pennsylvania Railroad's planned tubes under the Hudson, was brought on to head the work, which was underway

In a dramatic drawing for the September 1907 issue of *The Century Magazine*, artist G. W. Peters depicted the sinking of the foundations for the Hudson & Manhattan's great Hudson Terminal at Fulton and Canal streets in Manhattan. Author's Collection.

A drawing by artist H. M. Pettit showed the complex arrangement of tunnels and underground junctions that linked the Hudson & Manhattan's two Hudson River crossings with the railroad terminals on the New Jersey shore. Hagley Museum and Library (Neg. 76,383).

again by early summer of 1902. The old shield was put back into operation and the north tube was holed through on March 11, 1904, nearly 30 years after it had been begun. That day William McAdoo became the first person to walk from New Jersey to New York under the Hudson River. The south tunnel was drilled with a new shield and was holed through on September 25, 1905.

Meanwhile, McAdoo's company had developed much more extensive plans. These were launched by a separate company, the Hudson & Manhattan Railroad, which would later emerge as the operating company for the entire tunnel enterprise. The H&M planned a second crossing of the Hudson to lower Manhattan, extending from a new terminal at Exchange Place in Jersey City under the river in twin tubes to a new Hudson Terminal at Cortlandt Street in Manhattan, where an underground passage under Dey Street would connect with the new IRT subway at Broadway. Drilling of both tubes for the second crossing began in May 1905.

A planned north-south subway on the New Jersey side would connect both crossings to the passenger terminals of the Lackawanna, Erie, and Pennsylvania railroads, while on the New York side the upper Hudson crossing would be extended by a subway under Morton and Christopher streets and Sixth Avenue to a station at 33rd Street that would be linked with the Pennsylvania Railroad's planned new Pennsylvania Station.

Except for a segment of the original north tunnel, which was lined with brick, all four of the Hudson River tunnels were built with bolted cast-iron segments, forming tubes 15 feet 3 inches in inside diameter. Some particularly complex and difficult construction was required on the New Jersey side at the "Y" junction of the upper Hudson tubes with the north-south tunnels, where four tubes were interwoven on two levels to permit trains from either crossing to reach all three railroad terminals without the need for any crossings at grade.

The new rapid transit system was similar in its technical details to the IRT subway, with a 600-volt D.C. third rail power system that was supplied from a new power generating station in Jersey City. Fifty 48-foot, all-steel multiple unit cars designed by consultant L. B. Stillwell and built by the Pressed Steel Car Company and American Car & Foundry incorporated such advanced features as sliding end and center doors on each side for rapid loading and unloading, and an electric signal system that informed the motorman when all doors were fully closed.

By early 1908 the first two tunnels were ready for service between Hoboken and the station at 19th Street and Sixth Avenue in New York. At 3:30 p.m. on February 25 President Theodore Roosevelt pressed a button on his desk in the White House, signaling the start of an inaugural train from Sixth Avenue to Hoboken. A thousand guests had been invited for the inaugural run, and the train was so crowded that even Edward H. Harriman and Cornelius Vanderbilt III were straphangers. The train paused briefly under the river at a circle of red, white, and blue lights in the tube that marked the New York–New Jersey boundary, while governors Charles Evans Hughes of New York and Franklin Fort of New Jersey shook hands

A smartly uniformed train-man and policeman stood alongside a Hudson & Manhattan train beneath the coffered ceiling of one of the line's stations. Sliding side and end doors and an electric signal that informed the motorman all doors were fully closed were among the advanced features of the all-steel cars designed by L. B. Stillwell. Byron Collection, Museum of the City of New York.

Outbound from New York in June 1955, a Hudson & Manhattan train came to the surface at the tunnel portal west of the Grove Street station. The train was made up of D Class M.U. cars built by the Pressed Steel Car Company in 1911. Bruce Bente, Fred W. Schneider, III, Collection.

to celebrate the new link between the two states, and then continued the ten-and-a-half-minute journey to the Lackawanna Terminal in Hoboken, where a crowd of more than 10,000 waited in the square outside the station for the speeches that followed. The dignitaries celebrated with a dinner at Sherry's restaurant on Fifth Avenue that night, while the crowds queued up in the snow to wait for the opening of the tubes to the general public at midnight.

Both of the lower Hudson tubes were holed through on January 27, 1909, and the second crossing and the splendid new Hudson Terminal were opened on July 19, with the connecting tunnels on the New Jersey side opening a few weeks later. The subway up Sixth Avenue to 33rd Street was completed in 1910.

A 1906 agreement with the Pennsylvania Railroad further expanded the Hudson & Manhattan. The railroad was then building its new Pennsylvania Station in midtown Manhattan, and the rapid transit line agreed to operate a joint service between Hudson Terminal and a junction with the railroad's new line to Penn Station at Manhattan Transfer in Newark, providing travelers on the Pennsylvania a convenient connection to New York's financial district. Both companies provided track and equipment for the new service, which opened to Manhattan Transfer on October 1, 1911, and beyond to Park Place, Newark, the following November 26.

Meanwhile, New York was planning still other subway projects. Some work would begin sooner, but it would not be until 1913 that New York's next big round of subway construction got underway after nearly a decade of debate and mostly false starts.

The Rapid Transit Commission that had built the IRT was succeeded in 1907 by a new Public Service Commis-

Trains from Hudson & Manhattan's mid-town tunnels terminated at 33rd Street, not far from Pennsylvania Station. A train of the line's distinctive arch-windowed cars waited there in 1961. Richard Jay Solomon.

Hard rock tunnelers paused in their work on a Dual Contracts subway on February 25, 1918. New York Transit Museum Archives, Brooklyn (Neg. X8-514).

sion, which developed what was called the Triborough Subway System. This would have included a north-south trunk subway on Manhattan that would extend from South Ferry under Church Street, Broadway, Irving Place, and Lexington Avenue, with two elevated branches into the Bronx, and a crosstown line in downtown Manhattan that would cross the Manhattan Bridge to Brooklyn, where it would be linked with a Fourth Avenue subway already under construction. The Fourth Avenue line would be further extended to reach Bay Ridge and Coney Island. But even with some of the work already underway, the Triborough plan was superseded in 1913 by what became known as the Dual Contracts.

For the better part of two decades, New York's political leaders would debate the merits of municipally owned and operated rapid transit versus the model of private lessee operation of a system built with public funds established by the IRT. For the time being, the question was decided in favor of the latter.

The Dual Contracts were agreements between the city and its two rapid transit operators, the IRT and BRT, that essentially divided the city's planned new subway construction between the two private companies, and gave them favorable leases in return for financing part of the construction costs, as well as providing equipment for the new lines.

It was a subway construction project of unprecedented scale. All told, the projects planned under the Dual Contracts included 110 miles of new subway or elevated lines, comprising some 325 miles of single track main line, enough to double the size of New York's rapid transit system by 1917, when all the work was to be complete. Its $366 million estimated cost was almost equal to that of the Panama Canal, the largest public works project in history. Of this amount the City of New York was to assume $200 million, the IRT $105 million, and the BRT $61 million.

The IRT work under the Dual Contracts included the addition of third tracks on its Second, Third, and Ninth avenue elevated lines to permit rush hour express operation. The original "S" shaped IRT subway was to be divided at 42nd Street, with the lower part being connected with a new four-track Lexington Avenue subway up the East Side to the Harlem River, where it would divide into two separate routes into the Bronx. The upper part of the original route was to be linked to a new Seventh Avenue line, providing a through route up and down the West Side with direct service to the new Pennsylvania Station. The 42nd Street segment between Grand Central and Times Square would become a shuttle. The unused

Steinway Tunnel completed by August Belmont several years earlier under the East River at 42nd Street was to be extended west to Times Square and east to the east end of the Queensborough Bridge, where it would connect with new lines to Astoria and Flushing that would be jointly operated by IRT and BRT. Two branches from the IRT's Brooklyn extension would reach into the residential areas of Brooklyn. These and other extensions would give the IRT, in addition to its elevated lines, four branches into the Bronx linked with two four-track trunk lines extending the length of Manhattan and connected to two East River tunnels to Brooklyn. The subway distance on the IRT from the upper end of the Bronx to the ends of the lines in Brooklyn would be about 26 miles.

The BRT's portion of the Dual Contracts work in Brooklyn gave it various line extensions, two elevated line extensions to Coney Island, and the Fourth Avenue subway already under construction. The BRT gained an important new route into Manhattan, extending from the center of Brooklyn under the East River and then via Broadway and Seventh Avenue to 59th Street, the Queensborough Bridge, and to Astoria and Flushing. An already constructed Centre Street loop on Manhattan was to be linked with the BRT's new East River tunnel and the stub-end terminals of BRT lines across the Brooklyn, Manhattan, and Williamsburg bridges, allowing trains to circulate through Manhattan, arriving on one bridge and leaving by another.

Before very much of the BRT construction contemplated by the Dual Contracts had been completed, the company, caught between New York's rigid commitment to a five-cent subway fare[1] and the roaring inflation in its costs brought on by World War I, entered receivership in 1918. The receivership ended in 1923, when the company was reorganized as the Brooklyn-Manhattan Transit Corporation (BMT).

Construction of the various elements of the Dual Contracts continued through the end of the 1920s, but even before then the advocates of public ownership and operation got their way in what would be a third great wave of New York subway building. Still further expansion of the subways was becoming increasingly urgent, and in August 1922 New York Mayor John F. Hylan, who had long been a dedicated advocate of public ownership and operation of the city's subways, announced a plan for a new independent subway system that would be municipally owned and operated, and would compete directly with the IRT and BRT. Hylan's $575 million scheme included the "recapture" by the city of about a hundred miles of city-financed lines operated by IRT or the BRT, and municipal construction of 126 miles of new lines to serve growing areas of the city that needed better rapid transit. Unlike the existing subways, the new system would be operated by the city itself. Only three months earlier the New York Transit Commission, yet another transit planning agency created by the state government in 1921, had unveiled another, and far less ambitious, plan for 32.5 miles of new subway lines that would be financed by the city but operated by the private companies.

Efforts to reach a compromise between the two proposals went nowhere until 1924, when the state legislature passed an act that gave New York City a new authority to build and control new subways through a Board of Transportation. The new board was quickly formed under the chairmanship of John H. Delaney, a former state public service commissioner. Existing plans were revised and new ones made, and by the end of the year the Board had largely formulated its plans for the construction of 57 route-miles of new subways that were estimated to cost nearly $507 million. The Independent Subway scheme essentially consisted of a huge central loop, from which three tangents extended subway service to every borough of Greater New York except Richmond.[2]

---

1. The depth of this commitment can be illustrated by a statement made by New York Mayor John F. Hylan, who made the five-cent fare a centerpiece of his 1921 campaign for reelection. "My policy," Hylan declared, "has been the preservation of democracy and the retention of the five-cent fare."

2. Separated from the remainder of Greater New York by New York Harbor, the Borough of Richmond got its own modern rapid transit railway in 1925, when the Baltimore & Ohio rebuilt its steam-power subsidiary Staten Island Rapid Transit Railway into a third-rail rapid transit line built to standards virtually identical to those of the New York subway system.

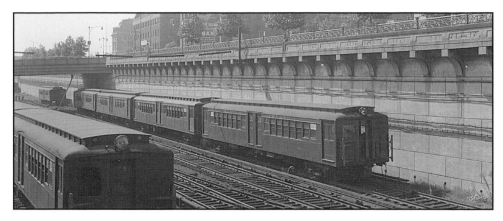

The new central loop was to consist of a crosstown subway in 53rd Street connecting with parallel Sixth and Eighth Avenue lines in midtown Manhattan that would join in lower Manhattan and tunnel under the East River to Brooklyn. From there, the line would loop northward to Queens Plaza and then tunnel under the East River again to connect back to the 53rd Street line. The three extensions off the central loop would include a long line up the West Side to Washington Heights, with a branch tunneled under the Harlem River to the Bronx; a line from Queens Plaza to Jamaica; and a subway in lower Manhattan that would connect with the loop near Houston Street and Sixth Avenue, paralleling the bottom leg of the loop through the East Side and extending under the East River to downtown Brooklyn and then on to a junction with the existing BMT Culver Line to Coney Island, which would be "recaptured" and added to the new Independent system.

Construction of the Eighth Avenue line of the new Independent Subway began with groundbreaking ceremonies on March 14, 1925. By the following year there were said to be ten thousand men at work on subway construction in New York. Most of the Independent system was built by the tried and true cut-and-cover method, varying from the practices of the original IRT construction only in a greater reliance on mechanical equipment than on pick and shovel labor. The planned new system would include six underwater crossings, three under the East River, and one each under the Harlem River and under Newtown Creek and the Gowanus Canal in Brooklyn. Except for about 4 miles of deep earth or rock tunneling, all of the remaining construction was to be cut-and-cover.

Municipal subway operation for New York finally became a reality at midnight on September 10, 1932, when seven-year-old Billy Reilly dropped the first nickel into a turnstile at the 42nd Street station to mark the opening of the new Eighth Avenue subway. Despite the great national depression, construction continued through the 1930s, much of it with the aid of federal funding. With the opening of the Sixth Avenue subway in December 1940, the principal elements of the Independent Subway system had been completed, at a cost of something like $650 million.

By this time, all of New York's subways were publicly owned and operated. After close to two decades of debate and negotiation, agreements were reached under which the city would buy out the IRT and BMT. The New York City Transit System took over operation of the BMT on June 1, 1940, while transfer of the IRT and its leased Manhattan Railway lines followed on June 12.

After a pause in subway construction during World War II, still more extensions were added to the system in the years immediately after the war. By 1954, on the fiftieth anniversary of the opening of the IRT, New York's subway system stood as the greatest anywhere in the world. Since work began on the IRT in 1900, the city had spent over a billion dollars to build 133 route-miles of underground and 72 route-miles of above-ground lines, with anywhere from two to six tracks, and more than 300 stations. Including the still-remaining nineteenth-century elevated railways, the New York City Transit System comprised a

New York finally got its own publicly owned and operated subway on September 10, 1932, when the Eighth Avenue line of the new Independent Subway opened. The year before, a test train of the city's new R1 cars for the IND made a station stop at Eighth Avenue in Brooklyn during a run over the BMT's Sea Beach line. Fred W. Schneider, III, Collection.

The Independent's first line along Eighth Avenue became the route for New York's "A Train" celebrated by Duke Ellington. A northbound A train stopped at the deep 181st Street station in Washington Heights in 1961. Richard Jay Solomon.

Alert to the line ahead, and wearing the traditional pin striped overalls of his occupation, a businesslike IRT motorman stood at the controls of his train. New York Transit Museum Archives, Brooklyn (Neg. X8-206).

total of 241 route-miles and 491 stations, and it transported more than four million passengers every day.

The effect of this extraordinary rapid transit system on the growth of New York City was profound. In the first half of the twentieth century New York's population grew from just over 3.4 million to almost 7.9 million, with almost all of that growth concentrated in the undeveloped areas of the Bronx, Queens, and Brooklyn that subway expansion had made accessible. While the population of Manhattan remained almost unchanged, that of Brooklyn more than doubled to over 2.7 million. The population of the Bronx increased more than sevenfold to more than 1.4 million, while Queens grew to a population of over 1.5 million, more than ten times what it had been in 1900. New York could not have become what it was without the subways.

Once part of the original dogleg IRT route that ran the length of Manhattan, the 42nd Street segment between Grand Central and Times Square became a shuttle after Dual Contracts extensions up Lexington Avenue and down Seventh Avenue converted the configuration to an "H." A mass of rush hour commuters boarded the busy shuttle at Grand Central. New York Transit Museum Archives, Brooklyn (Neg. X8-628).

In a few other major North American cities, too, subways were seen as a solution to their growing transportation problems. Boston, which had opened America's first subway in 1897, completed another under Boston Harbor to East Boston in 1904. Both of these were streetcar subways, but Boston soon had its first bona fide rapid transit subway. Operation of the Boston Elevated Railway's Main Line elevated trains through the Tremont Street trolley tunnel had presented a number of operational problems and limited the subway's utility for streetcar traffic, and the company was soon planning a separate downtown subway under Washington Street for its rapid transit line. Construction of the new tunnel began late in 1904 and it was put into service just four years later.

Within another year work had begun on a second rapid transit line, the Cambridge-Dorchester Subway. An initial 3.2-mile section between Harvard Square in Cambridge and Park Street in downtown Boston opened on March 23, 1912, utilizing two center rapid transit tracks in the handsome new Longfellow Bridge for the Charles River crossing. The subway was extended to Dorchester in several segments, finally reaching Andrew Square in 1918. Another extension a decade later took the line south to Ashmont.

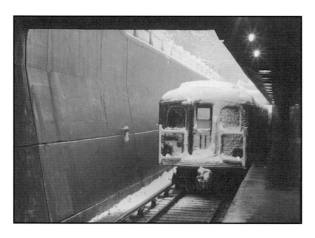

Philadelphia was close behind New York in getting started on subway construction. Work began in April 1903 for the city's first subway, which formed the eastern end of the east-west Market Street rapid transit line. Although the line was elevated elsewhere, the Philadelphia City Council had mandated that any downtown rapid transit line would have to be below ground east of the Schuylkill River. This subway section of the Market Street line included a four-track subway from the river to City Hall, with two tracks to accommodate streetcar lines from West Philadelphia, and a double track subway east of City Hall to Front and Arch streets. A portion of the tunnel was opened for streetcar traffic in 1905, while the Market Street rapid transit line began operation through the tunnel to 15th Street on March 4, 1907, and to 2nd Street on August 3, 1908. Unlike New York's subways, which were built largely with city financing, Philadelphia's first subway was financed entirely by the Philadelphia Rapid Transit Company, the privately owned operator of the city's transit system.

The subway provided reliable service in all weather conditions. Heavy snow was falling as a train of the BMT's durable standard cars entered the Prospect Park station in Brooklyn on the Brighton line. Henry Raudenbush, Richard Jay Solomon Collection.

Philadelphia's second subway, however, was publicly financed. This was a North Broad Street subway that was intended to be the north-south main trunk of an expansive system of subway and elevated lines laid out in a 1910 rapid transit plan developed by A. Merritt Taylor, the city's transit planner. Construction of the four-track subway began in 1915, but work was soon halted by World War I. It was not until 1924 that construction was restarted, delaying completion of the first six-mile segment between Olney Avenue and City Hall until September 1928. Attired in top hat, cutaway coat, and kid gloves, former Mayor W. Freeland Kendrick, who had gotten the project going again, operated the inaugural run out of City Hall station.

(Top) Boston's Cambridge-Dorchester subway came above ground to cross the Charles River on the West Boston Bridge, later known as the Longfellow Bridge. Children frolicked in the foreground as a two-car train of the Boston Elevated Railway's big steel cars headed out over the bridge on the way to Cambridge and Kendall Square in 1913, just a year after the line opened. Bradley H. Clarke Collection.

(Middle) This was the scene in Philadelphia's 8th Street subway station on July 30, 1908, as an assemblage of the city's leading citizens and helmeted police gathered at a dedication party for the subway section of the Market Street elevated subway. Planking was laid to allow the general public to walk through the new tunnel, and service began on August 3, 1908. Harold E. Cox Collection.

(Bottom) It was a festive occasion on September 11, 1915, when Philadelphia broke ground for the City Hall station for its new Broad Street subway. Presiding over the affair were Mayor Rudolph Blankenburg, at left with the shovel, and Director of Transit A. Merritt Taylor, at right with the pick. Unfortunately, it would be another 13 years before the subway finally opened. City of Philadelphia, Fred W. Schneider, III Collection.

In this view of construction in Philadelphia's Broad Street subway extension from South Street to Snyder Avenue, workmen are placing concrete around the track on November 26, 1937. City of Philadelphia, Fred W. Schneider, III Collection.

A second segment of the Broad Street line opened from City Hall to South Street in 1930, while still another southern extension opened to Snyder Avenue on September 18, 1938, extending the Broad Street subway to a total length of just over 8 miles. A 1.5-mile Ridge Avenue spur from the line began operation to 8th and Market streets in December 1932. A further 1.2-mile extension under Locust Street remained incomplete until 1953.

Philadelphia—and neighboring Camden, N.J., across the Delaware River—got another subway on June 7, 1936, when the Delaware River Port Authority opened a new rapid transit line between the two cities over its Delaware River suspension bridge. On the Philadelphia side a new subway connected the bridge line to the two PTC subways at 8th Street and Market, while a second subway on the Camden side extended from the bridge to Broadway.

Chicago, America's second largest city, talked a lot about subways but had trouble getting started. City Engineer John Ericson developed one of the earliest plans for Chicago subways in 1909. Intense surface congestion was severely limiting the capacity of the streetcar lines entering the central business district, while the elevated Loop was already operating at close to its full capacity during the rush hours. Instead of an independent rapid transit system like the New York subway, Ericson's plan proposed subways as a means of reducing street traffic congestion in the Loop by removing both streetcars and the obtrusive elevated structures from the streets of the downtown area. This was to be accomplished with new subways that intercepted both elevated and streetcar lines as they entered the central business district at four terminal stations on the boundaries of what was called the subway zone.

A $40 million first phase of the plan included a north-south subway under Wabash Avenue that was to extend between a terminal at Chicago Avenue and Franklin Street on

A Broad Street subway train paused in the new Walnut-Locust station shortly before it was opened to the public as part of the City Hall-South Street extension of the line on April 20, 1930. Permanent lighting fixtures have not yet been installed in the station. City of Philadelphia, Fred W. Schneider, III Collection.

One of Chicago's earliest subway plans, proposed by City Engineer John Ericson in 1909, would have placed both "L" and surface streetcar traffic below ground in the downtown area. Illustrated here in a drawing from the May 28, 1910, issue of *Scientific American* is the four-track subway under Wabash Avenue that was to carry north-south "L" traffic on the two tracks to the left, and streetcar traffic on the tracks at the right. Chicago's already-existing freight subway is shown below. Author's Collection.

the north and one at 22nd and Dearborn streets on the south. Streetcars would operate on two tracks of the four-track subway, while "L" trains would use the other two. Streetcars and "L" trains from the west side would enter another subway at either a northwest terminal at Halstead and Randolph streets, or a southwest terminal at Halstead and Van Buren streets. Two subway tubes from the northwest terminal would extend east under Washington and Randolph streets, turn south under State Street, and then return to the west under Adams Street and Jackson Boulevard to the southwest terminal. Typically, both streetcars and "L" trains would enter the subways, run through the downtown area to another terminal, and then reverse direction.

Later phases of the plan would have added additional loops and through routes, with a final phase that would have honeycombed the entire downtown area with two-, three-, or four-track subways under every street, enough to meet the needs of a 1950 Chicago population that was projected to reach six million.

Neither this nor any of several other plans that followed ever came to fruition. Chicago finally got its first subway more than three decades later, when the City, the U.S. Department of the Interior, and the Public Works Administration joined to finance the construction of two subways through the central business district. The first of these was a north-south route under State and Division streets and Clybourn Avenue that was strikingly similar in

The 5-mile State Street subway, connecting Chicago's North Side and South Side elevated divisions, finally opened in 1943 after five years of construction. This was a northbound train of PCC-type rapid transit cars at the State and Randolph station in April 1963. John Gruber.

Chicago's second subway, the 4-mile Milwaukee-Dearborn-Congress route, required this enormous concrete arched vault for the crossover at LaSalle and Congress streets. Krambles-Peterson Archive.

plan to the north-south route outlined in the 1909 Ericson plan. Instead of using the cut-and-cover construction commonly adopted in New York and elsewhere, the Chicago subway builders decided instead to build deep twin tubes 44 feet below street level that were excavated by tunneling. The 5-mile subway was completed and placed in service on October 17, 1943, diverting Ravenswood-Englewood and Howard-Jackson "L" trains from the congested Loop "L." Work began in 1939 on a second, 4-mile subway to the northwest under Milwaukee Avenue, and Dearborn and Congress streets, but completion was delayed by wartime material shortages, and the first section between Logan Square and LaSalle/Congress did not open until February 1951.

Other major North American cities considered rapid transit projects in the years before World War II. Cleveland, Los Angeles, Toronto, and Montreal were among those that conducted studies and made plans, but none ever materialized. With the inflated costs of labor and materials of every kind that followed World War I, static fare levels, and the advent of the private automobile, mass transit was no longer the profitable business it once had been, and the idea of public funding of mass transit had not yet gone beyond a few major cities.

Cincinnati, Ohio, came close to getting a subway. In 1916 voters approved a $6 million bond issue to build a 20-mile rapid transit system for the city. Construction began in 1920, and by 1927 4 miles of subway had been completed in the bed of the old Miami & Erie Canal when the project ran out of funds and was shut down. Work never resumed, and the subway remains there today, still unused.

Several cities built streetcar subways. The Municipal Railway of San Francisco completed a 2¼ mile Twin Peaks tunnel in 1918 that sped streetcar service to the southwestern part of the city. In 1927 the Pacific Electric Railway completed a mile-long subway under Bunker Hill that provided a fast entrance to downtown Los Angeles for a number of its suburban trolley lines. The same year Rochester, N.Y., opened an 8.5-mile subway for streetcars and interurbans in the bed of the abandoned Erie Canal, while the Public Service Company of New Jersey opened a similar, 3.8-mile City Subway for trolley cars in the bed of the old Morris & Essex Canal at Newark in 1935.

For almost all of the period before World War II, then, heavy-duty subway operation in North America was confined to just three eastern cities. In a much smaller way than at New York, the subways at Boston and Philadelphia helped to shape their city's development and eased congestion in the crowded downtown streets of these older cities.

Travel by subway was fast, but it was usually a crowded and not very comfortable experience. The cars were arranged to maximize standing room, and what seats were available were usually upholstered in such materials as rattan, more notable for their durability than their comfort. Floors and interior finishes, too, were specified with ease of cleaning and durability in mind.

New York's initial subway contract permitted the operator to charge more than the established five-cent fare by providing "additional conveniences for such passengers as shall desire the same," but on not more than one car per train, but neither the IRT nor any other subway ever did offer extra fare service. Somehow, first class accommodations seemed inconsistent with the mass transit nature of the subway, and bankers, doctors, and lawyers traveled together with day laborers, retail clerks, and janitors.

The Hudson & Manhattan offered another type of special car for a time. To shield women from the unwelcome attentions of men in crowded trains, the H&M operated a car at the rear of each rush hour train reserved for the use of women. Red signs pointed the way to the special car, and the trainmen assigned to the service wore a distinctive red cap.

Despite the density of traffic, the close headway operation, and the relatively high operating speeds, travel by subway was remarkably safe. The development of all-steel cars that paralleled the development of the first subways provided a much higher standard of fire safety and protection from collision for subway passengers, and the subway builders recognized that the highest standard of signaling and interlocking protection was needed. The New York subway system, for example, went from 1928 to 1970 without a fatal passenger accident on its trains, during which time it transported well in excess of 60 billion passengers. Virtually all of the passenger fatalities since the subway system opened were concentrated in two tragic crashes.

The first of them took place in wartime 1918 on the Brooklyn Rapid Transit Company's Brighton Beach line. Following a wildcat motormen's strike on the morning of November 1, the company pressed into service every available nonunion motorman and any other employees with experience at operating trains. One of these, a crew dispatcher named Edward Luciano, was assigned to a rush-hour run on the Brighton Beach line. Unfamiliar with the line, Luciano failed to make the necessary speed reduction to 6 mph on a sharp curve where the line made a transition from surface level to subway trackage at Malbone Street. The train entered the curve at a speed later estimated to be as high as 30 mph. The second car of the train derailed at the entrance to the tunnel and it was followed off the rails by three more cars. The BRT had not yet acquired all-steel cars, and the four-car train was made up entirely of wooden cars. Thrown against the tunnel abutment, in which heavy iron uprights had been embedded, three of them were torn open and one was demolished. At least 93 people lost their lives and more than 200 were injured.

The second occurred just short of 10 years later when the ninth car of a 10-car southbound express derailed at a defective switch south of the Times Square station on the IRT subway. The car swung diagonally across the track; and while the rear end was torn open against a concrete wall at one side of the track, the front end was smashed against a row of steel columns on the other side. At the same time, the tenth car of the train crashed into the wreckage. Seventeen passengers lost their lives and more than a hundred were injured.

As the subways became a part of the fabric of daily life, most notably in New York, they began to appear as a backdrop to literature and art that depicted life in the city. Illustrators like G. W. Peters and Charles Bauer depicted crowds of well-dressed New Yorkers boarding trains on the new IRT for the popular magazines. Somewhat later such artists as Lily Furedi, Fritz Eichenberg, Don Freeman, John Sloan, and Isac Friedlander created more realistic scenes of travel on the New York subways in woodcuts, etchings, and paintings.

The subway found its way into the new medium of film as well. Usually, these were background appearances in scenes of city life. Harold Lloyd and Gloria Swanson, for example, created comic scenes of travel on the crowded New York subway for the films *Speedy* and *Manhandled*, while Buster Keaton stood—improbably—alongside the immediately recognizable icon of an IRT kiosk on an Arctic lake in *The Frozen North*. In at least one case, the subway had what might be called a starring role. This

Fritz Eichenberg took a look at sleep on the subway in this 1934 wood engraving, "Sleep." Print Collection, Miriam and Ira D. Wallach Division of Art, Prints and Photographs, The New York Public Library, Astor, Lenox and Tilden Foundations.

In this 1936 lithograph, "Freedom of the Press," Don Freeman pictured the diversity of passengers on a crowded train. Collection of Lydia Cooley Freeman, University of Virginia Art Museum.

was in John Godey's 1973 novel, *The Taking of Pelham One Two Three*, and its 1974 film version, in which an IRT subway train and its passengers were taken hostage.

On the stage the subway's best-known appearance was undoubtedly in David Merrick's 1961 production of *Subways Are for Sleeping*. And in popular music the most memorable of subway-inspired tunes was without question Billy Strayhorn's "Take the 'A' Train" of 1941, which became a signature theme for jazz musician Duke Ellington. "Take your baby subway riding," sang Duke, "That's where romance may be hiding."

Appearing incongruously on a frozen Arctic lake, a New York subway kiosk was an instantly recognizable icon in the Buster Keaton comedy, *The Frozen North*. Museum of Modern Art/Film Stills Archive.

In the comedy *Speedy*, Harold Lloyd portrayed a passenger on a crowded subway train. The crush of New York's rush hour was only slightly exaggerated. Museum of Modern Art/Film Stills Archive.

The subway had a starring role in the 1974 thriller, *The Taking of Pelham One Two Three*. A terrified mother gathered her children around her in this scene from on board the hijacked train. Museum of Modern Art/Film Stills Archive.

Biographical Profile

WILLIAM BARCLAY PARSONS (1859–1932) was a native New Yorker, educated in Europe and at Columbia College, where he earned both arts and civil engineering degrees. After completing his studies in 1882 he joined the engineering staff of the Erie Railroad, leaving three years later to begin a consulting engineering practice at New York. Much of Parsons' practice was in railroad work, and in 1891, when he was just 32, he was appointed deputy chief engineer to the new Rapid Transit Commission that was planning a Manhattan subway. "Mr. Parsons, in addition to being an able engineer," Robert Ridgeway, later the New York Board of Transportation's chief engineer, wrote of him years later, "had the enthusiasm of a young man, and the judgment of one of mature age." The 1891 project was unsuccessful, but Parsons' work in developing the general plan for the subway brought him an appointment as chief engineer to a new rapid transit commission in 1894, and he went on to develop the plans for New York's first subway. When the project lagged, Parsons busied himself with service in the Spanish-American War, becoming chief of engineers for the New York National Guard, and conducting surveys for railroad

William Barclay Parsons. Library of Congress.

lines in China. Parsons returned to New York in 1899 to again take up his post as chief engineer for the Manhattan subway throughout the difficult years of construction.

His reputation made by the successful subway project, Parsons went on to a distinguished engineering career. Soon afterward he was appointed to the Isthmian Canal Commission and to an advisory board of engineers for the Royal Commission on London Traffic, and in 1905 became the chief engineer for the Cape Cod Canal. That same year he established a new consulting practice at New York that would later become the Parsons Brinckerhoff Quade and Douglas firm, which took on a wide range of rapid transit, hydroelectric, bridge, dock, and harbor work in the U.S., Canada, and Central America. Parsons interrupted his engineering practice to serve on the Western Front as an Army engineer officer in World War I. He later became a long-time trustee of Columbia University, and he was a prolific author on engineering subjects. Parsons was awarded the Norman Medal of the American Society of Civil Engineers, the Telford Gold Medal of Britain's Institution of Civil Engineers, and honorary doctorates from several colleges and universities.

While his engineering contributions were many, Parsons' greatest work was his planning and design of New York's first subway, which established the design standards and construction methods that guided successive generations of American subway builders. The engineering practice he founded remained a leading consulting engineering firm throughout the twentieth century, and—today known as Parsons Brinckerhoff—it has been one of the leading designers and builders of modern rapid transit systems.

The Chicago Transit Authority pioneered a new concept in rapid transit development in the 1950s with joint development of its new high-speed West Side rapid transit line with the new Congress (now Eisenhower) Expressway. Just west of the Loop a rush hour train headed down the expressway median toward the western suburbs in the gathering dusk of a winter evening in the 1960s. Sprague Library, Electric Railroaders' Association.

CHAPTER 4

RAPID TRANSIT AT MIDCENTURY

New Systems and a New Era

Metropolitan Toronto saw more new construction between 1954, when the first subway opened, and now, than was previously in existence during the first 120 years of incorporation of the City of Toronto. Since the formation of Metropolitan Toronto the rapid transit system has played an important role in determining the location of approximately $30 billion in new buildings.

—*Metropolitan Toronto: The Transit/Development Connection,*
Toronto Transit Commission, 1987

EXCEPT FOR A FEW CITIES, the period between wars was not a good one for North American rapid transit development. Boston and Philadelphia completed several substantial extensions to their systems, while Chicago finally began subway construction by the late 1930s. Only New York expanded its subway system substantially through the Dual Contracts and Independent Subway projects. And in all of North America there wasn't a single city that was able to complete a new rapid transit system.

For most cities, the prospects for major rapid transit investments were no better in the immediate postwar years. Transit operators did well enough during the war years, when shortages of gasoline and tires and a halt to the production of private automobiles had helped to generate record numbers of mass transit riders. This prosperity vanished quickly after the war, as costs went up and riders declined. By 1950 U.S. transit lines had lost 25 percent of the riders they had been carrying just five years before, and by 1955 they were down to less than half the wartime peak. The private transit companies were in no position to make major investments; most communities were far from ready to accept the idea of public investment in mass transit; and federal support for transit was still almost two decades in the future. In any event, most of America was convinced that the automobile represented the transportation future, and urban transportation investment was concentrated on new expressways and freeways.

But by this time, a few major cities had begun to move toward public ownership and operation of transit systems. New York, of course, had completed the transition to a public system before World War II. In Canada, the Toronto transit system had been publicly owned and operated ever since 1920, when the Toronto Transportation Commission (TTC) was formed to take over the city's transit companies. At Chicago, the Chicago Transit Authority (CTA) bought out the city's bankrupt surface and rapid transit lines in 1945. Just two

Although work was started before World War II, wartime material shortages delayed completion of Chicago's Dearborn Street subway until 1951. This view of a southbound Douglas Milwaukee train in the station at Monroe and Dearborn streets dates to 1964. By this time the lightweight PCC-type car had become the standard for Chicago Transit Authority "L" and subway lines. Krambles-Peterson Archive.

years later the new Metropolitan Transit Authority (MTA) acquired Boston's privately owned transit system. This move toward public ownership, operation, and support of mass transit, which over the next few decades would become virtually universal in North America, would provide the foundation for a new era of rapid transit development.

Regardless of whether the systems were public or still private, however, there was not much rapid transit development to talk about in the years after the war. In 1951 Chicago's new CTA finally managed to complete the first section of the Milwaukee-Dearborn sub-

An early project for Boston's new Metropolitan Transit Authority following its 1947 formation was an extension of its East Boston subway over the roadbed of the former Boston, Revere Beach & Lynn. A two-car train of PCC-type rapid transit cars operated over the line around the time of its 1952 opening as far as Suffolk Downs. Kevin T. Farrell Collection, from Fred W. Schneider, III.

way begun 12 years earlier. At Boston, an early project of the new MTA was the construction of a 6-mile extension of the short East Boston subway north over the roadbed of the abandoned Boston, Revere Beach & Lynn Railroad. The new line opened to Orient Heights and Suffolk Downs in 1952, and to its terminal at Wonderland in 1954. New York added only a few new route-miles to its subway system, and Philadelphia nothing at all, in the decade after the war.

Despite the generally gloomy outlook for transit investment in the immediate postwar years, two cities were able to begin new rapid transit systems.

The first to get started was Toronto, Canada's second largest city, which had been thinking about it for a long time. As early as 1910, when the city's population was only about 350,000, a report to the city council by New York consulting engineers Jacob and Davies had recommended that a system of subways be built, but a proposal for a Yonge Street line was soundly defeated in a municipal vote. The first concrete step toward rapid transit came just eight years later, when the Prince Edward Viaduct was opened across the Don Valley to link Bloor Street and Danforth Avenue. Anticipating a future subway, the city required that the viaduct be built with a lower deck for a rail line, little realizing that it would be almost a half century before it would be used.

By the 1940s, transportation problems had reached a critical stage on some of the city's principal thoroughfares. Probably the worst was Yonge Street, the principal north-south thoroughfare. During rush hours as many as 70 two-car trolley trains competed with heavy automobile traffic on the congested street. In 1942 the TTC had presented a rapid transit plan to the city council that called for a north-south subway under Bay and Yonge streets, extending from Union Station in downtown Toronto north to St. Clair Avenue, and an east-west subway through the downtown area. Both routes were to be operated with streetcars, which would continue on surface lines beyond the subway portals. The plan was rejected by the city council, but TTC was back with another in 1945. The idea of a north-south trolley subway had been given up, and the new plan proposed a 4.6-mile, high-capacity subway that would run north under Yonge to Eglinton Avenue. The alignment of the proposed east-west line was modified to a route under Queen Street, although it was still planned for use by streetcars.

On New Year's Day 1946 Toronto voters, by an 11 to 1 margin, approved the building of the Yonge subway. Design work was started almost immediately and the first construction began in September 1949. It was not an easy subway to build. The line was built largely by cut-and-cover construction under Yonge Street, and the builders had to carefully plan traffic diversions and maintain pedestrian access to the busy street. No less than 28 major diversions of the Yonge streetcar line were required in order to maintain service throughout the construction period.

Finally, all was in readiness, and the opening of Canada's first subway was marked with appropriate ceremony on the morning of March 30, 1954. The line was soon transporting a traffic approaching 39,000 passengers an hour. It was only the beginning of what would grow into one of North America's finest subway systems.

Next on Toronto's agenda was the east-west line. By the time a plan was approved in 1958, the idea of streetcar operation had been given up for this line too, and the route was now planned as an 8-mile heavy-duty subway under Bloor and Danforth streets, together with a 2.4-mile University line that looped back from a link with the Yonge line at Union Station to a junction with the Bloor-Danforth route at St. George Street. Work began first on the University line in 1959 and the extension was opened early in 1963. Bloor-Danforth construction began in 1962 and the line was opened early in 1966, finally making use of the rapid transit deck on the 48-year-old Don Valley viaduct.

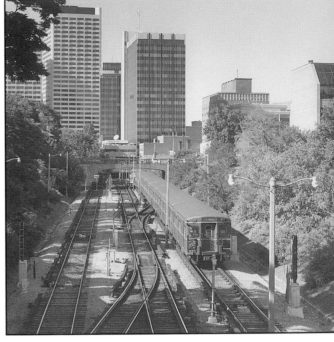

A train of TTC's durable original Gloucester-built cars headed north from Davisville toward Eglinton on the Yonge Street line in August 1984. The dense development surrounding the Eglinton station reflected the power of rapid transit to shape urban growth. William D. Middleton.

On a January night in 1966 snow cloaked the ground and the roofs of a train of TTC's Gloucester cars laid up on a storage track just north of the Yonge Street subway's Davisville station. John D. Thompson, Sprague Library, Electric Railroader's Association.

Westbound over Toronto's Bloor-Danforth subway in November 1984, a train has emerged from the subway portal in the distance to cross the Humber River and enter the Old Mill station. William D. Middleton.

Cleveland was not far behind Toronto in getting long-planned rapid transit construction going. And Cleveland, too, had been thinking about rapid transit for a long time. The city already had a rapid transit line of sorts. This was the Shaker Heights Rapid Transit, which had begun operation in 1920 as the Cleveland Interurban Railroad. Installed in the center median of divided boulevards or on private rights-of-way, the line was built by two Cleveland real estate developers, the brothers Oris P. and Mantis J. Van Sweringen, to provide fast trolley service between downtown Cleveland and their exclusive Shaker Heights development. The busy Van Sweringens also controlled the Nickel Plate and four other railroads, and were developing the great Terminal Tower and Union Terminal in downtown Cleveland.

The new terminal was to serve both main line passenger trains and a system of rapid transit lines the brothers planned to develop, in part on the rights-of-way of their railroads or those of abandoned interurban railways they had acquired. A 1929 map of the proposed Van Sweringen system shows no less than seven lines radiating from the city, in addition to the Shaker Heights line already in operation. Shortly before the new terminal opened in 1930, the Van Sweringens began some preliminary rapid transit construction for a Cleveland Heights line in the Nickel Plate right-of-way between East 55th Street and East Cleveland. Bridges were widened, catenary supports were erected, and the roadbed prepared. A widening of the Nickel Plate west of the terminal provided room for rapid transit in the right-of-way and on a new bridge over the Cuyahoga River. But this was as far as the Van Sweringens had gone when their financial empire ran afoul of the great depression that began in 1929. By 1934 the two brothers had lost control of their many real estate and transportation holdings, and dreams of rapid transit were set aside for another 20 years.

Rapid transit for Cleveland was again taken up at the end of World War II. An initial Reed-McCarter plan completed in 1944 outlined a comprehensive rapid transit system using PCC streetcars, while a revised plan completed the following year proposed instead a full high-capacity rail system with high-level platforms. A $29.5 million loan from the federal Reconstruction Finance Corporation financed the east-west line that was the principal element of the new plan, and construction began in February 1952.

Cleveland's rapid transit system was a long time in coming. On this section of the East Side line at Fairhill Road, trains operated under catenary structures that had been erected during 1927–1930, more than a quarter century before the line finally opened. The train of the line's original PCC-type cars was westbound from Windermere to Cleveland Union Terminal in 1957. Herbert H. Harwood, Jr.

In many ways the new east-west line reflected the Van Sweringen plan of more than 20 years earlier. The line operated through the Union Terminal, and followed existing railroad rights-of-way, even utilizing some of the preliminary construction completed by the Van Sweringens before 1930. The 13.1-mile line extended east from the terminal to Windermere, and west to West 117th and Madison streets. Opening of the east end of the line on March 15, 1955, was celebrated in grand style. Ohio Governor Frank J. Lausche and Cleveland Mayor Anthony J. Celebrezze led a political delegation that boarded an inaugural train for the run from Windermere to Union Terminal, which was followed by a civic luncheon at the Hotel Cleveland and speeches from a platform in the main concourse of the terminal. Continuous entertainment was provided throughout the first week of operation.

The remainder of the line opened five months later. A west-end extension to West Park followed in 1958, and a decade later Cleveland became the first American city with a rapid transit link to its airport when the line was extended to the city's Hopkins Airport.

Meanwhile, there were some pioneering developments on Chicago's rapid transit system. In 1953, the city began construction of a new high-speed West Side rapid transit route that represented the first U.S. example of joint rail rapid transit–expressway development in a grade-separated right-of-way. Located in the median of the new Congress (now Eisenhower) Expressway, the 10-mile line extended from a junction with the Milwaukee-Dearborn subway in the Chicago Loop to Forest Park in the western suburbs, replacing the Garfield Park elevated line. Thirteen island platform stations in the expressway section of the line were reached from roadway overpasses. The line opened on June 20, 1958, with the usual ceremony. Official guests traveled over the line in a special train and there were speeches by Chicago Mayor Richard J. Daley and CTA Chairman Virgil Gunlock at a dedication ceremony at the Morgan Street bridge, followed by a civic luncheon at the Palmer House. The following day 20,000 Chicagoans took advantage of free rides over the new line, which finally went into regular service the next morning.

A much different kind of Chicago rapid transit project with even greater implications for the future followed the 1963 abandonment of the Chicago North Shore & Milwaukee, an interurban electric railway linking Chicago and Milwaukee. At Howard Street on Chicago's North Side the North Shore, which reached the Loop over the "L," had switched to its own high-speed route through the Skokie Valley suburbs north of Chicago. The CTA bought 5 miles of line from the defunct North Shore, and

(Above)   The downtown Cleveland terminal for the city's new rapid transit system was the great Cleveland Union Terminal built by the Van Sweringen brothers. A westbound train dove toward the underground rapid transit platforms in June 1959. Fred W. Schneider, III.

(Left)   A westbound train rolled into Cleveland's East 55th Street station in 1959. The rapid transit line shared trackage at this point with the Shaker Heights Rapid Transit light rail line, which used the low-level center platform while the rapid transit trains used the high-level platforms on either side. Fred W. Schneider, III.

In 1968 Cleveland became the first North American city with a rapid transit link to its airport when the east-west line was extended to a new underground terminal at the Cleveland Hopkins International Airport. A westbound two-car train of the big Pullman-Standard "Airporter" cars acquired for the expanded service entered the short subway into the airport terminal in July 1979. Herbert H. Harwood, Jr.

Westbound to the airport, a train of Cleveland Transit System's original PCC-type rapid transit cars departs from Cleveland Union Terminal. Looming in the background is the city's landmark Terminal Tower. Fred W. Schneider, III.

A train of Airporter cars eastbound to downtown Cleveland and Windermere paused to board passengers at the Puritas station on Cleveland's West Side in July 1982. William D. Middleton.

Westbound from the Loop in the Congress Expressway median, a train of CTA's PCC-type rapid transit cars sped past four lanes of late afternoon commuter traffic at Sacramento Boulevard in 1959, just a year after the line opened. Chicago Transit Authority.

Abandonment of the Chicago North Shore & Milwaukee interurban line provided the CTA with the opportunity to create the innovative "Skokie Swift" high-speed rapid transit line on a section of the abandoned line linked to the "L" at Howard Street. This is an early rush hour scene at the line's Dempster Street western terminal. Traffic so exceeded expectations that within a half hour of the line's opening on April 20, 1964, the initial timetable was discarded in favor of more frequent service. Chicago Transit Authority.

101

Extension of the Chicago rapid transit system in the median of the Kennedy Expressway brought fast metro service to a northwest area of Chicago that had never had it before. A train to the airport hurried west past heavy expressway traffic just east of Cumberland Avenue station in August 1983. Art Peterson.

in April 1964 established a new "Skokie Swift" high-speed shuttle service between its Howard Street station and Dempster Street at Skokie. So successful was the service that in less than six months CTA had gone through seven schedule revisions, each increasing the frequency of service, and by the end of its third year the line was transporting 7500 passengers a day.

Perhaps the most notable feature of the Skokie Swift project, however, was its role as one of the first U.S. mass transit projects federally funded in partnership with a transit operator. Federal support was channeled to the Skokie Swift as a "demonstration" project under the National Housing Act of 1961, a program of federal transit support that over the next few years would evolve into the Urban Mass Transportation Act of 1964, which became a major source of the funding that would sustain a renaissance of U.S. urban mass transit over the next four decades.

As federal transit funding began to flow to capital projects, and with the successful West Side line as a model, Chicago planned similar projects for its growing expressway system. Two major new expressways incorporated center median rapid transit routes. The first of these was a new 10-mile rail line in the Dan Ryan Expressway to Chicago's South Side, completed in 1969, which extended South Side "L" service all the way to 95th Street.

Next came a new rail line in the median of the Kennedy Expressway that extended CTA rapid transit service into a northwest area of Chicago and its western suburbs that had never had it before. The long line was completed in several stages. An initial segment required both a subway and a complex expressway underpass to reach the new median right-of-way from the Logan Square "L" terminal. This first extension to Jefferson Park was completed early in 1970, while two subsequent extensions reached River Road in 1983, and a terminal at Chicago's busy O'Hare International Airport in 1984.

There was still one more major expansion project ahead for Chicago rapid transit. This was a 9-mile Southwest line from the Loop to the city's Midway Airport that would extend rapid transit service to another area of the city that had been without it. Constructed largely

By 1984 the CTA's northwest line in the Kennedy Expressway had reached an underground terminal at O'Hare International Airport. An arriving train had just discharged its passengers in June 1987. William D. Middleton.

in railroad rights-of-way, this new Orange Line began running to a new terminal directly linked to the airport terminal late in 1993.

Boston, too, took advantage of the new federal funding support for major extensions and improvements to its elevated and subway system. By 1966, the Massachusetts Bay Transportation Authority (MBTA), which had replaced the MTA two years previous, was ready to begin work on two major rail projects. The first to start was a 9.3-mile South Shore extension of the Cambridge-Dorchester Red Line along the right-of-way of the New Haven Railroad's abandoned Old Colony line to Quincy and Braintree. Trains began running to Quincy in 1971, and the full South Shore line was complete to Braintree in 1980. Still another Red Line extension west from Harvard Square in Cambridge to Alewife Parkway opened in 1985.

Simultaneous with the start of the South Shore work, MBTA contractors began work on a new subway tunnel from Haymarket Square in downtown Boston under the Charles River to Charlestown. This represented the first segment of a 6-mile Haymarket North project that would replace the north end of MBTA's Orange Line, the old Mail Line Elevated. The new line was open as far as Sullivan Square by 1975, and the entire extension to Oak Grove was in operation by 1977.

The south end of the Orange Line soon got similar treatment as part of the billion-dollar Southwest Corridor project, which utilized right-of-way acquired for an abandoned Interstate expressway project to build a new Northeast Corridor entry into Boston, and a new Orange Line alignment between downtown Boston and Forest Hills. Rapid transit trains

The most recent major addition to Chicago's rapid transit system was the 1993 completion of a new Southwest line from the Loop to the city's Midway Airport. Westbound to Midway Airport, a Southwest line train approached the Ashland station in April 1994. Visible through the girders of the parallel Burlington Northern Santa Fe truss bridge is the Chicago Loop's landmark Sears Tower. William D. Middleton.

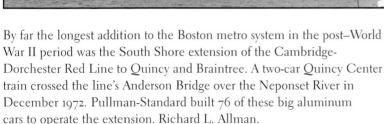

By far the longest addition to the Boston metro system in the post–World War II period was the South Shore extension of the Cambridge-Dorchester Red Line to Quincy and Braintree. A two-car Quincy Center train crossed the line's Anderson Bridge over the Neponset River in December 1972. Pullman-Standard built 76 of these big aluminum cars to operate the extension. Richard L. Allman.

En route to Braintree, a southbound train accelerated away from the station stop at North Quincy in September 1991. By this time the Red Line's once-silver Pullman-Standard cars had been refinished in red and white. William D. Middleton.

The most recent addition to MBTA's Red Line came in 1985, when trains began running over an extension from Harvard Square west to Alewife Parkway. A train of the Red Line's big Pullman-Standard aluminum cars discharged rush hour passengers at the completely rebuilt Harvard Square station in November 1985. William D. Middleton.

shifted to the new line in 1987, allowing the demolition of Boston's last remaining elevated line in Washington Street.

At Philadelphia, ambitious plans for subway expansion were proposed by a 1963 study, but only one project ever got built. This was still another extension of the South Broad Street subway south to a new terminal at Pattison Avenue that served three major sports arenas and the Navy Yard. Opened in 1973, the 1.2-mile line turned out to be Philadelphia's last subway extension.

A second project proposed by the 1963 plan almost made it. This was a 6-mile northeast subway branching from the North Broad Street subway at Hunting Park Avenue. A subway station that would have been served by the line was actually built by Sears Roebuck & Company in their northeast Philadelphia complex, but plans for the subway itself went on the shelf when bids came in far over available funds in 1970. The third projected extension, a 3.3-mile northwest extension from the north end of the Broad Street subway, never went anywhere at all. Instead of building new lines, Philadelphia turned its attention to a major rehabilitation of the aging and increasingly dilapidated Market Street and Frankford elevated structures.

At New York there were some sizable subway projects, but nothing like the heady days of the Dual Contracts or the Independent Subway construction. By far the biggest postwar addition to the subway system, and one of the longest New York subway extensions ever to open at one time, was an unusual project that took the subway across Jamaica Bay to Rockaway Park and Far Rockaway. Previously a Long Island Rail Road branch, the 11.6-mile line had been shut down after a 1950 fire

One of an earlier generation of North American metros, Boston's Main Line Elevated, now known as the Orange Line, was almost completely rebuilt after World War II. Reconstruction of the north end of the line to Oak Grove was completed in 1977. A four-car train crossed over the rebuilt line's Mystic River bridge between Medford and Somerville in July 1989. Fred W. Schneider, III.

destroyed much of the timber trestle across the bay. New York City Transit bought the line from LIRR in 1953 and began a $56 million reconstruction that included a new 4-mile concrete trestle and sand embankment crossing of Jamaica Bay. Opening of the line in 1956 gave New Yorkers a direct subway route to both the Atlantic beaches of the Rockaways and the Aqueduct racetrack. The new line also formed part of what was said to be the longest subway ride in the world, a 36.4-mile, 109-minute, rush hour "E" train routing between 179th Street in Jamaica and Far Rockaway via Manhattan.

Far more important in its impact on the subway system was the short Chrystie Street connection on Manhattan that opened in 1967. The new connection allowed trains from the former BMT lines over the Manhattan and Williamsburg bridges to reach the IND Sixth Avenue subway, substantially completing the physical unification of the three separate systems that had been merged in 1940.

By 1968 New York City Transit had become part of the Metropolitan Transportation Authority (MTA), which also had jurisdiction over all regional transportation. With the MTA came ambitious plans for subway expansion and modernization that were rolled out early that year. The first of these projects to get underway was a new Second Avenue subway, a line that had been promised to Manhattan's East Side residents ever since the Third Avenue elevated had been torn down in 1955. Work began in October 1972 with the customary groundbreaking ceremony, and construction continued for three years. Then, a victim of New York's severe financial crisis of the 1970s, the project was shut down and what subway had been completed was sealed up. It remains that way today.

Another ambitious MTA project fared only marginally better. This was a new two-level, four-track tunnel under the East River at 63rd Street that would provide both a new subway link to Queens and an entry to Manhattan's East Side for the Long Island Rail Road. The new subway connection was to link lines on Manhattan with a new express line across Queens. Work began in 1970, and the tunnel itself was finally completed in 1989, together with a new cross-town Manhattan subway linked to the Sixth Avenue line. But the new subway across Queens never materialized, and the new crossing was dead-ended at Queensboro Plaza. The new LIRR entry to Manhattan was stalled, too, and the lower level of the tunnel has yet to be used. Still other subway expansion outlined in the MTA's 1968 plan was never started at all. Instead, most of the money went to rehabilitation and modernization of the existing system, which had fallen on bad times after years of inadequate funding for maintenance and replacements.

(Above)   The final step in the Orange Line remake was the 1987 completion of the Southwest Corridor project, which relocated the south end of the Orange Line into a new alignment shared with Amtrak's Northeast Corridor. A southbound train for Forest Hills made a station stop at Massachusetts Avenue in November 1987. William D. Middleton.

(Left)   New York City Transit got an unusually lengthy addition to the subway system when it acquired a Long Island Rail Road line across Jamaica Bay to the Rockaways that had been closed by a trestle fire. Part of NYCT's rehabilitation of the line was this new concrete trestle across the bay south of Broad Channel. Outbound to the Rockaways, a long train of R10 cars crossed it in September 1969. Fred W. Schneider, III.

San Francisco's Bay Area Rapid Transit District set out to build a futuristic rapid transit system like no other before it, and succeeded handsomely. Traveling at close to 70 mph, an eastbound Concord Line train emerged from BART's 3.1-mile Berkeley Hills tunnel into Orinda in August 1974. William D. Middleton.

CHAPTER 5

NEW METRO TECHNOLOGIES

It's a flash of aluminum at 80 miles an hour, a comfortable seat in rush hour, a new panorama of the Eastbay.

That's BART, a four-letter word defining the most modern, fastest and probably most comfortable means of getting from here to there urban America has yet devised.

It's one of the most costly public works jobs on record in an era where the public rarely seems bothered about spending billions over 10 years to reach the moon, but is critical of allocating $1.4 billion in a decade to get from home to work and back, without ulcers.

BART is as colorful as the famed Moscow Metro, faster than any subway in the world, at least as spacious as jetliner first class space, quieter, smoother and better smelling than a bus, and less nerve-wracking than the Nimitz Freeway at 5:10 P.M.

—Harre W. Demoro, staff writer, *Oakland Tribune*,
BART opening day, September 10, 1972

BY THE 1960s, a growing number of North American cities were beginning to have second thoughts about their emphasis on an automotive solution to urban transportation needs. While the development of expressways and freeways had encouraged and facilitated a massive shift of urban population to the suburbs, no amount of road building ever seemed to be enough to meet the growing demand that it created. More and more, too, cities began to recognize the destructive effects of massive highway construction on the urban community. At San Francisco public opposition brought the waterfront Embarcadero Freeway to an abrupt halt. Boston cancelled a planned Southwest Freeway project. Vancouver, B.C., with more forethought than most North American cities, stopped the freeways cold at the city line.

By this time the shift to public ownership and operation of transit systems was nearly universal, and the idea of public support to transit as a basic public service was becoming more widely accepted. The first significant federal assistance to transit came through the National Housing Act of 1961, and the passage of the 1964 Urban Mass Transportation Act put in place a permanent program of federal support. Everything was now ready for an extraordinary renaissance of rapid transit in America.

Coincident with this new interest in the urban metro—as grade-separated rail rapid transit was coming to be known—was a proliferation of new technologies. Progress in electronics and computing technologies offered extraordinary promise for rapid transit applications. The needs of the aerospace industry had brought about the development of useful new materials and manufacturing techniques. And there were some promising new ideas in rapid transit technology itself. Over the next several decades all of these would come together to create a remarkable new generation of North American metro systems.

The first of these new metro technologies to reach regular service in North America came from France. This was the idea of subway trains operating on pneumatic tires instead of steel wheels. The basic idea had been around since about 1929, when the Michelin tire company developed a self-propelled rail car that ran on rubber tires. Steel flanges provided the necessary guidance. Both a smoother ride and better traction were claimed for the system. Michelin built a number of rail cars for the French rail system, and several were produced jointly by Michelin and the Budd Company for U.S. railroads during the early 1930s. The concept finally caught on in a big way when one line of the Paris Métro was converted to rubber-tired operation in 1957. In its Métro application subway cars were carried on trucks supported by rubber tires that ran on a concrete surface laid outside a normal track. Guidance was provided by small horizontally mounted wheels with pneumatic tires that pressed against guide rails mounted outside the running tracks. Normal flanged steel wheels mounted inside the rubber wheels dropped down onto the regular steel running rails in the event of a tire failure and also came into play to guide the train through switches.

This French technology came to North America in the early 1960s, when it was adopted by Montreal for the city's new Métro. Montreal had talked about developing a rapid transit system as far back as 1910, but nothing came of it until after World War II, when growing traffic congestion on the island city had reached daunting levels. In 1953 a Montreal Transportation Commission recommended a subway system for the city that would have both east-west and north-south lines operating under principal streets. Nothing happened—immediately—but the idea of a subway for Montreal became a major campaign pledge in 1960 by Jean Drapeau, a dynamic mayoral candidate who would head the city's government for the next 26 years. "Montreal cannot survive as a metropolis without a subway," he declared. "The city has no time to waste on ceremonies." Drapeau won, and was true to his pledge. On November 3, 1961, at the mayor's request, the Montreal City Council approved construction of a 10-mile Métro system based upon the routes recommended by the 1953 study. This was soon expanded to a 15.5-mile system with the addition of a third line that would cross the St. Lawrence River to serve St. Helen's Island, which had been selected as the site of Expo 67, the 1967 Montreal world's fair.

Design and construction of the Métro were carried out through the city's new Bureau du Métro, with technical assistance from the Parisian rapid transit system, La Régie Autonome des Transports Parisiens (RATP). Entirely underground, the new Métro was constructed largely by hard-rock tunneling or cut-and-cover tunneling in open cuts, with only a limited amount of soft-ground tunneling. The design of cars for the Métro limited their width to just 8 feet 3 inches, permitting the use of a narrower tunnel that could more easily fit within the width of downtown Montreal's narrow streets. Because of the good adhesion obtained with the pneumatic tire technology, engineers were able to design the Métro with unusually steep grades. Much of it was built with what was called a "humped station" profile, with rising or falling grades of up to 6.5 percent leading into or out of stations. This permitted construction economies by placing stations close to the surface, while the tunnels between stations could be excavated at a deeper level where drilling conditions were better and relocation of buried utilities could be avoided. The humped profiles also produced significant reductions in braking for trains entering stations, and in energy use for trains accelerating out of stations. Canadian Vickers, Ltd. supplied an initial Métro fleet of 369 rubber-tired cars, which operated in three-car motor-trailer-motor sets.

Montreal's new Métro, which opened late in 1966, was the first North American rapid transit system to adopt the French system of pneumatic-tired trucks. More important, it set new standards for subway amenities with its handsome cars and elegant station architecture. This was a train in the Rosemont station on Line 2 of the new Métro in 1966. *The Montreal Star*, from Canadian Vickers.

Transporting a weekday average of some 760,000 riders, Montreal's Métro has become one of North America's busiest subway systems. This scene of rush hour activity on Line 2 at the Berri-de Montigny station dates to September 1971. Fred W. Schneider, III.

The station at Lionel-Groulx provides a connection between Métro lines 2 and 7. En route from Côte-Vertu to Henri-Bourassa, a Line 2 train arrived there in August 1986. William D. Middleton.

In addition to the rubber-tired technology, the Montreal Métro brought to North America from Europe one of the first examples of a new automated fare collection technology using magnetically coded tickets that would become almost universal for North American rapid transit systems over the next several decades. Another French idea imported for the Métro that never did catch on in North America was the automatic platform gate, which closed as a train entered a station, blocking passengers from the platform while a train is in the station in order to prevent latecomers from holding the train doors open.

Métro construction began in May 1962 and the system's first two lines were opened with elaborate ceremony on October 14, 1966, just one week before Jean Drapeau successfully stood for reelection. Trains bearing many of the 6000 invited guests from every station on the Métro converged on the Berri–de Montigny station to join the mayor and the French Minister of State for the opening festivities. A brass band played, the Archbishop of Montreal blessed the new Métro, and at 4:30 p.m. it was opened to the public. Before the opening weekend was over, some one and a half million people had ridden their handsome new Métro. The third line opened early in 1967, in plenty of time for Expo 67 crowds.

The Montreal Métro's planners had recognized that modern rapid transit should appeal to potential riders who didn't have to use mass transit, and the interior appointments of the system's handsome blue and white cars and the dramatic architecture of its elegant stations set a new standard for North American rapid transit. In 1967, its first full year of operation, the Métro carried more than 136 million passengers, and the system quickly became a part of everyday life. Quite apart from easing Montreal's traffic problems, Métro played a key role in the evolution of a remarkable weatherproof underground city over the next several decades. A network of miles of underground pedestrian passageways, heated in the winter and air conditioned in the summer, was developed to link office buildings, hotels, theaters, banks, and retail stores all over downtown Montreal with each other and with Métro stations, creating a vibrant Montreal Underground that brought new life to the city center.

A first round of major expansion to the Montreal Métro was underway by the early 1970s, including both extensions to the two original routes and a new fourth route, which brought the system to a total of more than 40 route-miles and 65 stations. A third round of Métro expansion began late in 2001, when work began on an extension across the Riviere des Prairies to Laval that should open by the end of 2004.

Mexico City soon followed Montreal's example with the adoption of the same French pneumatic-tired technology. As the fast-growing Mexican capital's population soared past the 10 million mark in the early 1960s, the city began the development of a rapid transit system to help solve its massive transportation problem. The technology for the project came from a French consulting group through the Paris RATP, while French government loans helped finance an initial three-line system. Construction began in June 1967, and only 27 months later the system's first 9.4-mile line opened on September 5, 1969. The remaining two lines opened a year later. French manufacturers supplied an initial fleet of 536 cars.

Subway construction was almost entirely by cut-and-cover excavation in the soft soil of the old lakebed that underlies much of Mexico City. Lending unusual interest to the project were the remains of the city's old Aztec civilization unearthed by the work. Some 5000 Aztec artifacts were turned up during excavation for the initial three lines. Many were restored and put on display at Mexico's National Institute of Anthropology and History, but the largest—a gigantic Aztec pyramid—was incorporated into the imaginative redesign of the subway's Pino Suarez station. Distinctive, elegant architectural design distinguished the subway's principal stations.

Soon after the full three-line Sistema de Transporte Colectivo (STC) metro began operating in 1970 it was carrying a daily workday average of more than 850,000 passengers.

Mexico City's Sistema de Transporte Colectivo (STC) also adopted the French pneumatic-tired system for its new metro. In August 1976 a southbound STC Line 2 train approached its terminal at Tasquena, where the trains connected with Mexico City's only remaining light rail route. William D. Middleton.

Now transporting 4 million passengers every weekday, Mexico City's steadily growing metro system carries more passengers than any North American rapid transit system except New York's. This was a typically busy station scene on Line 3 at Hidalgo in August 1976. William D. Middleton.

A single variation from the pneumatic-tired, third-rail technology of the Mexico City metro is its Line A, completed in 1991, which employs a conventional steel wheel on steel rail technology and overhead catenary current collection. A Line A train is seen at Santa Marta in 1993. Jack May.

By 1976, when the initial three lines had been extended to a 26-mile system, this had more than doubled to a daily average of nearly 1.9 million and the city was getting ready to add still more lines to the system. Construction has been almost continuous ever since, and with the opening of the last segment of Line B late in 2000, STC had grown to an 11-route system with 175 stations and more than 125 miles of line. Except for a single line completed in 1991 with a conventional steel-wheeled technology and overhead current collection, the entire STC system employs the French-originated pneumatic tire technology. With a daily traffic of 4 million passengers in a city that is now approaching a population of 20 million, Mexico City's metro has become one of the busiest in North America, exceeded only by New York City.

Despite the success of both the Montreal and Mexico City systems, the French pneumatic-tired technology found no other takers in North America. Other new technologies were on the way that would prove to have a much wider application.

Chief among these was the concept of automated operation of trains, an idea that would become increasingly feasible through advances in computing and electronics. The earliest major test of automatic operation came, fittingly enough, on a section of the original IRT subway at New York. Early in 1959 Charles L. Patterson, chairman of the New York City Transit Authority, had proposed the development of completely automatic rapid transit systems. Plans were soon in place to test the practicality of the concept by automating the Transit Authority's 42nd Street Shuttle operating between Grand Central Terminal and Times Square, largely utilizing such already available technology as automatic acceleration controls; cab signals and speed control; and telemetry and safety enforcement systems. Union Switch & Signal, General Railway Signal, and Westinghouse Air Brake agreed to provide the required wayside and car equipment, and engineering, while the Transit Authority would provide the necessary cars, installation work, and testing staff.

The basic concept developed by the two signal companies involved electromagnetic speed and stop commands transmitted through track circuits and detected by induction coils on the train. Fail-safe features included a programmed emergency stop at any time a speed code was not received, and a grade-time and train stop system just before each terminal station to prevent runaways.

Testing began on a section of the Sea Beach line in Brooklyn late in 1959, and by early 1961 fully automatic test trains were operating satisfactorily. The next step was to install the equipment on the 42nd Street line, and in early January 1962 the authority began regular automatic operation on one track of the shuttle with what was dubbed the Subway Automatic Motorman, or SAM. New York's experimental automated train continued to perform well in regular service for more than two years, until the train was badly damaged by an April 1964 fire in the Grand Central subway station. This brought automated operation to an end at New York, but meanwhile rapid progress was being made elsewhere in the development of advanced new signaling and train control systems for a new generation of metros. While most of these new computer-based systems would stop short of driverless operation, they would permit virtually automatic operation, leaving little more than door closing and starts in the hands of the train operator.

Even as the SAM tests were proceeding at New York, equipment, signaling, and train control suppliers had begun the development of even more advanced concepts for automated rapid transit. In November 1961 General Electric demonstrated fully automatic operation on its Erie (Pa.) test track with a former Washington, D.C. PCC streetcar that automatically made station stops, opened and closed its doors, and accelerated quickly to its programmed speed.

In 1963 the Westinghouse Air Brake Company and its Union Switch & Signal subsidiary began similar automation tests with a specially equipped Pittsburgh Railways PCC streetcar. Automatic Train Operation (ATO) equipment developed through the Pittsburgh tests and later tested in regular service on Chicago Transit Authority got a practical application on the Expo Express, an intra-fair rapid transit system built for Montreal's Expo 67.

This specially equipped ex-Washington (D.C.) PCC trolley was employed by General Electric in a series of automated operation tests conducted late in 1961 on GE's Erie (Pa.) test track. A continuous trackside communication system fed information to equipment aboard the car that automatically started and stopped the car, and opened and closed its doors. General Electric Company.

Automated control equipment got an early test on the Expo Express at Montreal's 1967 World's Exposition. Eight of these six-car trains operated over line serving the Expo 67 grounds under the control of an Automatic Train Operation system developed by the Union Switch and Signal Division of the Westinghouse Air Brake Company. Except for the novel cab design, the big aluminum cars were near duplicates of Toronto's newest subway cars. Ted Liontos Photography, from Sprague Library, Electric Railroader's Association.

Linking the fair's main gate with the fair grounds located on islands in the St. Lawrence River, the 3.1-mile line was operated with a fleet of big aluminum cars built by Hawker Siddeley's Canadian Car Division. The WABCO/US&S ATO equipment provided fully automated speed control and stopping, and the trains' attendants had little more to do than push a start button at the proper time.

In 1961 Westinghouse Electric unveiled something quite different. This was the Skybus, a system of small, fully automatic vehicles operating on rubber tires over a fixed guideway under the control of a central computer. Most of the system's train control functions were placed in computerized wayside controllers at each station location, with minimal control circuitry on the vehicle itself. Control and communications signals were transmitted between the wayside controllers and vehicles by means of inductive loop circuits along the guideway and antennas mounted beneath each vehicle. Although the Skybus concept varied materially from a typical heavy rapid transit application, its control system ideas were readily adaptable to rapid transit applications.

An experimental Skybus installation operated successfully for several years. Although a planned transit installation at Pittsburgh never materialized, the Skybus technology proved well suited to "people mover" systems transporting large numbers of passengers between central terminals and gate locations at large airports, and the automated Westinghouse systems were soon in use all over the world.

In 1965 the Illinois Central Railroad began the pioneering installation of still another automatic system that would prove to have wide application for urban metro systems. Using equipment supplied by Advanced Data Systems, a Litton Industries division, this was an automatic fare collection system for the IC's Chicago suburban service. Automatic ticket vending and change making machines were installed at each station, while magnetically encoded tickets operated automatic entrance and exit gates.

Many of these new ideas for automated rapid transit soon found their way into practice on a remarkable new suburban rapid transit line in southern New Jersey. This new line was a project of the Delaware River Port Authority (DRPA), formed in 1952, which had inherited from the predecessor Delaware River Joint Commission the Philadelphia-Camden High Speed Line operated over the authority's Benjamin Franklin Bridge across the Delaware River. Among its powers the DRPA had the authority to operate rapid transit in Philadelphia and New Jersey within a 35-mile radius of Camden. By 1954 the DRPA had begun the first of a series of studies that by 1962 had evolved into a plan for a 14.5-mile line from downtown Philadelphia to suburban Lindenwold, N.J., which would replace rapidly vanishing commuter rail services. The fully grade-separated line would operate over a reconstructed Bridge Line and a new line installed largely in the right-of-way of the old Pennsylvania-Reading Seashore Lines.

Engineers were engaged in 1962 to design what would prove to be a prototype for a new generation of modern, highly automated rapid transit systems, and the first construction began two years later. A fleet of 75 stainless steel cars supplied by the Budd Company in-

New Jersey's Port Authority Transit high-speed line was the prototype for a new generation of modern highly automated rapid transit systems. A six-car train of PATCO's Budd-built stainless steel cars was westbound east of the Haddonfield (N.J.) station in the evening rush hour of October 11, 1971. Fred W. Schneider, III.

corporated such amenities and advanced features as air conditioning and air suspension, and were capable of high acceleration and deceleration rates and a maximum operating speed of 75 mph. Automatic train operation enabled a high performance level and one-person operation of trains of any length. Automatic ticket vending and fare collection equipment permitted the system to operate with unmanned stations, while closed circuit television equipment provided security oversight. All suburban stations were air conditioned, and an initial 4400 park-and-ride spaces were provided for suburban commuters.

Operation began between Lindenwold and Camden on January 4, 1969, and the full line into Philadelphia was in service by mid-February. Operated by the subsidiary Port Authority Transit Corporation, or PATCO, the Hi-Speed Line was an early success. By the end of the first year average weekday traffic had reached almost 30,000 passengers, and within five years PATCO was carrying an average daily load of about 40,000.

While PATCO would be the first such system to begin regular operation in North America, the concepts of automatic operation would get a much more demanding—and much more visible—trial on a major new system already taking shape in the San Francisco Bay Area.

Bay Area geography had always presented major difficulties for transportation planners. San Francisco itself had developed on the northern tip of the peninsula that enclosed the western side of the Bay, while other major population centers had grown along the eastern shore. Until completion of the San Francisco–Oakland Bay Bridge in 1936, ferries had provided the transportation link between the two sides of the Bay. These were fed on the East Bay side by an extensive suburban electric railway system operated by Southern Pacific and the Key System. These rail services began operating over the Bay Bridge to a new San Francisco terminal in 1939, but in an ill-advised turn of events buses replaced the trains less than two decades later.

In any event, with or without the bridge rail lines, transbay transportation was becoming an increasingly serious problem for the region. Extensive economic and population growth in the postwar period had brought major development throughout the Bay Area, and its bridges and highways were growing increasingly congested. As early as 1947 a joint Army-Navy board reviewed the problem and concluded that an additional connecting link between San Francisco and Oakland would be needed; it recommended an underwater tube for high-speed electric trains. A San Francisco Bay Area

The San Francisco Bay Area had a rapid transit system of sorts following completion of the San Francisco–Oakland Bay Bridge, when trains from the East Bay suburban rail systems operated by Southern Pacific and the Key System began running across the bridge to San Francisco. This was the first test trip over the bridge by a train of the Key System's new articulated cars on September 23, 1938. Regular service began early in 1939. By 1958 additional highway lanes had displaced the tracks and buses had replaced the trains. Robert G. Lewis Collection.

Rapid Transit Commission, created by the California Legislature in 1951 to study the region's long-range transportation needs, recommended in its final report of 1957 the formation of a five-county rapid transit district to build and operate a high-speed rail network linking major commercial centers with suburban sub-centers. Thus was born the San Francisco Bay Area Rapid Transit District, or BART. Created by the Legislature in 1957, BART comprised the five counties of Alameda, Contra Costa, Marin, San Francisco, and San Mateo, and was given the power to levy taxes and issue general obligation bonds, with voter approval. A plan for this regional system completed in 1959 envisioned some 118 miles of line serving 52 stations in the five counties.

Marin and San Mateo counties withdrew from BART in the spring of 1962, but by the following November the district was ready to go to the voters in the remaining three counties for approval of a $792 million bond issue to build a truncated system that would link the City and County of San Francisco with the two East Bay counties via a 3.6-mile Transbay Tube. At a time before the availability of federal capital funding for transit this was asking for a remarkable commitment from Bay Area voters, and it very nearly didn't happen.

First, supervisors of the three counties had to approve the plan and put the bond issue on the ballot. Alameda and San Francisco county supervisors had done that and the decision came down to Contra Costa County. Two of five county supervisors had come out in favor of BART, and two against. The deciding vote would be that of Supervisor Joseph S. Silva, a farmer from the northeastern corner of the county who was thought to be against the project. On the morning of the vote, San Francisco Mayor George Christopher, Oakland Mayor John Houlihan, and BART Chairman Adrien J. Falk traveled to Martinez for a coffee shop meeting at which they tried to persuade Silva to support the project. California Governor Pat Brown called in from Sacramento to urge support. Silva kept his counsel until the last, but that afternoon he voted in favor of the project.

The public referendum for BART proved an equally close call. There was strong opposition, but when the votes were counted, the bond issue had won. By a little over one percentage point above the 60 percent approval margin required for the bond issue the voters had said "yes," and the Bay Area was ready to proceed with what would prove to be a new kind of rapid transit system.

The plan for the 71.5-mile, 34-station, three-county system was laid out in the form of an "X." From a central hub at Oakland, the four legs extended west and southwest through San Francisco to Daly City, southeast to Fremont, east to Concord, and north to Richmond.

General engineering consultants and construction managers for the system appointed in 1959 were a three-member consortium that included Parsons, Brinckerhoff, Quade & Douglas, the firm founded by pioneer subway engineer William Barclay Parsons; Tudor Engineering Company; and the Bechtel Corporation. The system they set out to design and build would be unlike any other before it, intended to provide a standard of service and comfort that would draw commuters out of their automobiles and off the region's crowded freeways and highways. Breaking almost completely with traditional practice, the engineers established design criteria for the system that pushed rapid transit technology to unprecedented levels. This pioneering would not be without its price, for BART would face many, and often intractable, problems in its first years of operation, but its ultimate success would set the standard for a whole new generation of modern rail transit systems.

The entire system was designed for high-speed operation, with a maximum of 80 mph. Track construction was with continuously welded rail on prestressed concrete ties or directly attached to concrete slabs on elevated structures and in tunnels, with a nonstandard 5 foot, 6 inch wide gauge to provide greater stability and smoother operation at high speeds. BART's stations were widely spaced, with an average separation of more than 2 miles, allowing average terminal-to-terminal operating speeds of close to 40 mph. Aerospace technology produced a sleek, extremely lightweight BART car of aluminum and molded fiberglass, with such amenities as air suspension, wide, tinted windows, upholstered seats, carpeting, and air conditioning that promised a whole new level of performance, passenger comfort, and aesthetic appeal. A central computer-controlled system provided virtually fully automatic operation, with train operators responsible for little more than door closing and starts. Fare collection was fully automatic, with magnetic stored value fare cards and gates that coded the cards for the entry station and deducted the correct fare at the exit station.

BART construction began on June 19, 1964, when President Lyndon B. Johnson presided over a groundbreaking ceremony for a 2-mile Mt. Diablo test track at Concord on which BART would develop the technical specifications for its car fleet. The first subway construction for the system began early in 1966 at Oakland.

While its innovative new technology drew most of the attention, the building of BART was—more than anything else—a civil engineering and construction venture of exceptional difficulty and unparalleled magnitude. Altogether, BART required the construction of some 25 double-track route-miles at grade level, another 23 miles of elevated structure,

Laboratory car "B," one of three built for BART by the Budd Company, raced over the Mt. Diablo test track in a long series of tests of trucks, motors, and control systems for the revolutionary BART rail car. Bay Area Rapid Transit District, from Sprague Library, Electric Railroaders' Association.

Building the 6-mile Transbay Tube was the largest single BART construction effort of all. The twin tube underwater section of the crossing was built by the trench-and-tube method, in which pre-fabricated sections of tunnel were floated into position and then sunk into place in a trench dredged in the bottom of the Bay. Here, one of the twin tube sections is being launched at a Bay Area shipyard. Bay Area Rapid Transit District.

Elevated sections of the BART system were carried on prestressed, precast hollow concrete box girders spanning T-shaped reinforced concrete piers. An 80-foot girder was lifted into place on a half-mile section of aerial structure built as part of the Mt. Diablo test track and later incorporated into the completed system. Bay Area Rapid Transit District, from Sprague Library, Electric Railroaders' Association.

and 23 miles of underground construction, including the 3.6-mile Transbay Tube and a 3.1-mile hard rock tunnel through the Berkeley Hills. Track construction totaled some 160 miles. Major structures included the 34 stations, a headquarters and operations building at Oakland, and three car maintenance and storage facilities. The requirement for earthquake-resistant design and the construction difficulties inherent in building in a congested urban area added to the magnitude and complexity of the task.

For eight years the massive BART construction effort was a major force in the Bay Area economy. In 1968, one of the peak construction years, there were a hundred separate BART construction contracts underway, and new contract awards during the year totaled $81 million. Some 4500 construction workers were employed in building the system, and the monthly construction payroll for BART work ran to $4 million.

One of the earliest construction tasks begun was also one of the most difficult. This was the drilling of twin 16,100-foot tunnels through the Berkeley Hills for BART's Concord line. Geologic complexities for the site included tunneling through 19 distinct rock formations, all of them extensively folded and sheared by past geologic and seismic activity, as well as the need to tunnel through the Hayward Fault, which had produced two major earthquakes during the nineteenth century. In addition to the threat of earthquake movement along the fault, the Hayward Fault was also subject to a phenomenon known as "tectonic creep"— a continuous movement averaging a fraction of an inch a year between the two faces of the fault.

BART's engineers helped to reduce the unknowns in the tunneling work by first awarding a contract in 1964 for drilling small exploratory tunnels into the hills from both sides, permitting firsthand inspection of the conditions. Contracts for drilling and lining the twin tunnels were awarded in 1965, and the job took four years to finish. The parallel tunnels were bored through the hills 100 feet apart. Heavy steel ribs and timber lagging were installed as soon as excavation was complete, and the tunnels were later lined with 18 inches of concrete. In order to permit realignment of the track in the event an earthquake distorted the tunnels, the inside diameter of the tunnels was extra large—17½ feet instead of the 16½ feet used elsewhere on the system. The use of wood crossties in the tunnel, instead of bolting the rails to a concrete slab, was another measure designed to facilitate track realignment in case of earthquake disruption.

Work on the largest BART project of all, the Transbay Tube linking San Francisco and Oakland, started early in 1966. Including its approach tunnels, the Bay crossing was some 6 miles in length, while the twin tube underwater tunnel itself was 3.6 miles long. The tube was built by trench-and-tube methods similar to those developed more than a half-century earlier for the construction of the Michigan Central Railroad's Detroit River Tunnel, and also used for several early subway crossings of the East and Harlem rivers at New York.

At the San Francisco end of the crossing a large steel caisson 108 feet high was floated into place in the Bay opposite the Ferry Building at the foot of Market Street. As concrete walls and floors were placed, the structure gradually sank into place on the bottom of the Bay to form a ventilation structure and end point for the underwater tube. Later, two shield-driven approach tunnels were constructed inward from the caisson to link the tube with the BART subway under Market Street. At the Oakland end the approach tunnels were built in the open, behind cofferdams.

The Transbay Tube itself was designed to "float" on soft alluvial deposits on the bottom of the Bay to insulate the structure against earthquake shocks. Seismometers were buried in the bedrock and overburden under the Bay six years before construction started in order to study the effects of earthquake vibrations, and the analytical design for the tube structure was tested on a large "shake table" at the University of New Mexico. Elastic joints permitted movement between the tube and the ventilating structures at each end.

A 40-foot-deep trench for the tube was dredged in the soft material at the bottom of the Bay, and a 2-foot foundation course of sandy gravel was placed to support it. The tube itself was built in 57 separate sections at a South San Francisco shipyard. Each section consisted of a structural steel shell anywhere from 330 to 350 feet long, 48 feet wide, and 24 feet high, providing sufficient space for two parallel 17 foot tunnels for tracks, flanking utilities, and ventilation tunnels. After "launching," each of the sections was lined with concrete, floated into position over the trench, and then lowered into place. Divers guided each section into place; it was then welded to its neighbor, and the concrete lining completed. Sand backfill and, where necessary, a blanket of heavy rocks were then placed over the tube. The first section of the Transbay Tube was floated into place in February 1967 and the final one was lowered into position off Yerba Buena Island in April 1969. The entire structure was completed four months later.

BART subway construction in San Francisco, Oakland, and Berkeley involved several different tunneling methods. Much of the work was carried out in soft earth by shield tunneling, while at several locations the contractors employed huge 93-ton tunneling machines, with cutting heads of revolving or oscillating teeth that bored into the soft earth, while conveyer belts removed the excavated material from the cutting face. As the tunneling equipment moved forward, workers bolted together heavy steel tunnel liner sections behind them. At some locations high ground water levels necessitated the use of compressed air at pressures as high as 40 pounds per square inch to keep water out of the excavations. Another 9 miles of tunneling, including subway stations, was built by cut-and-cover construction.

Everywhere they worked, the subway builders were confronted with the problems of supporting or relocating buried utilities, rerouting street traffic, underpinning neighboring buildings, and disposing of the excavated material. Under Market Street in San Francisco and at two locations in Oakland a special "slurry trench" method was used to avoid the problems presented by water-saturated soils. With this method contractors first excavated a deep trench, in some cases as much as 100 feet deep, around the station or subway site between previously driven steel piling. As the trench was excavated it was kept filled with a heavy bentonite slurry, which formed a barrier to water seepage from the adjacent

A key figure in the successful development of BART was B. R. Stokes, whose turbulent 11 years as the authority's general manager saw the project through design, construction, and start-up. A former Navy destroyer officer and *Oakland Tribune* reporter, Bill Stokes became BART's first employee when he signed on in 1958 as its director of information. By 1963, a year after BART's successful bond issue, he had moved up to the general manager's position, where he skillfully moved the project ahead through all of the controversies and crises that accompanied the building of BART and the start-up problems that followed. Bay Area Rapid Transit District.

soil. The trench was then filled with concrete, placed through "tremie" tubes, which displaced the slurry from the bottom up. The concrete walls placed in this manner became a permanent part of the subway or station structure. Once the wall was complete, the site was excavated to its full depth. A special problem encountered at the downtown San Francisco stations was the effect of tremendous hydrostatic pressures against the completed structure from the water-saturated soil. Foundation slabs as much as 7 feet thick were needed to offset the upward thrust of this pressure.

BART's 23 miles of elevated structure was constructed with standardized concrete sections. The design developed by BART's chief architect, Donn Emmons, employed T-shaped concrete piers supporting pairs of concrete box girders, which carried the tracks. Particular attention was given in the design of the structure to minimizing the massive visual impact characteristic of most elevated structures. The piers were built with a hexagonal cross section, to reduce shadow width in cross lighting and to give a variation in tones. The box girders supporting the track were built with a trapezoidal cross section, with tapered faces that reduced the bulky appearance. By placing the tracks on two separate girders, sunlight was permitted to shine on the supporting columns, and the shadow area beneath the structure was broken up. A notable design innovation for the project was the development of landscaped "linear parks" beneath this elevated structure wherever possible.

Typically, the elevated structure employed 70-foot spans 15 feet above grade, but the spans ranged up to 100 feet and as much as 35 feet above the ground. The prestressed, precast hollow concrete box girders were 4 feet deep with an 11-foot wide deck. Some were built at the construction site and then lifted into place, but most were fabricated in a huge casting yard at Richmond, Calif.

BART's 34 stations were divided among 13 elevated stations, 7 stations at grade, and 14 subway stations. While BART's engineering consultants did the engineering design for all of them, architectural design contracts were awarded to 15 different Bay Area architectural firms. The result was a wide diversity, which was just what BART intended, and the imaginative, handsome stations that emerged from this approach were among the system's most noteworthy design achievements.

Financial problems dogged BART from the very beginning. The successful referendum for BART in November 1962 was immediately followed by a taxpayers' suit attempting to block the project. BART won, but the suit delayed a start to work for six months. The delay only helped a high rate of construction cost inflation to begin eating away at the budget, and the project was soon receiving intense and unremitting political and press criticism. The many financial crises provided regular topics for a "Bartman and Robin" series originated by *San*

Among BART's distinguished early passengers were President and Mrs. Richard M. Nixon, shown with General Manager B. R. Stokes during their trip between Fremont and Oakland on September 27, 1972, just two weeks after the line had opened. Bay Area Rapid Transit District.

Located at the junction of the Concord and Richmond lines, MacArthur station is always a busy place during the daily rush hours. A northbound Fremont to Richmond train loaded at an outer platform during the evening rush period of March 26, 1975. William D. Middleton.

A notable design concept for the BART project was the idea of landscaped "linear parks" that were placed beneath elevated sections wherever possible. This linear park example is at Marin Avenue in Berkeley. The train was inbound from Richmond in July 1989. William D. Middleton.

Delayed by numerous and complex problems, BART finally began operating through the Transbay Tube on September 16, 1974, to place the full 71.5-mile system in service. Just four days later an eastbound train made a passenger stop at the Powell Street station en route from BART's Daly City terminal in San Francisco to Concord. William D. Middleton.

Francisco Chronicle editorial cartoonist Bastian. Proposals to reduce the scope or quality of the system were beaten back, and additional sources of local, state, and federal funding were finally found to complete what turned out to be close to a $1.6 billion system.

Design for a BART car fleet was based upon an extensive test program carried out at the Mt. Diablo Test Track with three laboratory cars built by the Budd Company, and a production contract for an initial 250 cars was awarded in 1969 to the Rohr Corporation, a Southern California aerospace firm. Ten prototype cars were completed during 1970–71, while deliveries of regular production cars began late in 1971. Extensive testing of both cars and the automatic train operation system followed, and on September 11, 1972, BART began transporting revenue passengers over an initial segment of the system between Oakland and Fremont, while the remainder of the system went into service over the next two years.

It quickly became apparent that BART's sophisticated new technology was not as ready for regular service as it should have been. As Parsons Brinckerhoff historian Benson Bobrick put it, "public and political pressure forced service to begin prematurely, and the six-month shakedown period, provided for in the original schedule, was dropped. The ribbon was cut, and all the debugging was done in service, and on page one of the newspapers."

The radical new cars proved particularly troublesome. There were problems with overheated motor bearings and flashovers. Doors sometimes opened at speed, or on the wrong side of trains, or not at all. Onboard train control equipment often failed, public address systems didn't work, and a large number of air conditioning compressors were early casualties. Wheels began to move laterally on their axles. Reliability was abysmal. Almost two years after the first segment of the system opened, cars available for service averaged less than 60 percent of the total fleet, and train failures were averaging five or six daily out of a total of 22 in service.

The car problem was forcefully brought to public attention only three weeks after BART opened, when a two-car train—quickly dubbed the "Fremont Flyer"—failed to stop at the Fremont station and plunged off the end of the line to land on its nose in the station parking lot. The accident was traced to a defective crystal oscillator in an automatic train operation circuit on the car; the installation should have been fail-safe, but wasn't. Almost two years later the opening of service through the Transbay Tube was enlivened by a motor flashover that disabled one of two inaugural trains carrying dignitaries through the Tube. Guests on the disabled train became standees on the other inaugural train. A train fire in the Transbay Tube early in 1979 that took one life and shut down the tube for three months led to an extensive fire safety program for the entire system and a costly retrofit of the entire BART car fleet with more fire-resistant materials.

The automatic train operation, or ATO, system proved to have major problems. "Ghost trains" sometimes showed up on the central control board, while others disappeared altogether. Trains sometimes stopped inexplicably between stations, accelerated when they should have decelerated and vice versa, passed stations without stopping, or stopped without opening their doors. For a time safe operation was maintained only by placing attendants in a booth on each station platform to operate a primitive telephonic block signal system, advising the preceding station that a train had arrived, and that it was safe to release another. This was later replaced with several versions of a more sophisticated interim computer-controlled system, but it was several years before the ATO system was operating anything like it was supposed to.

For a time it seemed that the solution to one problem was always followed by the emergence of another. Public and press criticism was relentless (one critical 1967 piece in the *San Francisco Chronicle* was headlined simply "The BART Mess"). The BART district filed suit against its engineers, who countersued in return. The suits were settled out of court, and finally the problems began to recede. In the end, BART worked pretty much the way it was supposed to, and it changed life in the San Francisco Bay Area beyond all recognition.

BART transformed downtown San Francisco. Within only a few years some 40 new high-rise office buildings had been put up in the downtown area around BART's four

Market Street stations, and by 1992 more than 40 million square feet of new office building space had been built in the vicinity of the four stations. If less dramatic, similar new development was soon clustered around BART stations in Oakland and other East Bay communities. Well over a third of BART's riders were former automobile commuters, and there was soon an appreciable reduction in peak period congestion on the overburdened Bay Bridge. By the end of the decade BART was transporting a weekday average of nearly 175,000 daily riders.

By the beginning of the 1990s BART had begun an ambitious expansion program that would add more than 23 miles of new line and five new stations to the system well before the end of the decade. East Bay additions to the system included a 7.8-mile Concord-West Pittsburg extension and a new 14-mile branch from Bay Fair to Dublin/Pleasanton, while a 1.6-mile extension from Daly City on the San Francisco side added an important intermodal station at Colma. By this time San Mateo County, which had dropped out of the BART district in 1962, was back in, and construction began in 1997 for an 8.7-mile, four-station extension into the county from Colma that by the end of 2002 would take BART passengers right into a new international terminal at the busy San Francisco International Airport and to an intermodal terminal at Millbrae that would connect with the Caltrain regional rail service serving the San Francisco peninsula communities.

Operators in Central Control at BART's Lake Merritt headquarters in Oakland can follow the progress of every train on the system on video screens. Central computers manage such tasks as train dispatching, station dwell time, and performance commands required to maintain schedules. This view of the center dates to 1974, and its first generation computer equipment has long since been replaced by even more advanced technology. William D. Middleton.

Almost without exception, BART traffic has grown steadily every year from the day it opened, from some 4.5 million passengers in its first year to well over 90 million at the turn of the century, with an average weekday traffic that often reached as many as 375,000 passengers. The Bay Area's leap of faith into a new era of rail transit technology has paid off handsomely indeed.

The BART example was quickly followed with the initiation of similar new generation rail systems in other American cities.

The next major system to get started was an even larger regional rail system for the Washington metropolitan area. The idea of a modern rail transit system for the region went as far back as the National Capital Planning Act of 1952. An initial rail plan was completed

Soaring high above the rooftops of San Francisco, a westbound train accelerated away from the station stop at Balboa Park on the way to Daly City in May 1991. By this time, the dramatic front-end design of BART's original cars had begun to give way to practicality. The flat-faced design of these new "C" cars permitted two cab cars to be coupled together, something that had not been possible with the original sloped-end design. William D. Middleton.

in 1959, but it was another decade before the District of Columbia and the neighboring states of Maryland and Virginia had organized the Washington Metropolitan Area Transit Authority (WMATA) to build and operate a regional system, and all of the federal, state, and local funding sources were in place to begin construction of a 103-mile, 83-station Metrorail system based upon a plan adopted in 1969. Centered on downtown Washington, the system included six routes extending beyond the District of Columbia boundaries into suburban Maryland, and another three into the Virginia suburbs.

Consultants selected for the project in 1966 included DeLeuw, Cather & Company (later Parsons Transportation Group) as general engineering consultants and Harry Weese & Associates as architectural consultants. The first construction got underway with a ceremonial groundbreaking at Judiciary Square in downtown Washington on a cloudy December 9, 1969.

President Lyndon B. Johnson had urged that the system be designed to "take its place among the most attractive in the world." Like BART, it was to offer a standard of performance and comfort that could lure the affluent commuter away from his automobile.

Moved forward by 20 hydraulic jacks, a 150-ton earth tunneling shield drilled a 21-foot-diameter subway tunnel under Washington streets. Washington Metropolitan Area Transit Authority, from Sprague Library, Electric Railroaders' Association.

Much of the Washington subway tunneling was done by open face drilling and blasting, followed by placement of sprayed-on concrete on the rock walls, a process known as the New Austrian Tunneling Method. This was open face tunneling on WMATA's Red Line subway near Wheaton, Md., in May 1985. Phil Portlock, Washington Metropolitan Area Transit Authority.

Easily the most notable feature of WMATA's 47 underground stations was their column-free, vaulted arch design by architect Harry Weese. One of the splendid arches neared completion in the construction of the DuPont Circle station in April 1975. Paul Myatt, Washington Metropolitan Area Transit Authority.

WMATA's consultant team fulfilled that mandate with a design vision for the system that set it apart from all others. This was nowhere more evident than in the approach developed by architect Harry Weese, who designed all 83 stations. In the antithesis of the diversity in station architecture pursued by BART, Weese employed a common range of materials—granite, red quarry tile, concrete, glass, and bronze—to unify the system's stations. Broad, straight platforms and flashing platform edge lights to alert passengers to approaching trains became signature features of the stations. Easily the most notable Metrorail station design element was Weese's splendid column-free, vaulted arch design that gave the system's 47 underground stations a grandeur not normally associated with subways. For most of the subway stations these distinctive vaulted, coffered ceilings were heavily reinforced, cast-in-place concrete structures, while in others the ceilings were free standing elements erected from precast concrete segments inside the tunnel.

With just over 50 miles—nearly half the system—in subway, Washington's Metrorail ranked as one of the greatest tunneling projects of the last half of the twentieth century. The subway tunnelers faced difficult groundwater conditions and everything from soft earth to hard rock in the difficult and varied geology of the Washington area. Almost 21 miles of subway was built by the traditional cut-and-cover method, and another 14 miles of soft earth tunnel was excavated with open face digger machines followed by the installation of bolted steel liner rings and a concrete liner, or by massive tunneling machines that operated as a continuous train, placing precast concrete tunnel liners as they went at a rate of as much as 85 to 90 feet a day. At one location constrained by narrow streets, the subway tunnels were drilled through soft earth one above the other. Some 15 miles of tunnel was excavated through hard rock, usually by open face drilling and blasting, usually followed by placement of a sprayed-on concrete on the rock walls in a process known as the New Austrian Tunneling Method. Downtown Washington buildings, most of them on shallow foundations, required extensive underpinning, and buried utilities had to be temporarily supported or relocated as the tunnelers came through.

Subway stations were built either by cut-and-cover construction or by rock tunneling. One, in 14th Street at Columbia Heights, was built by a unique "top down" method. Slurry walls were first put down along the curb lines. Half the width of the street was then excavated to the station roof level and a concrete roof slab placed and tied into the slurry wall. The half-width of the street was then replaced and the process repeated on the opposite side. When both sides were complete, station excavation was completed beneath the roof level.

Free rides for all helped to attract throngs of opening day passengers for Washington's new Metrorail subway on March 27, 1976. This was the scene at the Red Line's Rhode Island Avenue station. Fred W. Schneider, III.

Imaginative lighting contributed to the dramatic effect of Washington's Harry Weese subway station design. Two opening day trains met at the Red Line's Judiciary Square station. Phil Portlock, Washington Metropolitan Area Transit Authority.

The graceful arch of the concrete canopy over the platforms at Metrorail's Rhode Island Avenue station framed a view of one of Washington's elegant new subway trains and the National Capitol. It was June 18, 1976, less than two months after the trains had begun running between Rhode Island Avenue and the downtown Metro Center. Fred W. Schneider, III.

At its outer end, WMATA's Orange Line into suburban Maryland paralleled Amtrak's high-speed Northeast Corridor line. Outbound from downtown Washington on the way to the line's suburban New Carrollton in October 1979, an Orange Line train passed the high voltage substation at Landover, Md., that fed the electrified Corridor. William D. Middleton.

The eastern leg of WMATA's Red Line into Montgomery County, Md., follows the right-of-way of the CSX Transportation main line west—the former Baltimore & Ohio—for much of its length. In September 1990 a train southbound from Wheaton, Md., emerged from subway at Silver Spring, Md., to follow the CSX line into the District of Columbia. William D. Middleton.

At the Franconia-Springfield (Va.) terminal of Metrorail's Blue Line, a train had just arrived from downtown Washington in October 2000 and its passengers headed for the stairways and escalators. William D. Middleton.

127

Metrorail closely paralleled—or improved upon—BART in most of its technical features. The Washington car design bore many similarities to the BART car, and Metrorail employed an almost identical stored value magnetic card automatic fare collection system. WMATA's computer-based central control system was designed to permit fully automatic operation, although it was later decided there should be an operator on each train. Included were automatic train protection, operation, and supervision subsystems. In addition to providing for fully automatic speed and braking commands, and programmed station stops as on BART, the system was capable of a fully automatic operation capability on either track in either direction, and could automatically route trains in and out of terminals and turnback tracks as well as receiving and dispatch tracks at storage yards. The system also permitted manual operation of trains at a full performance level whenever necessary.

Unlike BART, which completed its entire initial system as an integral undertaking over a relatively short period, the Washington system was developed incrementally over nearly 30 years of construction. An initial 4.6-mile, six-station segment of the system opened for service between Rhode Island Avenue and Farragut North on March 27, 1976, and it was almost 25 years later when the opening of a final 6.5-mile, five-station segment of Metrorail's Green Line into suburban Maryland on January 13, 2001, marked the completion of the full planned system.

Over that 25-year period Metrorail had grown into a system transporting nearly 700,000 daily passengers—second in the U.S. only to the New York subway system—and it had transformed daily life and altered the shape of population and economic growth for the national capital region in profound ways that could hardly have been imagined when the project was launched almost 30 years before. Arlington County and Alexandria in Virginia; Montgomery County, Maryland; and downtown Washington had all experienced phenomenal growth oriented to their Metrorail stations. An Urban Land Institute study in the late 1990s had projected that the rail system would account for $20 to $25 billion in economic development when the full system buildout was complete.

Fast-growing Atlanta followed close behind Washington with plans for a modern rail system. Rapid transit had been on its agenda ever since the 1950s. A plan for a system built and operated by a state agency was defeated in 1962, but just three years later the four counties in the Atlanta metropolitan area joined together to form the Metropolitan Atlanta Rapid Transit Authority (MARTA). An initial plan for a 40.3-mile rail system was voted down in 1983, but MARTA was back in 1971 with a new plan for a 56-mile system financed by a sales tax. In November 1971 voters in Fulton and DeKalb counties approved the plan, while those in the other two counties rejected the plan and dropped out of MARTA. The result was a revised plan for a 53-mile, 40-station system within the two remaining counties that incorporated North-South and East-West lines intersecting at Five Points in downtown Atlanta. By early 1972 MARTA had the same Parsons, Brinckerhoff-Tudor-Bechtel[1] consultant team that had built BART at work on the project, and the first construction for a 13.7-mile, 17-station first phase of the system was underway early in 1975.

Much of the planned system was to be located on elevated structures or at-grade within existing railroad rights-of-way to help keep costs down, but the initial segment included 4.5 miles of difficult subway tunneling, much of it in the heart of downtown Atlanta. Most of the subway work was done by cut-and-cover construction, but twin 2700-foot North-South line bores were drilled northward from Five Points under Peachtree Street to avoid disrupting traffic in Atlanta's principal downtown thoroughfare. Most of this tunneling was through hard rock, but one 950-foot-long section was driven through mixed soil and rock, or clay, with compressed air shields. A pilot tunnel drilled through the rock became the crown of the system's Peachtree Center station, and the station itself was carved out of rock.

---

1. Bechtel Corporation withdrew from the project several years later.

Most of the elevated structure was constructed with cast-in-place concrete box girders, but for two long sections of the North-South line MARTA contractors pioneered the use of precast, post-tensioned segmental concrete box girders for rapid transit or railroad work. These were built with precast trapezoidal box girder units 10 feet long, 7 feet deep, and weighing about 32 tons. "Wings" on each side of the box girder gave the sections an overall width of 30¼ feet for the double track rail line. Employed for spans of 70 to 143 feet, these segments were lifted by cranes into position on temporary steel assembly trusses or "launching girders" spanning between supporting piers. Once a complete span was in place and post-tensioned, the erection trusses were removed and moved forward to the next span. The innovative procedure permitted the completion of as many as four spans a week.

In the standards for its automatic train operation system, fare collection systems, equipment, and stations, MARTA followed closely in the path blazed by BART and WMATA, and profited greatly from the experience of the startup problems experienced by both systems. MARTA's order for an initial fleet of 120 75-foot aluminum cars went to French car builder Société Franco-Belge.

An initial section of MARTA's East-West line began operating between Avondale and the Georgia State station in downtown Atlanta on June 30, 1979, and the entire first phase of the system was in service by December 1981. Construction continued without interruption over the next two decades as MARTA built steadily toward the full system envisioned in the 1971 referendum that had launched rapid transit for Atlanta. An important milestone was reached in June 1988, when North-South line trains began operating into a southern terminal at Atlanta's busy Hartsfield International Airport.

As it had in the San Francisco Bay Area and Washington, modern rail transit dramatically reshaped daily travel patterns and urban development at Atlanta. New development was drawn to sites convenient to MARTA stations. One 27-story office building was built directly over the tracks of the North-South line adjacent to the Lenox station. A massive

Construction was in full swing on MARTA's South Line in March 1981. Visible in the distance in this northward view from just south of Interstate 20 are the Georgia State Capitol and the downtown Atlanta skyline. William D. Middleton.

The Peachtree Center station on MARTA's North Line was blasted out of solid rock, and its architects and engineers left much of it exposed to create the system's most dramatic subway station. North- and southbound trains met there in October 1984. William D. Middleton.

Underground Atlanta entertainment area, opened in 1989 next to MARTA's Five Points station, drew thousands of new riders to the system. By December 2000, when MARTA opened two new stations and a 2-mile extension of its North Line to North Springs, the Atlanta rail system had grown to a three-route, 47.6-mile network that was transporting a weekday average of more than 280,000 passengers. MARTA was making a dent in the region's formidable traffic congestion, and still further extensions were planned.

Two more Eastern Seaboard cities were soon embarked on metro construction. Baltimore began serious consideration of a modern metro system in the 1960s, when consultants identified a 28-mile first phase extending to the northeast and south from downtown Baltimore. Lack of political support in Anne Arundel County led to deletion of the south leg, but by 1976 Maryland's Mass Transit Administration (MTA) had a federal funding commitment for an initial 8-mile segment of Baltimore's northwest line. That was very nearly lost when highway proponents in the Maryland General Assembly launched an eight-day filibuster to block approval of the state funding needed for the project. Rapid transit survived by a narrow margin, and construction was underway by December 1976 for Baltimore's version of a modern metro.

The first 4½ miles of the line was in subway through downtown Baltimore, where narrow streets and underground work in close proximity to old buildings and other structures gave the metro builders some of their most difficult construction problems. The twin subway tubes were drilled with the invert, or bottom, of the tube typically at depths of 60 to 70 feet below the surface, although the depth reached over 100 feet at some locations. A little more than 3 miles of subway was driven, with the work about equally divided between shield-driven soft earth tunneling under air pressure, and hard rock tunneling that was accomplished by drilling and blasting. The remainder of the tunneling was by cut-and-cover work. A pioneering feature of the Baltimore tunneling work was the trial use, the first in the U.S., of precast concrete tunnel liners for some 1700 feet of soft earth tunnel. The

Like all of its rapid transit contemporaries, Baltimore's new subway featured innovative station architecture. One of the best was the Lexington Market station, where artist Patricia Alexander decorated the beams traversing the station with ceramic tiles in ethnic designs. An inbound train loaded at the platforms in April 1988, while an outbound train accelerated out of the station in the distance. William D. Middleton.

liners were bolted together from segments to form 30-inch wide rings that were placed immediately behind the tunneling shield as it advanced. The successful trial led to wide use of the technique on other subway projects.

The six subway stations were built by cut-and-cover work, three of them with a slurry wall technique. At several points, buildings were underpinned by augured piles. Other buildings and two old nineteenth-century masonry railroad tunnels under which the subway passed were stabilized by injecting a chemical grout into the soil beneath their foundations. At several downtown stations, the available subway right-of-way was so narrow that portions of building foundations had to be removed after first stabilizing the soil with chemical grout. For the most difficult of these, at Charles Center, about 25 percent of the foundations for a 33-story bank building were removed to make room for the station.

The balance of the line was either at grade or elevated construction in the right-of-way of the Western Maryland Railroad. The 2½-mile elevated section was constructed with precast, prestressed concrete box girder sections similar to those employed for the BART system and ranging in length from 48 to 99 feet.

Baltimore Metro trains began running on November 21, 1983. A second segment of line, opened four years later, extended service another 6 miles northwest to Owings Mills, while a 1.5-mile downtown subway extension eastward to the Johns Hopkins University Medical Center began operating in 1995.

Running close behind Baltimore was a modern metro project for Miami and Dade County, Florida. Beset by rapid growth that was pushing the metropolitan area population toward a million, the region began its first serious rapid transit study in 1964. A 1971 study recommended a rail system, and only a year later Dade County voters approved—by a two-to-one margin—a bond issue that would finance a local share of the cost for a 20.5-mile, 20-station system extending southwest from downtown Miami to Coral Gables and Dadeland, and north and west to Hialeah. Within another two years preliminary engineering was complete, and Dade County had a federal commitment to fund an 80 percent share of the project cost. Then—late in 1977—the project was very nearly derailed by an anti–rapid transit referendum that would have repealed the voters' 1972 approval of bonds for the local share of costs. Rapid transit survived by the narrowest of margins, and construction began in 1979.

South Florida's high water table made subway construction impractical for the Metro-Dade system, and virtually the entire line was built on elevated structure, about half of it within existing city streets and the remainder in a former Florida East Coast Railroad right-of-way south of downtown Miami. Engineers for the system developed an innovative design for a precast, prestressed double-T concrete girder for the elevated structure. Supported

A second segment of the Baltimore metro extended service to Owings Mills in suburban Baltimore County in 1987. Inbound to downtown Baltimore soon after the extension opened, an eastbound train accelerated away from a stop at the Old Court station in Pikesville. Fred W. Schneider, III.

In downtown Miami, the Metrorail line soared high above the Miami River on a prestressed concrete box girder span. A southbound train sped over the structure in January 1994. William D. Middleton.

Metrorail trains met just outside the Brickell station on the south side of downtown Miami in October 2001. Joseph M. Calisi.

by concrete piers, these were 12 feet wide and 5 feet, 2 inches deep, and were used for spans ranging from 40 to 80 feet. Longer spans were built with more conventional concrete box girders. Borrowing a popular idea from BART, areas below the elevated structure in the former railroad right-of-way were landscaped as "linear parks."

The south end of Miami's Metrorail system began running on May 21, 1984, and the full system was in service a year later. Although Miami and Dade County voters proved reluctant to approve local funding for a number of major extensions to the system, a 1.5-mile extension completed in 2002 took Metrorail west from its northern terminal to a new intermodal rail-highway terminal at the Palmetto Expressway.

In such characteristics as overall performance standards, automatic train operation installation, fare collection, and passenger amenities, the Baltimore and Miami systems were generally comparable to the earlier BART and WMATA metro projects. Wary of the kind of startup problems that had accompanied new technologies on these earlier systems, planners for both deliberately set out to design systems that were based almost entirely upon proven, already available components. Both systems also chose a lower level of automatic operation than that of either BART or WMATA. Under this "semi-automatic" operation, operators made station announcements, opened and closed doors, and started trains manually.

Of all the North American cities that have begun the construction of new generation metro systems, none has taken longer or had a more difficult time than Los Angeles. Given the area's notorious traffic congestion—arguably among the worst in North America—getting started on a rapid transit alternative would have seemed an easy decision for the region to make, but it wasn't. Beginning even before World War II, Los Angeles had de-

Much of the Los Angeles subway was excavated with huge 200-ton, 185-foot-long tunnel boring machines that were capable of advancing anywhere from 60 to 100 feet a day. One of the big machines headed into the tunnel heading at Westlake/ MacArthur in December 1991. Linda Salzman, Los Angeles County Transportation Commission.

veloped an extraordinary system of urban freeways that was supposed to provide unparalleled mobility and convenience for the region. It didn't quite work out that way, but Southern California's freeway dream was hard to relinquish. Aggravating any effort at regional decision-making was a Byzantine patchwork of political jurisdictions and conflicting interests that made the formation of a consensus or the setting of priorities exceedingly difficult. As Jack R. Gilstrap, the one-time head of the Southern California Rapid Transit District, once said of rapid transit for Los Angeles: "No area needs it more—no area has more political hurdles to clear to get it."

Ironically, the Los Angeles metropolitan area had largely developed around the framework of the Pacific Electric Railway, a Southern Pacific subsidiary that was the largest of all North American interurban electric railway systems. While PE developed an enormous rail traffic, transporting more than 100 million annual riders at its peak, rail passengers proved to be an unprofitable business, and PE had begun a shift to bus services even before World War II. What was left of the company's passenger business was sold to a bus operator in 1953, and the last of the PE rail lines closed in 1961.

Some studies of rapid transit for Los Angeles dated as far back as the 1920s, but the subject began to assume increasing urgency after World War II as road congestion grew steadily worse in the fast-growing region, and air quality declined to dangerous levels, largely as the result of automotive exhaust emissions.

A study of a rapid transit line for the San Fernando Valley–Los Angeles–Long Beach corridor completed in 1954 went on the shelf, but it did result in the formation of a public agency that continued rapid transit studies and eventually took over operation of the region's principal transit lines. More studies and plans followed over a period of more than two decades, but rapid transit for Los Angeles went nowhere.

Three times in less than a decade—in 1968, 1974, and again in 1976—Los Angeles voters went to the polls only to reject financing measures that would have permitted a start to ambitious regional systems. Finally, after years of political debate over routes, the region's Southern California Rapid Transit District pulled together a plan for an 18.6-mile "starter line" that would extend from downtown Los Angeles via Wilshire Boulevard and Hollywood to the San Fernando Valley, and would represent the first phase of a regional system. Some preliminary engineering began in 1980, but the project was soon sidetracked by the virtual disappearance of federal funding under a Reagan administration hostile to new rail starts. Finally, enough federal funding was forthcoming to begin a 4.4-mile, five-station Wilshire corridor segment of the project, and a jubilant Los Angeles Mayor Tom Bradley, who had made rapid transit a campaign pledge, presided over a September 29, 1986, groundbreaking ceremony that marked a start to a long-awaited Los Angeles subway. That first segment began carrying passengers in January 1993, and subsequent extensions added service in increments until trains began running over the full route to North Hollywood in the San Fernando Valley in June 2000.

Construction of this first Los Angeles subway had proved to be one of the most difficult, and the most costly, anywhere. Built in the earthquake-prone Los Angeles basin, and across three major fault lines, the line had required a number of special design features to assure earthquake safety. Some of the worst problems were created by petroleum deposits, and pockets of methane, hydrogen sulfide, and other gases, encountered at several points where the route passed through old oil field sites. The potential danger was illustrated by a 1985 methane gas explosion and fire in a Fairfax District department store that injured 21 people. To avoid similar problems in the subway, the planned alignment was shifted away from the most hazardous areas, and special protective measures were adopted to minimize the risk of gas explosions during construction or in the completed subway.

There were some costly mishaps. In 1990 timber lagging caught fire in the tunnel near Union Station, causing a section of tunnel to collapse. In 1994 subsidence over the tunnel construction sank a several-block-long section of Hollywood Boulevard by as much as a foot, and the work was shut down for nearly five months. The following year a huge sink-

Deep below Wilshire Boulevard, construction workers built the Red Line subway's station at Western Avenue in September 1992. The subway tunnels were drilled with big tunnel boring machines, while the station was being built by the cut-and-cover technique. The street above was carried on a temporary deck of timber planking and steel beams while the site was excavated and the station constructed. The horizontal tubes in this view braced the station walls against the earth pressure. William D. Middleton.

The completed Los Angeles subway looked like this. A train of Red Line metro cars built by Italy's Breda Costruzione Ferroviarie is in the tunnel between Pershing Square and the 7th Street Metro Center in downtown Los Angeles. Kelly Harriger, Los Angeles County Transportation Commission.

hole opened up in the Boulevard, collapsing a section of tunnel and causing millions of dollars in damage. On the Fourth of July weekend in 1996, one of the huge tunneling machines being used to drill the line's twin tunnels through the Hollywood Hills celebrated by getting stuck. It was six weeks before the machine was finally freed to continue tunneling.

Criticism of the project was relentless (one sample *Los Angeles Times* headline in 1998: "L.A. subway project on its death bed"). There were charges of mismanagement and corruption. The work fell behind schedule, and costs kept rising. By the time the 17.4-mile, 16-station line was complete the original $3.4 billion budget had grown by almost 80 percent to $6.1 billion. Instead of representing the end point for a subway "starter line," the opening of service to North Hollywood may well have marked the end to any more Los Angeles subway construction for the foreseeable future. In 1998 subway opponents had managed to put on the ballot—and Los Angeles voters approved—a measure that banned the use of county sales tax revenues for subway tunneling. But despite all of the problems in getting it built, and however doubtful the future of subway construction for Los Angeles, the city finally had a subway, and at least the traveling public thought it was a great alternative to the traffic-clogged freeways. Within weeks of the subway's opening, people were complaining about the full parking lots at the Valley stations, and within a year Southern Californians were taking an average of 150,000 trips every day on their new subway.

By the turn of the century, Tren Urbano, the newest North American metro, was taking shape at San Juan, Puerto Rico, with service expected to begin by fall 2003. With a population that was approaching the 1½ million mark at the turn of the century, San Juan was one of the largest U.S. cities without a rail transit system, and the fast growing metropolitan area was confronted with some formidable traffic congestion.

After more than two decades of study, Tren Urbano emerged as a firm project of Puerto Rico's Highway and Transportation Authority in the early 1990s. Planned as the first phase of an extensive system serving the entire metropolitan San Juan area, the initial project follows an L-shaped alignment linking the densely populated western community of Bayamon with Guaynabo and Rio Pedras, where it turns north to Hato Rey and Santurce. Except for a 1.1-mile subway under the historic community of Rio Pedras and the University of Puerto

Rico, the entire line is built at grade or on elevated structures, much of it in existing highway medians; one long section of line employs a right-of-way originally acquired for a highway that was never built.

Tren Urbano construction got underway in 1996, and the work has seen some innovative engineering. Almost all of the elevated structure was built with precast, post-tensioned segmental concrete box girders that were erected from launching girders. The subway was built with a combination of bored tunnel with a tunneling machine, cut-and-cover construction, and the New Austrian Tunneling Method. At Rio Pedras, a subway station was built without disturbing historic structures directly above it with what was called a "stacked drifts" procedure. Successive "drifts" 10 feet square were driven through the length of the station and filled with concrete to gradually form the arch of the station structure, which was then excavated and the station completed.

Like other recent U.S. systems before it, Tren Urbano will be capable of virtually fully automatic operation. Although trains will be manned, the operator's duties will normally be confined to opening and closing doors. A fleet of 82 75-foot stainless steel cars supplied by Siemens is very much in the modern metro model of high performance equipment with such passenger amenities as air conditioning, comfortable seating, and large, panoramic windows.

While these highly automatic modern metros were taking shape in U.S. cities, Canadian engineers were taking the next step toward fully automatic rapid transit. This was a new Advanced Rapid Transit (ART)[2] technology developed during the late 1970s by Canada's Urban Transit Development Corporation (UTDC),[3] which had evolved from a government financed research, development, design, and marketing organization set up by the Province of Ontario in 1973.

UTDC's goal had been to develop a transit technology that could fill the gap between high-cost, high-capacity heavy rail rapid transit and low-cost, low-capacity light rail technology. Incorporating such technical innovations as a linear induction motor propulsion system, steerable trucks, an automatic close-headway control system, and lightweight car bodies, ART represented the most comprehensive application of new transit technology in a single system since the development of the BART system a decade earlier. The choice of these technologies was reached through a systems approach that examined all the available or possible technologies, and chose those which provided an optimum combination for ART.

For cost reasons, ART was designed as an above-ground system, and to best meet Canada's severe winter operating conditions the engineers chose a conventional steel wheel on rail technology. The same concern for all-weather reliability led to the adoption of the linear induction motor propulsion system with regenerative braking, which provided predictable all-weather performance by eliminating dependence upon wheel rail adhesion for either acceleration or braking.

The linear motor technology chosen for ART in effect placed half of the traction motor in the track. A linear motor, which corresponded to the flattened stator of a conventional rotary motor, was suspended under each truck with a clearance of only a fraction of an inch above a foot-wide continuous steel reaction rail placed between the running rails. This

A pair of the handsome stainless steel cars that will operate San Juan's Tren Urbano stood outside the line's maintenance shops at Martinez Nadal during pre-startup test operation. Tren Urbano.

The Toronto Transit Commission's Scarborough Rapid Transit line was the first to begin operation with the Urban Transit Development Corporation's Advanced Rapid Transit technology in 1985. In May 1988 a two-car train loaded for the return trip from Scarborough Centre to the eastern terminal of the Bloor-Danforth subway at Kennedy station. William D. Middleton.

2. Originally called Intermediate Capacity Transit System, or ICTS.
3. UTDC has since been acquired by the Bombardier Corporation.

reaction rail corresponded to the rotor of a conventional motor, flattened and laid continuously in the track. Power was supplied to trains from a two-rail power supply system mounted on vertical supports beside the track.

The steerable truck developed for ART carried each axle in yokes, connected at a pivot point to establish a radial system. The design greatly reduced both wheel-rail wear and the flange-rail squeal characteristic of conventional trucks on curved tracks.

UTDC's designers adopted a SELTRAC train control system developed in Germany that was capable of providing both fully automatic operation and close headway operation with trains operating as little as 40 seconds apart.

Taking full advantage of this close headway capability, UTDC's designers chose a small train/frequent service approach for ART with small cars typically operating in trains of four or six cars. The extremely lightweight cars developed for ART were built of aluminum, with honeycomb roofs and floors, and fiberglass ends. The use of wheels only 18 inches in diameter helped to hold the overall height to only 10 feet 3 inches. Less than 42 feet long and a little over 8 feet wide—about the size of a standard transit bus—each car could carry a maximum of about 100 seated and standing passengers.

UTDC began an extended prototype and test program at its Kingston, Ont., development center in 1976. The first regular service test of the ART technology came with its adoption for the Toronto Transit Commission's Scarborough Rapid Transit line, although TTC elected to use train operators rather than employ the system's capability for fully automatic operation. Connecting with the eastern terminal of TTC's Bloor-Danforth subway, the 4.3-mile line began operation in March 1985.

The first large-scale application of the fully automatic ART technology went into service less than a year later, when British Columbia Transit opened its 13.3-mile, 15-station SkyTrain metro system between downtown Vancouver and New Westminster in January 1986, in time for the city's Expo '86 international transportation and communications exhibition. BC Transit had originally planned a light rail line, but had shifted to the ART technology when studies indicated that it would provide the greater capacity needed for future growth at a lower overall cost.

Much of the line was located on elevated structure placed in the right-of-way of an abandoned rail line, while some ingenious engineering gave SkyTrain a ready-made 1.2-mile downtown Vancouver subway. The small profile of the ART cars permitted the engineers to fit two tracks into an abandoned single-track Canadian Pacific tunnel by stacking them one above the other. By 1994 subsequent additions had expanded SkyTrain to an 18-mile, 20-station line that reached suburban Surrey over a crossing of the Fraser River on an innovative 1968-foot-long, cable-stayed SkyBridge that ranks as one of the most dramatic structures anywhere on North American rapid transit.

An initial fleet of 114 41-foot Mark I ART vehicles was later expanded to a total of 150, and the fully automatic system has established an impressive performance record for BC Transit, now the Greater Vancouver Transportation Authority, or TransLink. Trains normally operate in a fully automatic mode, with radio-equipped attendants on duty to provide coverage of trains and stations, conduct proof-of-payment fare checks, assist passengers, and respond to problems. Trains operate at a normal maximum speed of 50 mph, with base service at a frequency of 5 minutes or less, while peak period headways average 2 minutes, 30 seconds. From an annual total of a little more than 20 million passengers in its first few years of operation, SkyTrain traffic had grown to 40 million a year in 2000. Reflecting the benefits of automatic operation, the system's cost per passenger has steadily declined to an operating cost per passenger mile of about a third of that for bus service.

By late 1999 TransLink had begun construction of a second ART technology line, a 13-mile east-west Millennium Line that links Vancouver Community College southeast of downtown Vancouver with New Westminster via Lougheed Mall. Opening in three segments between late 2001 and late 2002, the extension has given Vancouver one of the world's longest fully automatic metro systems.

Westbound to downtown Vancouver, B.C., a fully automatic SkyTrain approached a stop at the Stadium station in September 1995. Just beyond the station the train will enter the former Canadian Pacific tunnel that carries the line through the downtown area. William D. Middleton.

Metrotown, in Burnaby, is perhaps the most notable result of the coordinated transportation and growth planning that have helped Vancouver to concentrate much of the city's development around the "nodes" created by SkyTrain stations. An eastbound train departed from the Metrotown station in September 1995. William D. Middleton.

Easily the most spectacular piece of engineering on Vancouver's SkyTrain system is this innovative 1968-foot cable-stayed bridge that carries the line over the Fraser River between New Westminster and Surrey, B.C. The train was eastbound from Vancouver to Surrey in September 1995. William D. Middleton.

During 2001–02 the Greater Vancouver Transportation Authority opened the new ART technology Millennium Line between Vancouver and New Westminster via Lougheed Mall. A test train of Bombardier's larger Mark II ART vehicles ran up the north bank of the Fraser River at New Westminster. Visible beyond the train are Canadian National's truss bridge crossing of the river, the steel arch, high level highway bridge, and SkyTrain's cable-stayed crossing to Surrey. Bombardier Transportation.

UTDC's Advanced Rapid Transit technology was also adopted for a Detroit downtown "people mover" system completed in 1987. A two-car ART train passes the city's Renaissance Center on the system's elevated loop. Bombardier Transportation.

The ART technology was also adopted for a "people mover" system completed by the Southeastern Michigan Transportation Authority (SEMTA) at Detroit in 1987. This fully automatic 2.9-mile elevated system operates as a one-way loop serving 13 stations in Detroit's Central Business District. More recently, the Port Authority of New York and New Jersey selected a turnkey design-build-operate consortium to construct a fully automatic, 8.1-mile AirTrain rail line at New York's John F. Kennedy International Airport that will use Bombardier's ART technology. A loop segment of the elevated line will link the airport's eight terminals, another segment will link the terminals with rental car and parking facilities, and the Howard Beach subway station, while a third segment will link the system with the Long Island Rail Road and three subway lines at Jamaica. Bombardier Transportation is supplying 32 Mark II linear motor powered cars for the project. Much larger than the original ART vehicle, these are 57-foot, 9-inch cars capable of carrying as many as 205 seated and standing passengers. AirTrain construction began in 1998, with the first two segments of the system opening in 2002, and the full system to be in operation a year later.

Beginning in the 1960s, Westinghouse and other manufacturers, both in the U.S. and abroad, had begun the development of a variety of fully automatic, pneumatic-tired tran-

140

sit systems operating on some kind of fixed guideway. Several of these systems had been widely adopted for such specialized applications as "people mover" links between airport terminals, and by the 1980s some were being applied to more conventional rapid transit applications as well.

One of the most successful of these for airport installations, the automated transit system developed by Westinghouse (now part of Bombardier Transportation), was adopted for a 1.9-mile, nine-station elevated Metromover installation that served as a downtown distributor for Miami's Metrorail system. Employing the same basic technology originally developed for the Westinghouse Skybus more than 20 years earlier, the Miami installation employed electrically powered, rubber-tired vehicles operating over a guideway structure with a center guide beam. Switching was accomplished by means of either pivoting or rotating guide beam switches. Each of the 100-passenger, 16-ton aluminum vehicles was carried on two single-axle trucks and powered by a single traction motor. Four horizontal rubber-tired guide wheels on each truck bore against the center guide rail, while a horizontal metal safety disk below the top flange of the guide beam provided a positive assurance against derailment. Opened in 1986, Miami's Metromover was expanded to a 4.4-mile system with the opening of two extensions in 1994.

VAL (for Vehicule Automatique Leger, or automatic light vehicle) was a similar system developed by France's Matra Transport. First installed in 1983 for an automatic rapid transit system at Lille, France, VAL was subsequently adopted for a number of other airport or rapid transit installations in Europe, Asia, and North America. In Florida, the Jacksonville Transportation Authority (JTA) chose VAL for its Skyway Express, a fully automatic elevated transit system that was planned to link the city's downtown area with bus services and parking lots on the periphery. An initial 0.7-mile segment began carrying passengers in 1989. An extensive 2.7-mile VAL installation completed at Chicago's O'Hare International Airport in 1993 linked the airport's several terminals with parking areas. Both the Jacksonville and Chicago systems adopted a 45-foot lightweight aluminum vehicle with a maximum capacity of 114 passengers and capable of operation in trains of up to three cars at a maximum operating speed of 50 mph.

"People mover" technology took up a major role in urban transit with its adoption for a Metromover downtown distribution system for Miami's new metro system. Opened in 1986, the fully automated Metromover was based on Westinghouse Skybus technology introduced in 1961. One of the 100-passenger, pneumatic-tired guided vehicles turned a corner on the guideway at S.E. 2nd Street and Biscayne Boulevard in January 1994. William D. Middleton.

By the end of the twentieth century, even that perennial favorite of nineteenth-century inventors and writers for Sunday supplements and popular magazines—the monorail—was beginning to get a little attention.

Still more monorail ideas had begun to emerge after the Second World War. Several short suspended monorails were installed in parks or fairgrounds at Houston, Dallas, Los Angeles, Tokyo, and elsewhere. The most nearly successful monorail design, however, was the Alweg system developed by the Swedish industrialist and inventor Axel Lennert Wenner-Gren. This was a supported monorail, with a car that straddled a supporting precast concrete girder, or beamway. Rubber-tired drive wheels ran on the top of the beamway, while horizontal guide wheels bore against each side of the girder. Demonstration Alweg installations were built in Germany in 1952 and 1957, and a short line was completed for California's Disneyland amusement park in 1959.

The system got a major test in regular rapid transit service when it was adopted for a line linking downtown Seattle with the site of Century 21, the 1962 Seattle World's Fair. "Gleaming, stream-lined trains will rush overhead almost silently on rubber-tired wheels running on

narrow beamways of concrete—transporting 10,000 passengers an hour to and from Century 21 while they sit in deep-cushioned luxury next to huge view windows overlooking the city, Puget Sound, and the spectacular exposition site," promised an Alweg brochure.

The 1.2-mile elevated line consisted of two parallel concrete beams, 3 feet wide and 5 feet deep, supported by a single row of concrete columns. Two 120-foot-long, four-car trains, each capable of carrying as many as 450 seated and standing passengers, shuttled back and forth over the line. A highly popular feature of the 1962 fair, Seattle's Alweg monorail continued to operate after the fair was over.

For a time, monorail fever was everywhere. In the years after World War II upwards of two dozen proposals for monorail transit systems for North American cities were put forward. One that was seriously considered was in Los Angeles, where in 1953 the newly formed Los Angeles Metropolitan Transit Authority completed a study for a monorail system that would have extended from the San Fernando Valley through downtown Los Angeles to Long Beach. No money was available to build the system, however, and the modest Seattle installation was to remain the only North American example of monorail as a rapid transit technology for almost 40 years.

Installed for Seattle's 1962 World's Fair, the 1.2-mile Alweg monorail has remained a novel feature of the city's transportation system. One of the line's two 120-foot straddle-beam trains arrived at the downtown terminal in July 1964. William D. Middleton.

Monorail technology took on a new task in late 2001 when the Newark Airport's internal monorail system was extended to link the airport with a new Northeast Corridor rail station. This was a view of monorail trains at the new station from Haynes Avenue in November 2001. Joseph M. Calisi.

By the end of the twentieth century, however, monorail was back. AEG Monorail Systems (now Bombardier) was selected to install its beam-straddling monorail system for a 3.9-mile system linking terminals, car rental agencies, and parking lots at the Newark International Airport that opened in 1996, while a mile-long extension completed late in 2001 linked the airport with a new rail station on Amtrak's Northeast Corridor.

Monorail technology got another major boost in Florida in 1994, when the Jacksonville Transportation Authority selected Bombardier Transportation's UM III Monorail System for a buildout of the 2.5-mile Skyway Express that had begun operation of a short section with the Matra VAL technology in 1989. The fully automatic Bombardier system employed a straddle beam technology, with the vehicles supported and guided by rubber tires riding on the top and sides of the supporting beam. An initial segment of the Skyway Express monorail opened late in 1997, and the full system was in operation by November 2000.

And at Seattle, dreams of monorail came to life in a surprising way in the November 2000 election. Despite an already existing regional transit authority with approved funding to build a light rail and commuter rail system, Seattle voters approved a referendum that established a new public development authority to build and operate a 40-mile monorail system linked to the existing mile-long Century 21 line, although a funding source for the system remained to be found. The dream of futuristic monorail trains, silently and swiftly whisking passengers above the city's crowded streets on their daily journeys, was an enduring one.

The most extensive monorail system operating in rapid transit service anywhere in North America is Jacksonville's Skyway Express. The fully automated Bombardier UM III straddle beam monorail in downtown Jacksonville is linked to peripheral parking and bus lines, and—potentially—to future light rail lines. En route to the Kings Avenue terminal, a train approached the Riverplace station in October 2001. Joseph M. Calisi.

Cleveland's Shaker Heights Rapid Transit was among the earliest examples of the technology that has come to be known as light rail transit. Operating in private rights-of-way or boulevard medians, the line provided a fast trip downtown for residents of the Shaker Heights community. A second generation of light rail rolling stock for the line arrived shortly after World War II in the form of modern PCC streetcars equipped for multiple-unit operation. An eastbound four-car Van Aiken Express is seen leaving the subterranean Cleveland Union Terminal in 1956. Herbert H. Harwood, Jr.

CHAPTER 6

LIGHT RAIL TRANSIT: NEW LIFE FOR AN OLD TECHNOLOGY

. . . a "light-rail vehicle," as transportation experts define it, is a "go anywhere vehicle"; that is, a kind of railroad car that can run down a street in mixed traffic or through a subway tunnel or along an elevated track or on the ground over its own separate right-of-way. Nor is that the limit of its versatil-ity: a light-rail vehicle can operate independently, or several L.R.V.s can be hooked together to form a train.

Tony Hiss in *The New Yorker*, March 6, 1989

FOR MANY SMALLER North American cities new rail rapid transit systems seemed be-yond reach, no matter how great the need, for they were enormously expensive. Constructed largely during the 1960s, the 71.5-mile BART system had cost some $2.6 bil-lion, or more than $36 million a mile, to build. The 103-mile Washington metro cost $9.4 billion over a 30-year construction period. That was an average of more than $91 million a mile, with some of the system's most difficult subway sections costing as much as $300 million a mile.

For cities that couldn't afford—or didn't need—that kind of costly, high-capacity metro system, a lower-cost alternative called light rail transit (LRT for short) came on the scene in the 1970s. If the name was new, the technology wasn't. Light rail transit was essentially an updated streetcar technology, and it represented a compromise form of electric railway operation somewhere between the extremes of a conventional streetcar operation in public thoroughfares and a full-fledged metro system. As the Transportation Research Board's Committee on Light-Rail Transit once defined it: "Light-rail transit is a mode of urban transportation utilizing predominantly reserved but not necessarily grade-separated right-of-way. Electrically propelled rail vehicles operate singly or in trains. LRT provides a wide range of passenger capabilities and performance characteristics at moderate costs."

Streetcar technology dated all the way back to the end of the nineteenth century, when the electric railway emerged as the primary mode of urban transportation for almost ev-ery North American city. Beginning with a few pioneering installations in the 1880s, electric railways grew into an enormous industry in only a few decades. By the time the industry reached its peak physical expansion in 1917, there were well over 60,000 streetcars in op-eration on some 26,000 miles of street railway trackage in the U.S.; and the streetcar com-panies were transporting close to 11 billion passengers a year. Over the next several decades, however, growing private automobile usage and rising costs made the business increasingly uneconomical. By the mid-1920s some transit companies had begun to convert a few streetcar lines to motorbuses, which could be operated cheaply and didn't require the heavy expenditures needed to maintain and renew track and power systems. By the end of the 1930s streetcars had vanished from most smaller cities.

In 1929 an organization of street railway executives had formed the Electric Railway Presidents' Conference Committee, which conducted a five-year research and development effort that produced the standardized design for a new PCC (after the committee's initials) streetcar of radically improved appearance and performance. Despite the purchase of nearly 5000 of these modern PCC cars, even the large city systems began to disappear rapidly after World War II. By 1955 buses were hauling six times as many passengers as the streetcars, and the street railway era was essentially over.

From the ruins of the street railway industry emerged a few hardy survivors. One of the principal reasons for the decline of the industry after World War II had been the effect of steadily worsening street traffic congestion, which prevented most streetcar operators from realizing the superior earning potential of the advanced PCC cars. Almost without exception the surviving lines were ones that incorporated many of the attributes of what came to be called light rail. Typically, these were lines that carried a heavy traffic and that operated, at least in part, in reserved rights-of-way that permitted higher operating speeds and avoided the delays of traffic-congested streets.

By then part of the Greater Cleveland Regional Transit Authority, the Shaker Heights line was rebuilt to modern light rail standards and re-equipped with a new generation of articulated light rail vehicles during the early 1980s. Inbound to Public Square from the Shaker Boulevard Green Line, a Breda light rail vehicle made a passenger stop at Warrensville Road on a snowy January day in 1986. William D. Middleton.

Boston's Tremont Street streetcar subway of 1896 formed the downtown trunk of the Massachusetts Bay Transportation Authority's extensive Green Line light rail system. Inbound from Riverside, a Type 8 articulated light rail vehicle built by Japan's Kinki Sharyo unloads passengers at the Park Street station on Boston Common. The Riverside line itself is MBTA's newest light rail route, having been established in 1959 on a former Boston & Albany rail line. William D. Middleton.

Perhaps the best early example of the light rail concept was afforded by the Shaker Heights Rapid Transit line completed at Cleveland by the Van Sweringen brothers in 1920. The inner portion of this 15-mile line was built in private right-of-way, while two outer branches were laid in broad boulevard medians, enabling the Shaker Heights line to provide fast, reliable service between the suburb and downtown Cleveland. The line was operated with standard Cleveland streetcars equipped for multiple-unit operation in trains.

At Boston, the pioneer Tremont Street trolley subway, completed in 1896, and its later extensions provided a traffic-free entry to the congested downtown area for the city's Green Line system of streetcar lines. Philadelphia's downtown Market Street trolley subway, built as part of the Market Street subway-elevated project in 1905, provided a similar fast trip to the downtown center at City Hall for a 31-mile, five-route system of West Philadelphia subway-surface streetcar lines. Another three suburban lines operating largely in private rights-of-way extended into the western suburbs from a connection with the Market Street El at 69th Street Terminal. At Newark, N.J., the 5-mile City Subway reached the downtown area through a trolley subway constructed in the bed of the abandoned Morris & Essex Canal in 1935. Pittsburgh retained a South Hills trolley system that had both extensive reserved right-of-way operation and a fast entry to downtown Pittsburgh through the mile-long Mt. Washington tunnel. San Francisco retained five trolley routes that had substantial reserved median operation, while four of them reached a Market Street entry into downtown San Francisco via the long Twin Peaks or Sunset tunnels. At both New Orleans and Mexico City, surviving streetcar lines enjoyed traffic-free running over extensive reserved medians. Only Toronto continued to operate a significant system of conventional streetcar lines in urban streets.

All of these surviving lines had been updated with modern PCC car fleets in the years after World War II with the exception of New Orleans, which had formed a sentimental attachment to its lumbering 1923–24 vintage Perley A. Thomas streetcars. At Boston, a new light rail line had even been created in 1959: the 12-mile Riverside line, installed in the right-of-way of an abandoned Boston & Albany rail line, reaching downtown Boston via the Tremont Street trolley subway.

Much like Boston's light rail system, surface lines from West Philadelphia had a fast subway route to the Philadelphia city center. Inbound from Route No. 13, Darby, a modern light rail vehicle built by Japan's Kawasaki arrived at City Hall station in December 1985. William D. Middleton.

The Newark (N.J.) City Subway line reached the downtown area through a subway built in an abandoned canal bed. One of the PCC streetcars that operated the line for nearly half a century made a station stop at Norfolk Street on an inbound trip to the line's Penn Station terminal in May 2001. Modern light rail vehicles finally replaced the PCC cars just three months later. Herbert H. Harwood, Jr.

(Top) The long Mt. Washington Tunnel and extensive private right-of-way that gave riders on Pittsburgh's South Hills trolley lines a fast trip to downtown ensured their survival into the modern light rail era. A major modernization begun in the early 1980s included new cars, a downtown subway, and a new crossing of the Monongahela River over the former Pennsylvania Railroad Panhandle Bridge. A modern light rail vehicle crossed the bridge soon after the new line opened in 1985. Port Authority Transit.

(Middle) A new Market Street subway built as part of the BART rapid transit project gave San Francisco's Municipal Railway the foundation for modernization of its surviving streetcar lines into the Muni Metro light rail system. Muni Metro trains unloaded morning rush hour passengers at the subway's Embarcadero terminal at the foot of Market Street in January 1988. William D. Middleton.

(Bottom) Alone among surviving surface rail systems, the Regional Transit Authority at New Orleans declined to upgrade its equipment fleet with modern light rail vehicles, electing instead to carry out a major overhaul of the city's beloved 1923–24 vintage Perley A. Thomas streetcars. Seen from Audubon Park, one of them passed the Tulane University campus in July 1987 on an outbound trip on St. Charles Avenue. William D. Middleton.

148

With the advent of federal transit support in the 1960s and a growing interest in rail solutions to urban rapid transit needs, these early light rail precursors became candidates for rehabilitation and modernization programs that would upgrade them to modern light rail transit technology. San Francisco's BART rapid transit project of the 1960s included a second subway tunnel under Market Street for the Municipal Railways' light rail system, and the city carried out an extensive rehabilitation and modernization program for the balance of the system. The systems at Boston, Newark, Philadelphia, and New Orleans completed extensive rehabilitation of track and power supply systems during the 1970s and 1980s. During the early 1980s, Cleveland's Shaker Heights system and a first phase of Pittsburgh's South Hills lines were completely rebuilt to modern light rail standards. By the end of the decade Mexico City had completed a similar reconstruction of its surviving Xochimilco trolley line into a modern light rail line.

During the 1980s almost all of these surviving lines were also reequipped with new fleets of modern light rail vehicles. Some came from North American manufacturers, but European or Japanese suppliers built most. Instead of acquiring new cars, New Orleans chose

Two street railway lines of Mexico City's Servicio de Transportes Eléctricos (STE) survived as feeders to the Tasquena line of the city's metro system. Both were upgraded to modern light rail standards in 1986 and reequipped with modern articulated light rail vehicles, some of them rebuilt with old PCC car components. One of STE's modern articulated light rail vehicles, built by Mexican car builder Concarril, is seen at Huipulco Junction in 1993. Jack May.

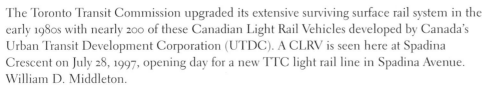

The Toronto Transit Commission upgraded its extensive surviving surface rail system in the early 1980s with nearly 200 of these Canadian Light Rail Vehicles developed by Canada's Urban Transit Development Corporation (UTDC). A CLRV is seen here at Spadina Crescent on July 28, 1997, opening day for a new TTC light rail line in Spadina Avenue. William D. Middleton.

UTDC development of the single unit CLRV was followed by an articulated version. The Toronto Transit Commission acquired 52 of the big cars. Their prodigious crowd-swallowing capacity is demonstrated here by a TTC Route 501 car at Humber Loop in 1990. William D. Middleton.

to rebuild its beloved Perley A. Thomas streetcars for the city's St. Charles rail line, while in the late 1980s New Jersey Transit elected to overhaul its City Subway PCC car fleet for another decade or more of service. Modern light rail vehicles finally replaced these well-kept cars, by then well past the half-century mark, in August 2001. With that, PCC cars continued to operate in light rail service only at Boston, where the Massachusetts Bay Transportation Authority was once again overhauling a small fleet of the enduring cars for continued service on the 2.6-mile Ashmont-Mattapan high-speed line.

Before the end of the 1970s, North American cities were beginning to plan entirely new light rail systems. The first to complete a new system was Edmonton, Alberta, where new rail lines had been proposed as part of an integrated urban transportation system for the

Edmonton, Alta., opened the first entirely new North American light rail system in 1978. A three-car train of German-built Siemens-Duewag articulated light rail vehicles crossed the North Saskatchewan River bridge to the University station in June 1994 over an extension to the original line completed in 1992. Fred W. Schneider, III.

Calgary, Alta., was close behind with its own new C-Train light rail system, which opened in 1981. A single Siemens-Duewag articulated car was photographed at 5th Avenue and 4th Street S.E. on a run from the City Centre to Whitehorn in June 1994. Looming on the horizon is the Olympic Saddledome on the grounds of the Calgary Stampede. Fred W. Schneider, III.

fast growing city as early as 1963. Planning for an initial 4.5-mile light rail route extending from downtown Edmonton to the city's northeast sector began in 1974 and the line opened in April 1978. Typical of almost all new light rail systems that followed, design and construction of the Edmonton line were characterized by an emphasis on simplicity that helped both to limit construction costs and to provide an installation that could operate efficiently and reliably. Except for a mile-long subway that was needed to avoid downtown traffic congestion, the entire line was constructed within a Canadian National right-of-way. Standard ballasted track was employed, with a 600-volt D.C. overhead catenary power supply and a simple two-aspect block signal system. Initial equipment for the line was a fleet of 14 standard articulated light rail vehicles built by Germany's Siemens-Duewag. Subsequent extensions north to Clareview and south across the North Saskatchewan River to the University of Alberta expanded the line to a total length of 7.8 miles that was moving an average of 36,000 daily passengers by the turn of the century.

Calgary, another fast-growing Alberta city, was close behind Edmonton with a similar light rail "C-Train" line that opened in May 1981. Built in a 7.8-mile South Corridor, it operated largely in a Canadian Pacific right-of-way, and in a 7th Avenue transit and pedestrian mall in the downtown area. Track and power supply were similar to those at Edmonton, and Calgary acquired a fleet of the same Siemens light rail vehicles adopted at Edmonton. Subsequent extensions added lines to the northeast and northwest from downtown Calgary, expanding the system to a total of 20.3 miles by the end of 2001, when it was transporting a weekday average of close to 188,000 passengers.

In July 1981, San Diego became the first U.S. city to open a new light rail line. Championed by then state Sen. James R. Mills, an indefatigable light rail advocate, the first lines of the San Diego system were built largely on lines of the San Diego & Arizona Eastern Railway, a former Southern Pacific subsidiary acquired by San Diego's Metropolitan Transit Development Board, or MTDB. For an initial 16-mile route between downtown San Diego and San Ysidro at the Mexican border, MTDB rehabilitated the SD&AE line and installed the necessary power supply and stations. Freight service was continued, with freight trains operating only after the light rail trains had shut down for the night. The entry to downtown San Diego was made over city streets. Once again, a standard Siemens articulated vehicle was chosen for this newest light rail system. The San Diego Trolley, as it was called, was an immediate success, and MTDB was soon embarked on its expansion

San Diego's first light rail line was established at relatively low cost by acquiring the existing San Diego & Arizona Eastern freight rail line between San Diego and the Mexican border at San Ysidro and rehabilitating it for light rail operation. Freight operation continued at night, after light rail service was shut down for the day. A northbound train from San Ysidro to downtown San Diego made a passenger stop on the line at 24th Street in National City in June 1982, a year after the line opened. William D. Middleton.

The light rail metro that opened at Buffalo in 1984 operates largely in subway, with a pedestrian and transit mall route through downtown Buffalo. A train loaded passengers at the Amherst Street subway station in May 1988. William D. Middleton.

into a regional rail system for the entire San Diego metropolitan area. By the end of the century, a long line to the east had been installed on a former SD&AE branch, a second route completed through downtown San Diego, a north line opened as far as Old Town San Diego, and the first phase of an east-west line completed through the Mission Valley, with construction underway on a second segment that would complete the line.

In 1984 Buffalo completed a 6.4-mile light rail metro, which incorporated elements of both a typical light rail system and a full-scale metro. Trains operated through the city center on the surface in a Main Street transit and pedestrian mall, while the remainder of the line operated through subway.

Portland (Ore.) was next with a 15-mile Eastside MAX—for Metropolitan Area Express—light rail line that was built, in part, with funds diverted from a cancelled freeway project. Opened in 1986, MAX quickly proved to be another light rail success story, and the region has since expanded its LRT network into a 33-mile system with the completion of a long Westside MAX and a light rail link to the Portland airport, with still another 5.6-mile Interstate extension into north Portland under construction.

Plagued by growing traffic congestion, still more fast-growing California cities turned to light rail. By 1987 new lines were operating in both Sacramento and San Jose, and both cities have continued to develop additional lines as part of planned regional rail systems. By 1990 Los Angeles had completed a 22-mile light rail Blue Line between downtown Los Angeles and Long Beach, while a second, 20-mile east-west Green Line light rail route between Norwalk and Hawthorne opened in 1995. By 1994 some construction had begun for a third, 13.7-mile route that should add light rail service to Pasadena by 2003.

Mexico, too, added new light rail systems at two of its largest cities. The first to begin operation was at Guadalajara, Jalisco, where the Sistema de Tren Electrico Urbano (SITEUR) opened a 9.3-mile north-south surface and subway line in 1989. A second, 5.3-mile east-west subway route was added in 1994. At Monterrey, Nuevo Leon, regional transit agency Metrorrey completed an 11.5-mile, elevated Line 1 of a regional light rail metro in 1991, while a second 3.1-mile Line 2 subway was completed three years later.

Still more new U.S. light rail systems followed in the 1990s. In 1992 Maryland's Mass Transit Administration completed the first segment of a Central Light Rail Line at Baltimore that has since grown to a total length of 30 miles. A year later the Bi-State Development Agency at St. Louis opened an initial section of a 17-mile MetroLink light rail line extending from the St. Louis International Airport through downtown St. Louis and across the Mississippi River to East St. Louis, Ill. A 17.4-mile extension to Belleville, Ill., opened in 2001, while construction was underway for a further 8.8-mile extension to Scott Air Force Base. Denver's Regional Transportation District (RTD) completed a 5.3-mile Central Corridor light rail line in 1994. An 8.7-mile Southwest Line extension to suburban Littleton opened in 2000, while construction was in progress for a Central Platte Valley Spur and Southeast Line that will add almost 21 additional miles to the RTD rail system.

In 1996 Dallas Area Rapid Transit (DART) began operating initial segments of a planned regional light rail system that quickly gained enthusiastic support from one of America's most automobile-centered cities. A full 20-mile "starter" system that was completed by 1997 included lines from downtown Dallas north to Park Lane, south to Ledbetter, and southwest to Westmoreland. Construction scheduled for completion in 2002–03 included a North Central line to Plano and a Northeast line to Garland that would add almost 24 miles to the DART rail system. Late in 1999 the Utah Transit Authority

The East Side MAX light rail line at Portland (Ore.) was built, in part, with funds from a cancelled freeway, and the line was placed in a corridor shared with the Union Pacific and the rebuilt Banfield Freeway. A westbound train approached the 60th Street station in November 1990. William D. Middleton.

Sacramento's RT Metro light rail line runs through the heart of downtown Sacramento in a K Street transit mall. A train en route to the line's northern terminal at Watt/I-80 turned into 12th Street at the end of the mall in June 1994. William D. Middleton.

Passengers on RT Metro's Folsom line get an experience akin to a roller coaster near 65th Street, where the line was threaded under the U.S. 50 freeway and then over the Union Pacific tracks. The train was eastbound to Butterfield from downtown Sacramento in January 1988. William D. Middleton.

Demonstrating light rail's versatility, a southbound Santa Clara Valley Transportation Authority Guadalupe Corridor light rail train rolled quietly through the streets of downtown San Jose. VTA's initial fleet of 50 articulated light rail vehicles was built by Canada's Urban Transit Development Corporation. Santa Clara Valley Transportation Authority.

The first Los Angeles light rail line opened between downtown Los Angeles and Long Beach in 1990, operating almost entirely in a Southern Pacific right-of-way that was itself a former Pacific Electric interurban electric railway route between the two cities. In January 1991 a southbound train to Long Beach made a passenger stop at the Del Amo station. William D. Middleton.

Operating in the median of busy Avenue Colon, a northbound train had just left the Santa Filomena station on Line 1 of Guadalajara's Sistema del Tren Eléctrico Urbano light rail system in August 1994. The domed structure in the background is the Santa Filomena church. William D. Middleton.

Guadalajara's second light rail line was an east-west subway Line 2 that opened in 1994. An eastbound Line 2 train loaded at the Juarez II station in August 1994. William D. Middleton.

The first line of Monterrey's Metrorrey light rail system was an L-shaped elevated Line 1 that linked the city center with districts to the north and east. In July 1994 a westbound Line 1 train approached the central Cuauhtémoc station, where the line would connect with Metrorrey's Line 2 subway, then still under construction. William D. Middleton.

opened its 15-mile, north-south TRAX light rail line between downtown Salt Lake City and suburban Sandy, south of the city, while a 2.5-mile east-west line between downtown and the University of Utah campus was completed late in 2001 in time for the 2002 Winter Olympics at Salt Lake City. In April 2000 New Jersey Transit's Hudson-Bergen Light Rail Transit System became North America's newest light rail line when its first 7.5-mile section began operation between Bayonne and Jersey City. Subsequent extensions are gradually expanding the Hudson-Bergen line over a full 20.1-mile route that should be complete between Bayonne and the Vince Lombardi park-and-ride facility in Bergen County by 2010. Construction was also in progress for the first segment of an 8.8-mile Newark-Elizabeth light rail line that will be linked to NJ Transit's Newark City Subway route.

In October 2001, the first North American example of diesel light rail transit, a new kind of low-cost, "cordless" light rail, began operation over a 5-mile route at Ottawa, Ont. Instead of operating from an overhead power supply, the line's three European-designed articulated light rail vehicles were powered from their own diesel-electric power plant. A similar NJ Transit diesel light rail line was under construction over a 34-mile route between Trenton and Camden in southern New Jersey.

In every case, the builders of these new systems were able to employ the extreme flexibility inherent in light rail technology to fit the lines into a wide variety of available and economical alignment opportunities. As at Edmonton and Calgary, the new light rail lines at Portland, Sacramento, Denver, Salt Lake City, and on New Jersey's Hudson-Bergen LRT—in part—shared space in the same right-of-way with main line railroads. At Los Angeles, the new LRT Blue Line to Long Beach shared a right-of-way with a Southern Pacific freight line that had once been the route for the Pacific Electric Railway's Long Beach interurbans. Portions of the Dallas system were built in the rights-of-way of abandoned railroad lines, and—in one case—in a utilities corridor.

Much of Baltimore's Central Light Rail Line follows former railroad lines. North of Baltimore the line was installed in the roadbed of the Pennsylvania Railroad's one-time main line from Baltimore to Harrisburg. A two-car train of the line's big ABB Traction articulated light rail vehicles crossed the line's bridge over an arm of Lake Roland in May 1992. John J. Bowman, from Fred W. Schneider, III.

The innovative Bi-State Development Agency at St. Louis took maximum advantage of available rail infrastructure to establish the MetroLink light rail line. West of downtown St. Louis, the line was installed on the former Wabash Railroad main line, where freight service was continued at night after the end of light rail operations. A westbound train approached the Forest Park station in July 1993. William D. Middleton.

(Top) Denver's Regional Transportation District opened the first section of its MAC—for Metropolitan Area Connection—light rail system in 1994. The impressive downtown Denver skyline was in the background in August 1994, shortly before the line opened, as a westbound test train approached the Colfax Avenue viaduct. William D. Middleton.

(Middle) The first two Dallas area Rapid Transit light rail lines to open linked the downtown area with points to the south and southwest. With downtown Dallas looming in the distance, an outbound Blue Line train took the line to the south at the junction of the two lines in September 1996. The Red Line southwest to Westmoreland continued off to the left. William D. Middleton.

(Bottom) Bold and dramatic architecture in keeping with the Texas city's brash image characterized DART station design. This was the newly opened Mockingbird Lane station at the north end of the system's subway under the North Central Expressway in January 1997. The train was northbound to Park Lane. Dallas Area Rapid Transit.

Ready to begin its 15-mile run southward to Sandy, Utah, a Utah Transit Authority TRAX light rail train waited at the line's Delta Center terminal in South Temple Street in downtown Salt Lake City in 2000. In the background is the former Union Pacific passenger station. G. Mac Sebree.

New Jersey Transit's Hudson-Bergen light rail line serves the communities along the New Jersey side of the Hudson River opposite Manhattan. A southbound train ran west in Essex Street, Jersey City, in May 2000, just a month after the first segment of the line began carrying passengers. Until the tragic events of September 11, 2001, the twin towers of New York's World Trade Center loomed large on the horizon. Herbert H. Harwood, Jr.

A new kind of light rail transit for North America was introduced at Ottawa, Ontario, in October 2001, when three of these diesel light rail vehicles began operating over a Canadian Pacific rail line as part of the Canadian capital's OC Transpo transit system. OC Transpo.

Transit malls have often proved a low-cost means of providing traffic-free light rail routes through congested urban areas. Buffalo's Main Street was converted to a light rail and pedestrian mall to provide a downtown entry for the city's light rail metro. An inbound train stopped at the Huron Street station on the mall in May 1988. William D. Middleton.

Major portions of the Baltimore and St. Louis systems and Ottawa's new diesel LRT route have shared track arrangements similar to San Diego's, with freight railroads operating service over the same tracks when the LRT trains were not operating. Similarly, NJ Transit's Southern New Jersey diesel LRT line will occupy track space shared with a freight railroad during its non-operating hours.

Another frequent alignment choice placed new LRT lines in the center medians of freeways or boulevards. Much of San Jose's initial Guadalupe Corridor line was placed in the center median of existing boulevards or at the center of a new Guadalupe Expressway. Similarly, substantial segments of Portland's Eastside MAX LRT line were located in boulevard medians or in a corridor shared with the rebuilt Banfield Freeway and a Union Pacific main line. Major portions of the Sacramento Regional Transit District's RT Metro light rail system went into rail corridors or a right-of-way originally acquired for a freeway that was never built. At Los Angeles, the center median route of the east-west Green Line light rail line was constructed as an integral part of the new Century Freeway. Substantial sections of the light rail systems at Portland, Sacramento, San Jose, Baltimore, Salt Lake City, and Newark shared downtown streets—streetcar style—with other traffic. Buffalo, Sacramento, and Dallas, much like Calgary, put portions of their systems in downtown malls or transitways shared with pedestrian traffic.

For some lines, subways or tunnels proved the best solution for parts of their routes. Except for its downtown transitway, Buffalo's entire light rail metro was in subway. The Los Angeles–Long Beach Blue Line entered downtown Los Angeles via a subway that gave it a direct link with the Red Line subway. For the Westside MAX at Portland, a 3-mile tunnel under the city's West Hills proved to be the best route out of downtown. At Dallas, the DART light rail route north from downtown Dallas was placed in twin tubes some 3½ miles long, drilled under the reconstructed North Central Expressway.

Perhaps the most innovative light rail routing of all was that adopted for the initial section of the MetroLink light rail line between the St. Louis airport and East St. Louis. Major portions of the line west of downtown St. Louis operated over a rebuilt Norfolk Southern line that continued to operate as a freight line after light rail operating hours ended. The line operated across the Mississippi River on the historic Eads Bridge, utilizing a rail deck that had been idle since 1974, and through downtown in a Washington Avenue–8th Street tunnel that had once linked the Eads Bridge with rail lines in the Mill Creek Valley south of the city center.

Most of these new generation light rail systems also limited their initial development costs with extensive stretches of single-track operation, planning later to install a second main track as traffic—and service frequency—made it necessary. Stations were typically simple shelters, with boarding from low level platforms.

As still another cost saving measure, these new light rail lines introduced the European concept of barrier-free, proof-of-payment fare collection, which sped service as well as reduced operating costs. Passengers simply boarded trains through any door with valid transfers or tickets purchased from vending machines on the station platforms, with periodic checks by roving ticket inspectors—and fines for riders without a valid ticket or transfer—to ensure compliance. Edmonton Transit became the first North American rail system to adopt the new system in 1980, and it became the standard for virtually every new light rail system, as well as several new metro systems.

The MetroLink light rail line at St. Louis crossed the Mississippi River on the historic Eads Bridge, utilizing a refurbished rail deck that had been idle for 20 years. An eastbound train for East St. Louis, Ill., stopped at the Laclede's Landing station at the west end of the bridge in April 1999. William D. Middleton.

The low-level platform boarding typical of light rail practice necessitated some innovative solutions to new requirements for accommodating passengers with disabilities. Several systems, among them the new lines at Edmonton, Calgary, Los Angeles, and St. Louis, met the need through the adoption of high-platform boarding, similar to metro practice. Others adopted wheelchair lifts, either mounted on the light rail vehicles or on platforms. Still others built short platforms, reached by ramps, at car floor level for access. A more recent solution, first adopted by Portland, has been the development of low-floor light rail vehicles, which a wheelchair passenger can board by means of a bridgeplate extended from the train.

By the end of the twentieth century light rail transit had become what was by far the fastest-growing U.S. transit mode. Over the two decades from 1980 to 2000, annual light rail passengers more than doubled to a turn-of-the-century total of more than 293 million. North American light rail expansion showed every sign of continuing at that high level well into the twenty-first century. With few exceptions, the existing LRT systems either had further extensions under construction or in planning. Entirely new systems were already under construction at Minneapolis and Houston, while planning and engineering were in progress for planned systems at close to a dozen other urban areas. For an old technology that had been near moribund only a few decades earlier, light rail transit was showing a remarkable vitality as it moved into its second century of transit service.

Rapid transit car design usually was utilitarian to an extreme. This was one of 400 R10 cars built for New York City Transit during 1948–1949 by the American Car & Foundry Company. Even a bright turquoise and white color scheme and a shiny TA emblem applied in the 1960s could do little for the homely front-end design. Sprague Library, Electric Railroaders' Association.

CHAPTER 7

CONVEYANCES FOR THE MULTITUDES

The Cars We Rode

"Pleasing to Eye and Ear"

This streamlined rapid transit car is the latest development in the design and equipment of cars for city rapid transit lines and is adaptable for operation on either subway or "L" lines of the BMT System. The most important advance to be noted by the passenger is the sharp reduction in the noise level due to the lighter weight of the new car and the use of rubber in the wheels and trucks.

The design and construction of this car, telescoping as it does a quarter-century of progress in the rapid transit industry, was made possible by utilizing the latest scientific and technical advances of the aviation, automotive, aluminum, rubber, transportation and electrical industries. The car embodies the latest methods of aviation structural design in the advanced use and assembly of aluminum alloys. The rubber industry contributes the most recent research developments of vehicle springing and mounting. The entire background of the automotive industry in precision manufacture and production is utilized, while very recent improvements in motors, controls and braking are contributed by the electrical industry.

—From a BMT brochure describing the experimental
"Bluebird" articulated PCC type rapid transit car, 1939

NEW YORK'S PIONEER ELEVATED RAILROADS reflected the steam railroad technology of their time, albeit on a reduced scale imposed by the weight limitations of the elevated structures and the need to negotiate the extremely sharp curves of El alignments that followed urban street systems.

Elevated railway passenger cars were typically lighter and smaller versions of the day coaches operated by the main line railroads. Some of the earliest cars built for the New York Elevated in 1872, for example, weighed only 9400 pounds. The first cars on New York's "Gilbert" elevated in 1878 were only 37 feet 10 inches long and 8 feet 9 inches wide, and were carried on two four-wheel trucks. Each car accommodated 48 passengers. Later El cars were somewhat larger, usually about 46 or 47 feet in length, and by the 1890s car weights had increased to anywhere from 30,000 to 40, 000 pounds. Frames and car bodies were of wood construction, with trussed sides as the principal load carrying members. Clerestory roofs provided interior ventilation. While a few cars were constructed with side doors that opened directly into the passenger compartment, almost all elevated cars were

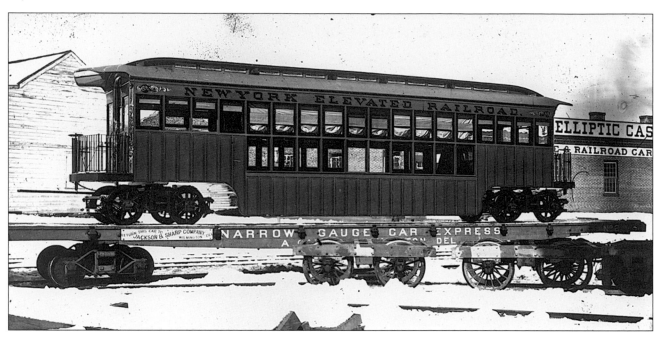

One of the New York Elevated's novel "shad belly" cars of 1872 was loaded on a flat car, ready for shipment from the Wilmington, Del., plant of the Jackson & Sharp Company. The drop center, low-center-of-gravity design was intended to reassure passengers who feared the cars would topple off the elevated structure. Jackson & Sharp Collection, Delaware Public Archives (Neg. Folder 11, No. 13).

built with open platforms at each end, similar to steam railroad practice. A major elevated railway variation, however, was the universal use of high-level station platforms to speed boarding and alighting. Consequently, no steps were required, and the platforms were provided with gates operated by trainmen.

A novel variation from this typical elevated car configuration was the "shad belly" car that turned up on the New York Elevated in 1872. Built by the Jackson & Sharp Company of Wilmington, Del., these were designed to reassure passengers who feared that the elevated cars might topple off the elevated structure. The 35-foot cars achieved a low center of gravity with a depressed center section between the trucks that was only four-and-a-half inches above rail level. The low-slung arrangement, however, slowed entrance and exit. Passengers soon got over their fear of falling, and the unusual cars were rebuilt into a more conventional arrangement.

Interior accommodations of these early cars tended toward the austere. Most of what seating was provided was in the form of longitudinal benches along each side of the car, leaving plenty of room for standing passengers and allowing clear access to the end doors. The interior arrangement soon evolved into a fairly standard one with longitudinal seating at each end of the car and several pairs of transverse seats at the center. Some early elevated cars were fitted with seating formed from wood veneer, but seats were usually upholstered in such materials as woven rattan, which made up in durability for what it lacked in comfort. Floors were usually covered with some kind of matting. Leather straps suspended from the ceiling were provided for the benefit of standees. Windows had shades or blinds. Oil or—later—gas lamps provided illumination.

Heating of elevated, as well as street railway, cars during winter weather was long a contentious issue in the industry, with many executives insisting that no satisfactory heating equipment was available, or that it was an unnecessary frill that a majority of their riders didn't want anyway. In July 1885, for example, the *Street Railway Journal* quoted Chicago street railway executive Jacob Rehm to the effect that "if you heat the cars, the next thing they will want is Axminster carpets and satin cushions." In the end, heating was usually provided with some sort of coal-fired heating stove.

Most elevated companies made up for what their cars lacked in comfort with elaborate decoration. Interiors were finished in decorative wood paneling and inlay work, with elaborate ceiling headlinings. Light fixtures were marvels of Victorian brasswork. Exteriors were finished in distinctive colors and decoration. The New York Elevated, for example, finished

An early attempt to introduce deluxe service on the elevateds was this elegant parlor car built by Jackson & Sharp for the New York Elevated in 1877. The closed ends and center entrance doors were variations from customary elevated car design. The exterior was finished in the road's claret red, with intricate gold lining and decorative work. The richly decorated interior featured carpeting and a coal-fired heating stove. Jackson & Sharp Collection, Delaware Public Archives (*Top*, Neg. Folder 12, No. 17; *Bottom*, Neg. Folder 1, No. 2).

Typical of elevated railway coaches of the steam era was Chicago's South Side Rapid Transit No. 33, shown ready for delivery from the Pullman Company in 1897. Wood construction was universal for rapid transit rolling stock until the early twentieth century. Passengers boarded and alighted from the gated end platforms, using station platforms at car floor level. Smithsonian Institution (Neg. P3820).

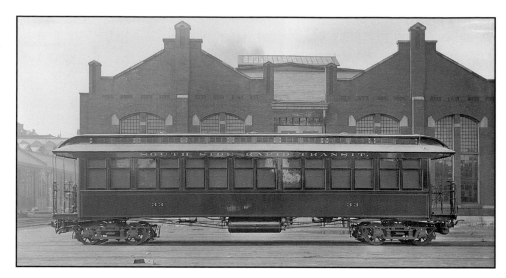

The interior arrangement of this South Side Rapid Transit car, built by Jackson & Sharp in 1892, was typical of early elevated railway equipment. There were several banks of transverse seats at the center of the car, while longitudinal seating at each end allowed ample standing room near the end entrance doors. Seats were upholstered in durable rattan, the floor was covered with sturdy fiber matting, and leather straps were provided for standing passengers. At the same time, the car was fitted with louvered shades on the windows and ornate brass lamps, and the ceiling headlining was finished in intricate gold lining and decorative work. Jackson & Sharp Collection, Delaware Public Archives (Neg. Folder 11, No. 21).

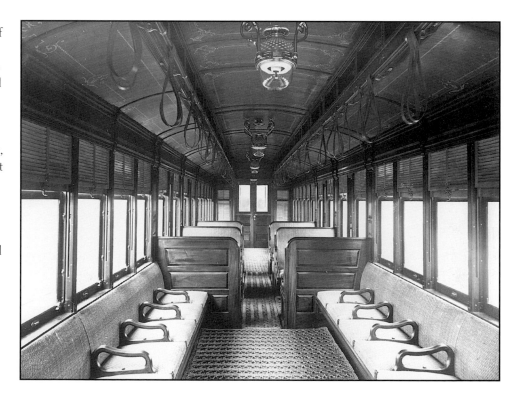

its cars in claret red, with ornate gold lining and decorative work, while cars of the rival Metropolitan Elevated were finished in apple green, with pea green and gold trim.

There were a few attempts to introduce more luxurious, extra-fare equipment on a few of the early elevated roads. In 1877 Jackson & Sharp built an elegant parlor car for the New York Elevated. Instead of the conventional open platforms at each end the car had entrance doors at the center, with rounded ends. The exterior was finished in the line's standard claret red, with unusually intricate gold lining and decorative work. The interior was richly decorated, with such extra amenities as carpeting on the floor and a coal-fired heating stove.

To help promote its service when it opened in 1878, the Metropolitan acquired a number of luxurious extra-fare drawing room cars. Built by the Pullman Palace Car Company, these were finished in oak and mahogany paneling decorated in the Queen Anne style, with archi-

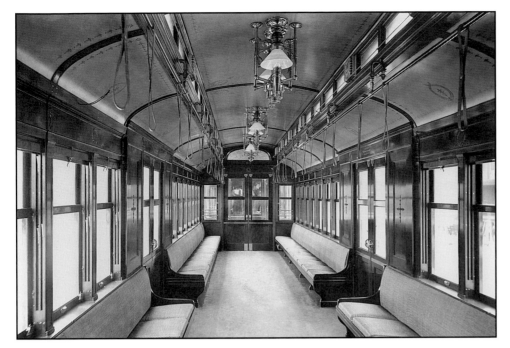

Also a common interior arrangement for elevated cars was an all-longitudinal seating configuration, represented here by New York & Brooklyn Bridge No. 93, completed by the Pullman Company in 1896. Considerably larger than most other elevated cars, the bridge cars were fitted with center entrance doors, as well as the usual end doors and platforms. Smithsonian Institution (Neg. P3285).

On a few elevated lines, open cars provided pleasant travel during the hot summer months. This open car, completed by Jackson & Sharp for the Manhattan Railway in 1901, is shown on shop trucks at the builder's Wilmington (Del.) plant. Passengers boarded at any point and sat in transverse seats that extended the full width of the car. The striped curtains could be pulled down in the event of rain. Jackson & Sharp Collection, Delaware Public Archives (Neg. Folder 7, No. 19).

tectural window cornices, and fitted with red leather seats, tapestry curtains, gilt kerosene chandeliers, and Axminster carpeting. While these elegant cars attracted plenty of attention, it soon became apparent that too few people were willing to pay an extra fare for first-class service on their relatively short daily journeys, and the deluxe service was soon given up.

While the closed car with open end platforms would remain the predominant elevated car configuration well into the twentieth century, it was far from an ideal arrangement for the heavy traffic and frequent stops of the elevated roads, for the need to enter and exit through the end doors and platforms greatly impeded boarding and alighting. Recognizing this, several of the Brooklyn elevated lines and the New York & Brooklyn Bridge acquired cars that incorporated large sliding center doors opening directly into the passenger compartment in addition to the usual end platforms.

The New York Elevated's first steam locomotives were little four-wheel, enclosed "dummy" machines. The Brooks Locomotive Works turned out No. 9, *Spuyten Duyvel*, in 1875. The metal cab was painted claret red and ornately striped. Smithsonian Institution (Neg. MAH-31638C).

Motive power for New York's first elevated road consisted of "dummy" steam locomotives enclosed in a car body that was intended to help them blend into the cityscape and avoid frightening the horses. The very first of these was the appropriately named *Pioneer*, designed by the New York Elevated's superintendent and master mechanic, David W. Wyman, and built by a local iron works in 1871. The four-wheel locomotive was fitted with a vertical boiler and a two-cylinder engine geared to one of the axles. Side rods transmitted power to the second axle. Weighing less than four tons, the *Pioneer* proved too light for elevated service, and was soon replaced by larger dummy locomotives. Also designed by Wyman, these were four-ton, four-wheel machines fitted with a horizontal boiler and driving the four driving wheels through a center crank axle and side rods. Water was carried in a tank draped over the boiler, while enough hard coal for each round trip was carried

The New York Elevated soon decided that enclosed dummy locomotives were unnecessary. No. 27, built by the Baldwin Locomotive Works in 1878, was more conventionally arranged. The colorful livery and fussy decoration of the earlier locomotives were retained, however. H. L. Broadbelt Collection.

(Top)   The Metropolitan Elevated Railway began operation in 1878 with dummy locomotives that were much larger than those of rival New York Elevated. This was one of 29 Class G 2-4-2 tank engines built by the Grant Locomotive Works in 1878. They were fitted with ornate car bodies built by the Pullman Company to match the line's passenger cars and finished in the same pea green highlighted with darker green-and-gold striping. The illustration is from the November 16, 1878, issue of *Scientific American.* Author's Collection.

(Middle)   Although Matthias N. Forney had patented his compact 0-4-4T double-ended tank locomotive design in 1866, it was not until 1878 that one of the New York elevated roads was persuaded to give it a trial. No. 39 was one of the New York Elevated's first Class B Forneys delivered by Baldwin in mid-1878. By early 1879 the road was operating a fleet of 70 of the sturdy little engines. The illustration is from the November 23, 1878, issue of *Scientific American.* Author's Collection.

(Bottom)   With her crew standing by, a Manhattan Railway Forney stood ready for a run over New York's Sixth Avenue El. No. 17 was one of 25 Class F Forneys built by the Rome Locomotive Works in 1886. New York Transit Museum Archives, Brooklyn (Neg. X4-239).

Forney No. 1 was the first of 46 built for Chicago's South Side Rapid Transit "L" by Baldwin in 1892–1893. Note the high- and low-pressure cylinders of the four-cylinder Vauclain compound design. Unlike Manhattan's elevateds, which employed only simple locomotives, the Chicago line operated nothing but compound locomotives. H. L. Broadbelt Collection.

in a coalscuttle. The entire locomotive was enclosed within a rectangular cab, painted claret red and ornately striped. As the road's elevated structure was strengthened over the next several years, it became possible to operate larger locomotives. The steam dummies *Liberty* and *West Chester*, built by the Baldwin Locomotive Works of Philadelphia in 1876, were much more powerful machines, each weighing 7½ tons.

The rival Metropolitan road opened in 1878 with a fleet of similar, but much larger, dummy engines. Built by the Grant Locomotive Works of Paterson, N.J., these were carried on four 39-inch driving wheels and two-wheel pony and trailing trucks. Each weighed just over 16 tons fully loaded, and was capable of pulling three loaded cars. The ornate wooden car bodies were built by the Pullman Palace Car Company and fitted with windows all around to resemble the passenger cars they pulled.

The steam dummy disguise was soon seen as unnecessary, and both roads began operating locomotives of more conventional appearance. In 1878 the New York Elevated became the first road to try a new type of double-ended tank engine designed by locomotive designer and technical journalist Mathias N. Forney, then editor of *Railroad Gazette*. These had four driving wheels under the boiler, a four-wheel truck under the cab and an extended frame for the water and fuel supply. The first Forney locomotives, built from the same plans by both the Baldwin works and the Rhode Island Locomotive Works at Providence, were mounted on 38-inch driving wheels and weighed just under 15 tons fully loaded. The Forney design proved extremely well adapted to the demanding stop-and-go service of the elevated railways, and soon became the standard for the New York and Brooklyn elevated lines. Nearly 400 of them were in service by the time the last one was delivered in 1894, while another 81 Forneys

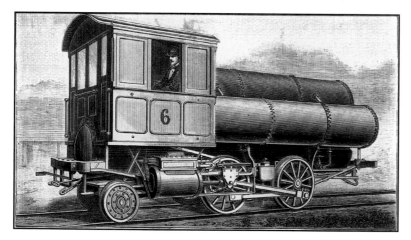

Among alternatives to steam for elevated railway motive power that were tried and found wanting was the compressed air locomotive. This was the Hardie compressed air locomotive tested on New York's Third Avenue elevated in 1881, shown in an illustration from the September 9, 1882, *Scientific American*. Author's Collection.

were built for Chicago's South Side and Lake Street elevated lines. As traffic climbed on the elevated lines, successive batches of the little locomotives grew steadily larger and more powerful to handle larger trains. The largest Forneys built for New York service, ten Class L locomotives built by Baldwin for the Suburban Rapid Transit in 1885–86, were mounted on 48-inch drivers and weighed 27½ tons. The largest of all—and the last built—were 35 Forneys completed for Chicago's Lake Street Elevated by the Rhode Island Locomotive Works during 1893–95, which were mounted on 44-inch driving wheels and weighed 30 tons in working order.

However well the Forneys performed, steam locomotives were far from an ideal choice for elevated railway motive power. They were inherently ill suited to the demanding requirements of the frequent stops and starts of elevated service, and their smoke, cinders, escaping steam, and noise made them unpopular with residents and businesses along the elevated lines.

A few early attempts to develop cable traction systems for elevated operation had not been particularly successful. Another early effort to come up with a better form of El motive power was a compressed air locomotive designed by Robert Hardie that was tested on New York's Third Avenue elevated in 1881. Looking much like a conventional steam locomotive, the Hardie locomotive had four big air reservoirs that were charged to a pressure of 600 pounds per square inch. Air was released through an expansion valve, and after passing through a small boiler where it was heated and moistened, drove the locomotive by means

Impressed by the success of the electrified Intramural Railway at the 1893 World's Columbian Exposition, Chicago's still a-building Metropolitan West Elevated cancelled its order for steam locomotives and completed the line as the first regular electrically powered elevated railway. On this early electrification a single heavy motor car pulled each train. No. 722, one of 55 motor cars built for the line by the Barney & Smith Car Company, headed a train of three trailer cars on the newly completed West Side "L." Author's Collection.

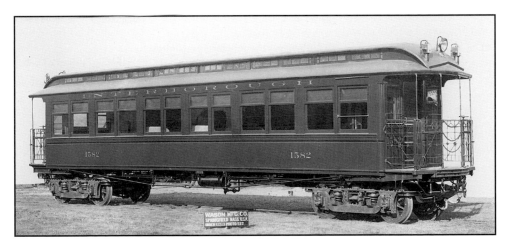

Even after the advent of all steel cars for its subway lines, New York's Interborough Rapid Transit continued to acquire wooden cars for the elevated lines it had leased from the Manhattan Railway. Except for the motors, control equipment, and other appurtenances required for electric operation, they were little different from the cars that remained from the steam era. No. 1582 was one of an order for 83 motor cars built for the IRT by the Wason Manufacturing Company of Springfield, Mass., during 1907–1908. Duke-Middleton Collection.

of a conventional reciprocating machinery. A novel feature of the locomotive was an arrangement whereby the cylinders could be used as air pumps, thus providing a means of braking. Although nothing came of the tests, a newer generation of Hardie compressed air locomotive turned up on the Manhattan Railway in 1897. This improved design was fitted with an air reservoir that could be charged to a pressure of 2400 pounds per square inch, and the compressor plant located near Rector Street was capable of fully charging the locomotive in about a minute. Once again, however, tests led to nothing more. By this time another and better solution to the elevated railway motive power problem was at hand.

By the time Chicago's Lake Street line's new Forneys had begun to haul passengers, the end was near for the steam-powered elevateds as electric traction came on the scene. The Columbian Intramural Railway had already conclusively demonstrated the superiority of electric traction on the grounds of the 1893 World's Columbian Exposition in Jackson Park. Another Chicago line still under construction, the Metropolitan West Side Elevated Railway, promptly cancelled its order for steam locomotives and began planning for electric operation. The Lake Street "L" was close behind with electrification plans, and steam lo-

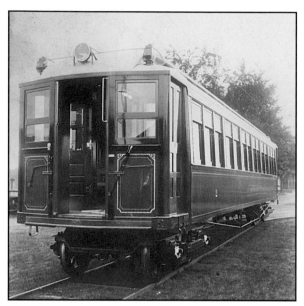

Before beginning production of 500 composite wood and steel cars for New York's first subway, the IRT ordered two sample cars from Wason that were used to test various design features for the production cars, as well as various amenities for a possible "first class" service. This was sample car No. 2, the *John B. McDonald.* Sprague Library, Electric Railroader's Association.

comotives made their final runs on June 13, 1896, less than a year and a half after the last of the Forneys had been delivered. Steam operation of the South Side elevated ended in 1898. Brooklyn's Els completed a conversion to electric power in 1900, and the last steam operation of the Manhattan elevateds ended in 1903.

The very first elevated railway electrifications of the Intramural and West Side lines involved the use of powerful motor passenger cars which acted as locomotives pulling several non-powered trailer cars. The motor cars built for the Intramural Railway by Jackson & Sharp were 46 feet long, weighed over 22 tons, and were powered by four 50 h.p. Thomson-Houston motors. Each motor car was capable of accommodating 84 passengers, and could pull trains of two to four similar trailer cars of identical capacity. The Metropolitan West Side began operation with a fleet of 55 motor cars built by the Barney & Smith Car Company of Dayton, Ohio. These were 47-foot, 32½-ton cars powered by two 125 h.p. General Electric motors, and capable of hauling trains of three or four trailer cars.

Following Frank Sprague's successful development of multiple-unit control for electrification of Chicago's South Side line, this became the standard form of electrification for both elevated railways and the new subways that soon followed. While some new rolling stock was also acquired, electric equipment for the former steam-operated elevateds consisted largely of their former trailer cars reequipped with trucks, motors and control equipment for M.U. operation.

The advent of subways brought new demands for rapid transit car builders. A principal concern with underground operation was the possibility of fire. For reasons of both fire protection and greater safety in the event of collisions, the use of metal passenger cars had long been advocated. Over the last half of the nineteenth century more than 30 patents had been granted to inventors for iron or steel passenger car construction, and a number of sample cars had been built. But, largely for reasons of economy, the industry had stayed with wooden car construction. By the first years of the new century, however, this was beginning to change as the Interborough Rapid Transit began building a great subway for New York, and the Pennsylvania Railroad and its Long Island Rail Road subsidiary began planning for electric operation into Manhattan through long Hudson and East river tunnels.

The IRT was interested in all-steel cars from the beginning, but when it came time to place its initial equipment orders in the spring of 1902 none had yet been built and there were still many design problems to be worked out. In any event, the car building industry was not yet ready to take on such a large order for metal cars. Instead, the IRT decided, as their 1904 publication on the construction and equipment of the subway put it, "to bend all energies to the production of a wooden car with sufficient metal for strength and protection from accident, i.e., a stronger, safer, and better constructed car than had heretofore been put in use on any electric railway in the world."

Consequently, orders for IRT's first 500 cars called for what was termed a composite or protected wooden car. Built by the Wason, St. Louis, Jewett, and Stephenson car companies, these were 51-foot cars constructed with all-steel underframes and anti-telescoping car bulkheads and platform posts. The wood used in their construction was impregnated with a fireproofing compound. Other fire protection features included such measures as copper sheathing over the wooden sides and asbestos sheets under the floor to protect against electrical fires, while the electrical equipment and wiring were enclosed in incombustible casings and pipes.

These composite cars weren't good enough for *Scientific American.* "Fire Peril on Underground Railroads," headlined the popular weekly over an August 22, 1903, editorial on the subject that was occasioned by a disastrous subway fire on the Métro at Paris, "in which nearly a hundred people were smothered like rats in a hole." More than a hundred were killed and three trains of wooden cars destroyed in the August 11 Paris blaze, which was apparently started from an electrical fault.

"It is absolutely imperative," commented the journal, "that the construction of the rolling stock be such that the burning of a car or train of cars will be rendered impossible. . . . We are well aware . . . that the new cars are to be very thoroughly fireproofed, and it must be admitted that on paper the precautions that are to be taken in the way of incombustible linings for the floors of the car, asbestos protection, the use of fireproof paint, etc. are among the most approved methods of protecting inflammable material. In the present case, however, the risks attendant upon the break-down of this system of fireproofing are so frightful that it should certainly be abandoned in favor of the only absolutely sure method of abolishing every particle of wood and making the cars, from trucks to ventilator, entirely of metal."[1]

In any event, the company by no means gave up its pioneering search for an all-steel car. While none of the car building companies was willing to take on the task, the Pennsylvania Railroad agreed to make its shop facilities at Altoona, Pa., available to manufacture a prototype all-steel car designed by consulting engineer George Gibbs. This first car was completed at the end of 1903, utilizing standard commercial steel shapes. After some design modifications incorporating special rolled and pressed steel shapes to reduce the weight of the car, 200—later increased to 300—all-steel cars were placed on order from American Car & Foundry in 1904. Only a year later the Long Island Rail Road followed suit with an order for 134 all-steel cars for its newly electrified lines. Also designed by Gibbs, these were virtually identical to the IRT cars in anticipation of a planned through operation of LIRR trains into Manhattan over the IRT's Brooklyn extension that never materialized.

Although they were about 4 feet longer than New York's standard elevated cars, the IRT's first subway cars were configured much the same way, with several pairs of transverse seats at the center of the car and longitudinal seats along the sides at each end. Seating was upholstered in the usual durable rattan, while floors were of "monolith" fireproof cement overlaid with slatted wearing strips. While entrance and exit was by means of platforms at either end of each car, a major improvement over the elevated cars was the use of an enclosed vestibule with sliding doors that were activated by means of mechanical levers by a guard located between each pair of cars.

A further 50 steel cars ordered in 1907 for the IRT's Brooklyn extension were generally similar to the original Gibbs cars, but the sliding doors between the interior of the car and the vestibules were eliminated and storm doors added at the outer end of the vestibule, allowing the platforms to be used by standing passengers. By this time, too, it had become clear that the heavy traffic volume of the subway required much better entrance and exit capacity, and these cars were designed to permit the addition of doors at the center of the car. In 1909 a test train was equipped with these additional doors, while another train was fitted with an arrangement recommended by the well-known electric railway engineer Bion J. Arnold. This involved the addition of two new sliding doors on each side, with one near each end of the car.

The additional door capacity permitted a one-third reduction in station dwell time, and the IRT subsequently adopted the single center door arrangement, in addition to vestibules and doors at each end, as its standard. Although extensive structural alterations were required, the entire original car fleet was retrofitted with the additional doors, while all later car orders conformed to the new standard.

Consulting engineer George Gibbs designed the first all-steel subway cars for the IRT, and they quickly set the standard for the New York subway system. By 1916 steel "Gibbs" cars operated all IRT subway services, and the original composite wood and steel cars had all been relegated to elevated service. Gibbs & Hill, Inc.

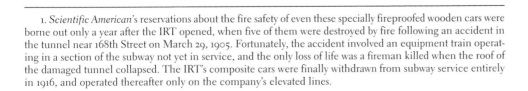

1. *Scientific American's* reservations about the fire safety of even these specially fireproofed wooden cars were borne out only a year after the IRT opened, when five of them were destroyed by fire following an accident in the tunnel near 168th Street on March 29, 1905. Fortunately, the accident involved an equipment train operating in a section of the subway not yet in service, and the only loss of life was a fireman killed when the roof of the damaged tunnel collapsed. The IRT's composite cars were finally withdrawn from subway service entirely in 1916, and operated thereafter only on the company's elevated lines.

The few attempts to develop an extra fare service on elevated or subway lines were soon given up, and high-capacity, no-frills cars operating in "one class" service made up almost the entirety of the subway and elevated fleets at New York, Boston, Philadelphia, and New York. There were a few interesting variations, however.

Decidedly different from the Interborough Rapid Transit's hundreds of austerely furnished subway cars was the *Mineola*, built for the company by Wason in 1904. Probably the only private car ever operated by a subway, the *Mineola* was built for the use of August Belmont, the IRT financier. The car was similar to the IRT's regular composite cars in overall size and its mechanical and electrical equipment, but there the similarity ended. The interior was finished in natural mahogany, artistically inlaid, with an arched Empire ceiling tinted pistachio green, with gold trim. The floor was covered with broadloom carpeting. Curved plate glass windows extending from the roof to the floor at each end provided an unobstructed view of the line, and there was an oval stained glass window in each side. An office compartment at one end was furnished with a roll-top desk and chairs, while a lounge at the opposite end had an upholstered settee set against the bulkhead, portable tables, and chairs. At the center of the car alongside a connecting corridor were a lavatory and a galley equipped with an electric grill, electric oven, refrigerator, pantry, and a well-stocked wine cellar.

Belmont used the car for inspection trips over the IRT, and sometimes, it was said, for trips to the races. For racetrack outings—if indeed there were any—Belmont and his party could have boarded the car on a side track to his Belmont Hotel on 42nd Street and then operated via the IRT to a connection with the Long Island Rail Road at Flatbush and Atlantic avenues, and thence over the electrified LIRR to the track at Belmont Park. The car was later used as a construction car, and then sold for junk. Rescued from a farm in New Jersey, it is now at a Branford, Conn., trolley museum.

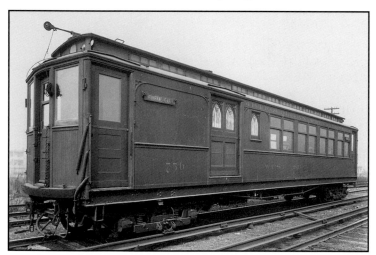

There was nothing in elevated railway service quite like the Metropolitan West Side's funeral car No. 756. Originally a standard "L" car, it was rebuilt for the Chicago line's special funeral service in 1906 with leaded, colored glass Gothic windows set into the doors and sides of the casket compartment. Mourners traveled in individual wicker seats in the main compartment. Krambles-Peterson Archive.

Even more unusual were the funeral cars operated by Chicago's Metropolitan West Side Elevated. The operation of funeral cars by street railways was relatively common early in the twentieth century, but the Metropolitan West Side was probably the only rapid transit railway to provide such a service. With many of Chicago's cemeteries located in the far western suburbs, a funeral could require a long and arduous trip by horse and carriage over the poor roads of the time, while the elevated could provide a fast and comfortable trip. One Metropolitan passenger car was modified for the service by removing all advertising from the car and installing dark green carpeting and portieres, while one window was modified on each side of the car to receive a casket. The car accommodated 34 mourners, and additional cars were provided from the regular service fleet to accommodate more, as required. The service operated from the line's Laflin Street station, where an elevator for handling the casket was available, to sidings at the Waldheim and Concordia cemeteries.

Additional cars were similarly modified for the service, and in 1907 car No. 756 was turned over to the Pullman company for more extensive rebuilding as a funeral car. A separate compartment with large baggage-type doors on each side was provided for the casket, with leaded, colored glass Gothic windows set into the door and sides of the compartment. The mourners' compartment was finished in polished weathered oak inlaid with narrow strips of black and light yellow, and a light yellow ceiling, while the floor was covered in a figured green carpet. Individual wicker seats for 28 were provided. After a number of years in funeral service, the car was reassigned to service as a medical examining station, still retaining the Gothic windows originally installed for funeral service.

With the successful introduction of the IRT's new steel cars, the wooden car era was soon over for North American rapid transit lines. All subsequent New York City car orders

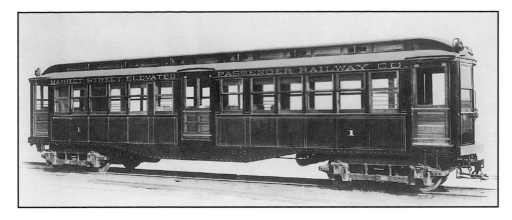

Philadelphia adopted a center door car design for its new Market Street Elevated. The design greatly speeded boarding and alighting, particularly if passengers boarded at the end doors and exited from the center door as the designers intended. Pittsburgh's Pressed Steel Car Company built 40 of these steel cars for the line in 1906. LeRoy O. King, Jr. Collection.

were for steel cars. The Hudson & Manhattan tubes, the Market Street subway-elevated at Philadelphia, and Boston's Cambridge-Dorchester Subway all began operation with steel cars. At Chicago, the Metropolitan West Side company had sent a wrecked wooden car to the American Car & Foundry Company for rebuilding with an all-steel body as early as 1904, and the last new wood cars built for the Chicago "L" system were 20 motor cars completed for the Chicago & Oak Park by the J. G. Brill Company of Philadelphia in 1909. The next new cars for Chicago, an order for 128 motor and trailer cars delivered in 1914 to the combined Chicago Elevated Railways, were all-steel cars built by the Cincinnati Car Company.

Several of the later subways were built to more generous clearance standards and with long radius curves that enabled them to operate unusually large and commodious cars. The first of these was Boston's Cambridge-Dorchester subway, which brought an innovative approach to subway car design when it opened in 1912. The line was built to standards that accommodated a roomy car 69 feet 2½ inches long and 9 feet 6 inches wide. Each of the 43-ton steel cars seated 72 passengers. Unlike earlier subway cars, the big Cambridge cars had no vestibules at the ends, and were fitted with three wide sliding doors on each side that opened directly into the passenger compartment. The Standard Steel Car Company built an initial 40 of the big cars, while another 115 similar cars followed from the Laconia, Pressed Steel, and Osgood Bradley car companies over the next 17 years.

Chicago's elevated system got its first steel cars during 1914–1915, when the Cincinnati Car Company delivered 128 of them for the combined companies. Although they were equipped with both end and center doors, the center door feature was never much used in Chicago, and it was omitted from follow-on orders for 205 additional cars received during 1922–24, represented here by motor car No. 4275. Krambles-Peterson Archive.

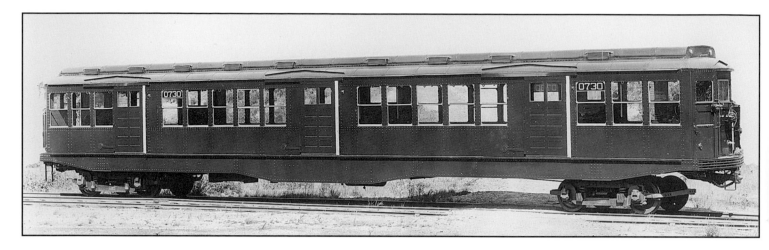

(*Top and right*) The Boston Elevated Railway pioneered in subway car design with the equipment for the new Cambridge-Dorchester subway in 1912. The largest subway cars yet built, these were over 69 feet long and 9 feet 6 inches wide. The end doors and vestibules of previous designs were eliminated, and three wide sliding doors on each side opened directly into the commodious passenger compartment. Seating for 72 passengers was provided on longitudinal wooden benches, with strap-hanging space for several times that number of standing passengers. No. 0730 was one of a later batch of cars completed by the Osgood Bradley Car Company of Worcester, Mass., in 1927. Author's Collection.

A formidable subway car was the big Standard car developed by Brooklyn Rapid Transit in 1914. These high capacity cars were 67 feet long and 10 feet wide, and weighed 45 tons. Almost a thousand were built for BRT over a ten-year period. A train of Standards traveled over the BMT Canarsie line around 1961. Richard Jay Solomon.

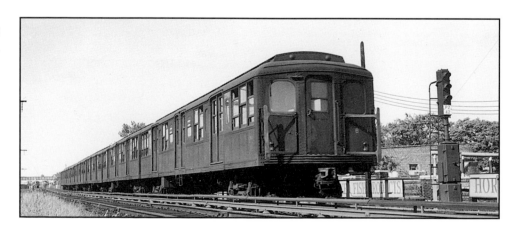

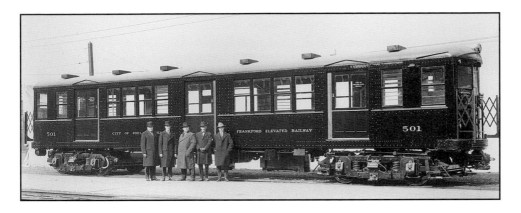

Philadelphia adopted a much larger steel car design for the additional cars required for the Frankford extension of the Market Street elevated line in 1922. Fitted with three wide sliding doors in each side, the big cars were 55 feet long and weighed 45 tons. No. 501, the first of the series, is shown with proud officials at the Philadelphia plant of builder J. G. Brill Company. Author's Collection.

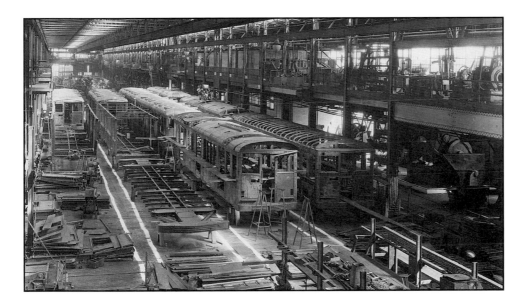

In August 1921 the J. G. Brill firm was hard at work on orders that would total 100 cars for Philadelphia's Frankford elevated extension. This view of the cavernous Brill plant provides an interesting look at the process of car body construction as the big steel cars are riveted together. Author's Collection.

At New York, the size of Interborough subway cars was—and still is today for cars operating on former IRT lines—restricted by clearances and curvature to a length of 51 feet and a width of 8 feet 9 inches. Wisely, when New York's Public Service Commission began developing what was called the Triborough Subway System in 1908, they established standards for width, height, and curvature that would allow the future operation of main line railroad suburban equipment in the subways. Although the idea of suburban train through routing never materialized, the more generous dimensions enabled the use of larger equipment on all New York subways built to the new specifications. These included Brooklyn Rapid Transit (BRT) lines started under the Triborough scheme and the Dual Contracts that superseded it, as well as lines built under the Independent Subway plan of 1924. At the same time, of course, it gave New York two sets of specifications that prevent—to this day—equipment interchangeability between the former IRT and other lines.

Taking full advantage of the new specifications, and influenced by the big Cambridge cars, the BRT designed a new high-capacity steel car that would be 67 feet long and 10 feet wide, and weighed 45 tons. An innovative design by consulting engineer Lewis B. Stillwell employed each side of the car to its full depth as a supporting truss to help meet weight restrictions imposed by existing sections of the BRT system over which the cars would operate. The cars incorporated such advanced features as automatic tightlock couplers, electric red and white tail lamps controlled from the cab, enclosed marker lights, cab signals, and automatic speed control. Electro-pneumatic controls operated three sets of double sliding doors on each side of the car. Each car provided 357 square feet of floor space, compared with only 187 square feet in a standard IRT car. Each car seated 72 passengers in an array of longitudinal and transverse seats, and the American Posture League helped the BRT design a more comfortable seat based upon measurements of several hundred people. An order was placed early in 1914 for the first 100 of a BRT steel car fleet that would eventually reach a total of 900 motor and 50 trailer cars. A remarkably successful design, these durable BRT Standards, as they were known, remained in service until 1969.

Philadelphia's Broad Street subway was another line built to generous clearance standards that allowed the use of large cars. The line opened in 1928 with a fleet of 150 steel cars built by the J. G. Brill Company that were 67 feet 6 inches long and 10 feet wide, weighed 55 tons, and seated 67 passengers each. Similar to both the large Boston and BRT cars, they were built without vestibules, with three pairs of large sliding doors on each side.

The Brooklyn-Manhattan Transit Corporation (BMT), which succeeded the bankrupt BRT in 1923, soon emerged as a leading innovator in rapid transit car design under the leadership of its superintendent of equipment, William G. Gove. The first new design to appear under BMT auspices was the "Triplex," a 137-foot, three-unit articulated car that weighed 104 tons. The car was mounted on four trucks, with adjoining units sharing a common truck. Four Triplex pilot models delivered by the Pressed Steel Car Company of Pittsburgh in 1925 proved successful, and orders were soon placed for additional units that brought the Triplex fleet to a total of 121 units by 1928.

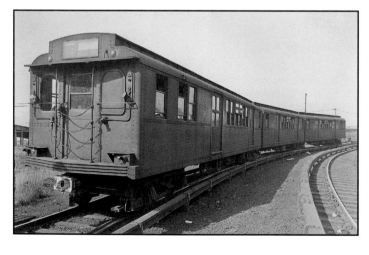

The first in a long line of innovative subway car designs by the Brooklyn-Manhattan Transit Corporation was the 137-foot, articulated "Triplex" introduced in 1925. No. 6046 was one of 121 Triplex cars built by Pressed Steel Car Company during 1925–28. Richard Jay Solomon Collection.

The BMT's next foray into advanced car design was a pair of lightweight trains ordered from car builders Pullman Car & Manufacturing Company of Chicago and the E. G. Budd Manufacturing Company of Philadelphia in 1933. The BMT's objective was to develop all-metal trains that provided the safety required for subway service, yet were light enough to operate on any of the BMT's existing elevated structures, and that could provide schedule speeds very much higher than any existing BMT equipment. Car bodies for both trains were to utilize materials and fabrication techniques developed by the builders for new streamlined passenger trains then being completed for main line railroads. Pull-

The Budd Company rolled out this innovative five-section articulated, or "multi-section," train for the BMT in 1934. Fabricated of welded stainless steel, the 168-foot, 6-inch train weighed only 80 tons. It is seen at the builder's Philadelphia plant ready for shipment to New York. The Budd Company, Donald W. Harold Collection, from Fred W. Schneider, III.

Interiors of the Budd train featured such unaccustomed subway amenities as cork flooring, ducted heating and ventilation, indirect lighting, and seats upholstered in full grain maroon leather. The Budd Company, Donald W. Harold Collection, from Fred W. Schneider, III.

Pullman's equally innovative lightweight articulated train design for the BMT was fabricated from aluminum alloy. The 170-foot train could accommodate 674 seated and standing passengers. An exterior finish in two shades of green gave rise to the train's "Green Hornet" nickname. Pullman Car & Manufacturing Co., Author's Collection.

man's lightweight, three-unit, articulated M10,000, *City of Salina*, for the Union Pacific was built of aluminum alloy, while Budd's three-unit, articulated lightweight *Zephyr* for the Chicago, Burlington & Quincy was fabricated from welded stainless steel, with a corrugated stainless steel skin.

Each of the BMT trains was made up of five articulated units, with adjoining units supported by a common truck, and was designed so that intermediate sections could be added or removed to make up an articulated train of anywhere from three to seventeen units. The Budd train was 168 feet 6 inches long, weighed only 80 tons, and seated 170 passengers, with standing room for another 470. The 170-foot Pullman train weighed 70 tons, and accommodated 184 seated and 490 standing passengers. The Budd train's interior accommodations represented a substantial improvement over the usual subway standards, with cork flooring, ducted heating and ventilation, indirect lighting, and seats upholstered in full-grain maroon leather. Electrically operated doors for the entire train could be controlled from the motorman's cab. The Pullman train was similar, with red-brown leather seats and an interior finish in two shades of blue-gray with a cream ceiling. The Budd train's stainless steel exterior was unpainted, while the Pullman train was finished in two shades of green, with an aluminum color for the skirt and roof, giving rise to the "Green Hornet" nickname, after the then-popular radio serial, that was soon attached to the train.

Although arranged differently, interior appointments of the Pullman "Green Hornet" were similar to the Budd train, with such features as indirect lighting and ducted heating and ventilation. Interior colors were two tones of blue-gray with a cream ceiling, while seats were upholstered in red-brown leather. Donald W. Harold Collection, from Fred W. Schneider, III.

Trucks, motors, and controls for both trains conformed to the performance criteria developed by the Electric Railway Presidents' Conference Committee (ERPCC) for the new-generation PCC streetcar, which was designed to provide improved acceleration and braking rates, smoother control, and better riding qualities. The much higher acceleration and braking rates available were expected to provide average schedule speeds in local service that were 40 percent greater than those with the company's existing equipment. Both trains were equipped with lightweight welded steel trucks. The Budd train was fitted with one 70 h.p. General Electric motor driving each axle through single-reduction helical gearing, while the control system was similar to that developed by GE for the PCC streetcar. Both standard air braking and an eddy current braking system were provided, with provision for the future addition of magnetic track brakes. The Pullman train had a similar propulsion and control system supplied by Westinghouse, with both air and dynamic braking.

The two trains entered regular service in the summer of 1934 and proved highly successful, remaining in service for a number of years. The Pullman train fell victim to a wartime aluminum scrap drive in 1943, while the Budd train continued to operate until 1954.

Based upon experience with the two prototypes, BMT placed orders with Pullman-Standard and St. Louis Car just two years later for a fleet of 25 five-unit, articulated "multi-section" cars. Propulsion, control, and braking equipment, and performance standards for the new cars were similar to the two prototypes, but the cars themselves were fabricated from low-alloy, high-tensile Cor-ten steel, and were more conventional in appearance. Interiors were much more austere than the prototypes, with rattan seating and bare bulb lighting. Ten St. Louis cars were fitted with Westinghouse electrical and braking apparatus, while 15 Pullman-Standard cars were equipped with GE equipment.

Next came what would be a final BMT initiative in the development of improved rapid transit equipment. This was a new car that closely followed the design concepts developed for the streamlined PCC streetcar. The BMT had been one of the principal supporters of the ERPCC, much of the committee's test work had been done on the BMT, and the company's surface lines subsidiary had been the first to place the new cars in regular service in 1936. In 1938, at the same time it was planning to acquire another 500 PCC streetcars, the BMT ordered a prototype three-section articulated aluminum rapid transit car from the Clark Equipment Company of Battle Creek, Mich., that would be equipped with standard PCC trucks, propulsion, and control equipment, adapted as necessary for rapid transit operation.

Passengers boarded a train headed by multi-section No. 7004 on the BMT's 8th Avenue line. Built of low-alloy, high-tensile steel, the 179-foot five-section cars weighed just over 91 tons. New York Transit Museum Archives, Brooklyn (Neg. X8-201).

Delivered early in 1939, the prototype car was 80 feet 4 inches long and weighed just 37 tons, making it the lightest rapid transit car for its size ever to operate in New York. The Clark B-2 trucks employed resilient wheels, hypoid gearing, and magnetic track brakes, and the car was fitted with all-electric GE control. The 1930s modern exterior was finished in medium and dark blue with white trim. The interior was stylishly finished in blue-green and aluminum, with blue tinted mirrors in each corner, "bull's-eye" light fixtures like those used in PCC cars, and seats upholstered in green mohair for 84 passengers. Only months after the new car was successfully tested, the BMT placed a production order with Clark Equipment for another 50 "Bluebirds," as the distinctive cars came to be known.

But the time for innovative lightweight cars for the New York subways was over. Long negotiations were finally completed, and on June 1, 1940, the City of New York took control of the BMT. Soon afterward the city moved to cancel the contract for the 50 Bluebirds, finally agreeing to take delivery of five cars already under construction. These five cars joined the prototype in 1941, and this small Bluebird fleet transported fortunate New York subway riders for almost 15 years before they were withdrawn in 1955.

While the BMT was experimenting with lightweight, articulated car designs, New York's two other subways systems stayed with standard, heavyweight steel cars. The first cars ordered by the City of New York for the new Independent Subway System in 1930 set a standard for big, heavy cars that was to endure for decades. Known by the city's Revenue Contract number under which it was procured, the R1 was a heavy steel car 60 feet 6 inches long and 10 feet wide, and weighing 42 tons. Each car was powered by two 190 h.p. Westinghouse motors mounted on one truck, while the second truck was unpowered. The commodious cars seated 60 in a combination of rattan upholstered transverse and longitudinal seating, and were capable of accommodating another 222 or so standing passengers. Four pairs of sliding doors on each side provided ample entrance and exit capacity. Exteriors were finished in dark green, with "CITY OF NEW YORK" lettered in gold on each side. Interiors were finished in a utilitarian dark green, with white ceilings and red concrete floors.

An initial 300-car R1 fleet was completed by American Car & Foundry during 1930–31, while the same builder, Pullman-Standard, and Pressed Steel Car built more than 1400 more essentially identical R6, R7, and R9 cars for the expanding Independent system over the next decade. What they lacked in aesthetic appeal, creature comforts, or innovative features was more than offset by their capacity and rugged reliability; and the sturdy cars went on to serve millions of New York subway riders for close to four decades.

The last, and surely the finest, in the long line of innovative BMT car designs was the lightweight aluminum "Bluebird" built by the Clark Equipment Company in 1939. Incorporating the radically improved electric railway technology developed for the PCC streetcar, the three-unit, articulated car was 80 feet 4 inches long and could accommodate 84 seated and 234 standing passengers. The prototype Bluebird delivered in 1939 is seen at 8th Avenue on the Sea Beach Line. Donald W. Harold Collection, from Fred W. Schneider, III.

Bluebird interiors were finished in blue-green and aluminum, with seats upholstered in green mohair. The car was illuminated with "bull's-eye" lighting fixtures and a pressure ventilating system delivered filtered air. Donald W. Harold Collection, from Fred W. Schneider, III.

With its car design for the Independent Subway, New York's first publicly owned and operated subway, the city began a long line of conservative, heavyweight steel car designs that would transport New Yorkers for decades to come. No. 100 was the first of 300 R1 cars completed for the IND in 1930–31 by American Car & Foundry. New York City Board of Transportation, Richard Jay Solomon Collection.

Generous clearance standards enabled the use of unusually large cars for Philadelphia's Broad Street subway. This was the first of 50 new cars built by the Pressed Steel Car Company for the South Broad Street extension of the subway in 1938. The design retained the same 67-foot 6-inch length and 10-foot width of the line's original equipment. The new cars featured an Art Deco color scheme and graphics, and such interior amenities as a red and gray finish, leather upholstered seating, stainless steel fittings, and recessed lighting. Fred W. Schneider, III, Collection.

The IRT placed only one order for new cars in the decade prior to the 1940 unification. This was with St. Louis Car for 50 cars to provide extra capacity for the anticipated crowds attending the 1939 World's Fair in Queens. While these "World's Fair" cars, too, were in the conservative heavy steel car tradition, they were configured in what had by now become the standard New York arrangement, without vestibules or end platforms, with three pairs of sliding doors on each side for rapid entrance and exit.

Following the 1940 unification of the Independent, BMT, and IRT into New York City Transit, the conservative, heavy car approach of the Board of Transportation that had produced the R1 and its successors prevailed, and it would be many more years before New York would again become an innovator or pioneer in subway car design.

After World War II, leadership in rapid transit car design shifted to Chicago, where the newly formed Chicago Transit Authority faced the daunting task of replacing an obsolete fleet of over 1600 rapid transit cars that averaged some 40 years in age. More than two-thirds of this fleet was made up of wooden cars, some dating as far back as 1893.

The need for new equipment was heightened by the requirement for all-steel cars for operation in Chicago's expanding subway. At the time the State Street subway opened in 1943, Chicago Rapid Transit had shifted its entire fleet of steel cars to this route, while still more all-steel equipment would be needed for the Dearborn subway.

CRT had begun to think about a new car design as early as 1939, when a full-size car body mockup was completed at the company's Skokie Shops. The design incorporated several features that would later become standard for Chicago's rapid transit fleet. Doors located at the quarter points provided efficient entrance and exit. Tapered ends permitted a car that was 4 feet longer than existing equipment, yet still met the tight clearances imposed by the elevated's short radius curves. Bulging concave-convex "fish belly" sides provided an 8-inch greater width at seat height while still meeting the system's 8-foot 8-inch width limit at platform level.

Chicago took up articulated lightweight car design where the BMT left off with the 1947–48 delivery of four prototype three-section articulated cars that incorporated all-electric PCC streetcar technology. Handsomely finished in maroon and aluminum, No. 5003 was loaded on a flat car for shipment from the plant of builder St. Louis Car Company in 1948. St. Louis Car Company, Author's Collection.

By the time the State Street subway opened, the company was contemplating an articulated aluminum car incorporating PCC car technology—much like the BMT's Bluebird. An order for 30 articulated cars was placed with the St. Louis Car Company in 1944, but was then cancelled because of financing problems. Ultimately, orders were placed for four prototype cars, two each from St. Louis Car and Pullman-Standard. Delivered during 1947–48, these were 88-foot 7½-inch, three-section articulated trains, with the adjoining sections sharing a common truck. Built of aluminum alloy with steel reinforced frames, the lightweight cars employed the curved side design developed for the 1939 mockup to provide a greater width at seat level. A pair of "blinker" type doors was provided at the center of each of the three articulated sections. Each car seated 96 passengers in transverse aluminum tubular frame seats upholstered in mohair. Crank-operated individual windows with adjustable curtains were provided at each seat. Interior fittings included aluminum handrails and stanchions, and modern "bull's-eye" lighting fixtures.

Trucks, electrical, and control equipment for the four cars incorporated the all-electric technology developed for the PCC streetcar. The Pullman-Standard cars employed Westinghouse electrical equipment, while the St. Louis Car units were fitted with GE equipment. A Cineston master controller combined both propulsion and braking controls in a single control handle. PCC type trucks were built by the Clark Equipment Company for the Pullman Standard cars and by St. Louis Car themselves for their units. These employed inside frames and roller bearings and were fitted with resilient wheels. Two 55 h.p. motors on each truck were mounted parallel to the car centerline with drive shafts that extended through the center bolster to drive the opposite axle through hypoid gearing. An electrically actuated drum brake was provided on each motor drive shaft, and magnetic track brakes were mounted between the wheels on each side of the truck.

The four prototype articulated units provided CTA with valuable experience during extensive tests and regular service operation on different parts of the elevated and subway lines. When the time came for its first major new car order, however, the authority chose a more conventional arrangement instead of the articulated design of the prototypes, although the same PCC technology was adopted. These new cars would be 48-foot single-end, double-

After a number of years in storage, Chicago's prototype articulated cars began 20 years of service on the CTA's high-speed Skokie Swift route. Pullman-built No. 51 operated over the Skokie line in October 1964, wearing the mercury green and croydon cream colors adopted for Chicago rapid transit in 1950. Chicago Transit Authority, Author's Collection.

When it came time for production orders for a PCC-type rapid transit car fleet, the Chicago Transit Authority decided upon "married pairs" of 48-foot cars instead of the articulated configuration of the 1947–48 prototypes. An eight-car train of the PCC-type cars made a passenger stop on a three-track section of the "L" around 1961. Richard Jay Solomon.

truck cars that would operate semi-permanently coupled in married pairs, which permitted significant economies by eliminating the need for automatic couplers between the two paired cars or control cabs at one end of each car. Each pair seated a total of 98 passengers.

Orders for 200 of the new cars went to the St. Louis Car Company in 1948 and 1950, and the first new equipment began entering service in August 1950. There still remained close to a thousand obsolete elevated and subway cars overdue for replacement, and changing conditions on the CTA's surface lines soon offered an unusual solution. During 1946–47, CTA had placed 600 new PCC streetcars in surface operation, but by 1950 this was looking like a bad investment, as street traffic congestion worsened and increasing numbers of riders gave up streetcars for their own automobiles. Plans were soon formed for a program under which buses would replace the streetcars, which would then be transformed into new rapid transit cars. The streetcar car bodies themselves were scrapped, while trucks, motors, control equipment, motor-generators, track brakes, and even such components as seats, light fixtures, and windows were reconditioned and installed in new body shells. St. Louis Car won a contract for the work, and over a five-year period from 1954 to 1959 a total of 570 streetcars were transformed into new PCC type rapid transit cars.

While Chicago thus became by far the largest user of PCC rapid transit cars, it was not the only one to adopt the advanced streetcar technology for subway-elevated operation. In 1950, Boston's Metropolitan Transit Authority (MTA) ordered 40 PCC type cars for the new

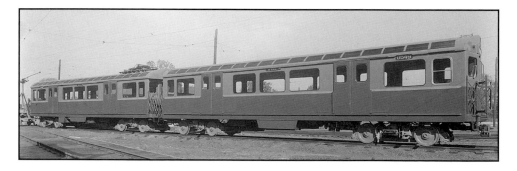

In 1950 Boston's Metropolitan Transit Authority acquired 40 of these PCC-type rapid transit cars, which operated in two-car pairs over a new rapid transit route built in the roadbed of the former Boston, Revere Beach & Lynn. A pair of the MTA cars was photographed at the plant of builder St. Louis Car Company. St. Louis Car Company, Author's Collection.

PCC-type cars were also introduced in high-performance versions for Boston's Main Line elevated and Cambridge-Dorchester subway. This is a two-car train of Pullman-Standard PCC-type cars on the Massachusetts Bay Transportation Authority's Orange Line elevated—originally known as the Main Line elevated—in Washington Street at Newton Street in August 1976. Herbert H. Harwood, Jr.

rapid transit line being built on the roadbed of the former Boston, Revere Beach & Lynn. Several years later another 100 "high performance" PCC type cars were ordered from Pullman-Standard to replace older equipment on the MTA's Main Line elevated. Employing components developed in tests at Chicago, they were fitted with 100 h.p. traction motors instead of the usual 55 h.p. PCC motors, and were capable of much higher acceleration rates and maximum speed than previous PCC rapid transit equipment. A further order for 92 similar, but larger, cars for the MTA's Cambridge-Dorchester line followed several years later. Cleveland's new rapid transit line opened for service in 1955 with a fleet of PCC rapid transit cars that reached a total of 88 by 1958. New York's Hudson & Manhattan Railroad became still another PCC car operator in 1958–59, when St. Louis Car delivered 50 new cars for operation through the Hudson Tubes between New Jersey and Manhattan that were notable for both their high performance characteristics and as the first air-conditioned rapid transit equipment. Toronto originally planned a PCC type car for its new subway, but eventually chose a more conventional car design.

New York's Hudson & Manhattan was another user of high-performance PCC-type cars, which also had the distinction of being the first air-conditioned rapid transit equipment. St. Louis Car built 50 of them in 1958. No. 1200 was one of 30 of the new cars owned by the Pennsylvania Railroad and used by H&M in their joint service between Newark and New York. St. Louis Car Company, Author's Collection.

Meanwhile, Chicago's CTA had been experimenting with ways to develop higher speeds and acceleration rates. Eight test cars were equipped with experimental truck designs, control systems, and other experimental equipment, and some were fitted with 100 h.p. traction motors. While the standard PCC elevated-subway cars were capable of 50 mph, several modified cars were capable of reaching a maximum speed of about 76 mph. The outcome of this work was a specification for a new generation of CTA high-speed cars that took shape in a 180-car order delivered by Pullman-Standard in 1964.

Some of the most advanced rapid transit cars of their time, the new cars made extensive use of extrusions and welding in their aluminum car bodies, and aircraft type floor panels laminated from balsa wood and aluminum sheet. Trucks were a new cast steel design, while the use of 28-inch wheels and four 100 h.p. motors on each car permitted a maximum speed of 65 mph

The CTA cars were notable, too, for a new emphasis on esthetics and passenger comforts. The use of molded fiberglass ends permitted the designers to incorporate an unusual sculptured look. Interiors were finished in light colors, with a light blue seat covering. The cars were fitted with fluorescent lighting, large "picture" windows, and—most important of all—air conditioning.

The 180 advanced Pullman-Standard cars set a new high performance standard for CTA that formed the basis for subsequent orders for more than 1200 additional cars from a variety of builders over the next three decades. Although incremental improvements were made to the design, all of the CTA's nearly 1400 high performance cars were capable of operating in trains with each other.

The Toronto Transit Commission soon established still another new direction in rapid transit car design. TTC had begun operation of its initial Yonge Street subway with a fleet of 57-foot conventional cars supplied by Great Britain's Gloucester Railway Carriage & Wagon Company. The first 100 of an initial order for 106 cars completed during 1953–54 were of all-steel construction and weighed nearly 43 tons. The balance of the order was built with all-aluminum car body construction, reducing the weight of each car by fully six tons. Another 34 cars delivered by the same builder during 1956–59 employed aluminum roof construction, which reduced the weight of each car by about four tons per car.

These 75-foot aluminum cars, built for the Toronto Transit Commission by the Montreal Locomotive Works in 1962, were the longest subway cars then in use anywhere in the world, and were the prototypes for hundreds of later Toronto cars. Headed by one of the 36 new cars, an Eglinton train loaded in the Bloor Street station of the Yonge Street subway. Eric Trussler Photograph, Toronto Transit Commission.

Based upon this experience with aluminum construction, TTC specified an even larger car of all-aluminum construction for its new University subway. Built by the Montreal Locomotive Works during 1962–63, these 74-foot 6-inch cars were almost 18 feet longer than the original Gloucester cars, yet they weighed less than 30 tons, almost 13 tons less than TTC's initial cars. They also represented the longest rapid transit cars then operating anywhere in the world, with the lowest weight per linear foot or square foot yet attained. These lightweight, high capacity cars provided impressive gains for TTC in performance characteristics, as well as reductions in weight, maintenance costs, and power consumption, and established the basic design for more than 800 more big aluminum cars acquired over the next 35 years.

Replacement car orders for the elevated and subway systems at Boston, Philadelphia, and Cleveland, and the New Jersey-New York Port Authority Trans-Hudson (PATH) incorporated many of the advances pioneered at Chicago and Toronto. In 1962 PATH acquired 162 modern cars from St. Louis Car that incorporated such features as stainless steel construction, air conditioning, and high performance components that permitted speeds of 70 mph. Almost 200 more similar cars followed over the next 22 years. A 76-car fleet built by Pullman-Standard in 1969 for Boston's new South Shore extension of the Cambridge-Dorchester Red Line adopted performance and passenger comfort standards similar to those for the CTA and PATH cars. The 70-foot cars incorporated aluminum body construction, air conditioning, and high performance controls, motors, and trucks that permitted a 70 mph maximum speed. Similar standards were established by MBTA for 242 new cars supplied by Canada's Hawker Siddely and UTDC for the authority's Orange, Blue, and Red lines during the 1980s.

The Chicago Transit Authority's 180 2000-series cars produced by Pullman-Standard in 1964 represented a major leap forward in rapid transit car technology. Capable of a 65-mph maximum speed, they featured an advanced car body design of aluminum extrusions, with lightweight aircraft-style floor panels and molded fiberglass ends. Passenger amenities included fluorescent lighting, "picture" windows, and air conditioning. A two-car train of the "New Look" cars is shown westbound on the Lake Street line at the Chicago River crossing in 1964, with the Merchandise Mart in the left background. Chicago Transit Authority, Author's Collection.

In 1960 270 Budd Company stainless steel cars replaced the original equipment on Philadelphia's Market Street elevated-subway, while another 125 stainless steel cars from Japan's Kawasaki replaced original Broad Street subway equipment in 1982. Reflecting Toronto's successful experience with extremely large cars, the Cleveland Transit System adopted a 70-foot car body for 30 stainless steel "Airporter" cars delivered in 1967 and 1970 for a rapid transit extension to the city's Hopkins Airport. Compared even to its earlier lightweight PCC equipment, CTS was able to gain a per-passenger weight reduction of nearly 25 percent through the use of a large car and lightweight materials. An even longer 74-foot stainless steel design was specified for a 60-car order from Japan's Tokyu Car Corporation that replaced the line's original equipment during 1985–86.

At New York, experimentation with innovative lightweight equipment had largely ended with the 1940 unification, and descendents of the heavy steel cars of the 1930s continued to roll off the car builders' assembly lines for the New York system by the hundreds through the end of the 1960s. A notable exception was a ten-car R11 order delivered by the Budd Company in 1949. These were handsome 60-foot stainless steel cars intended as prototypes for the long-planned Second Avenue subway. Innovative interior features included electrostatic dust filters and ultraviolet germ-killing lamps in the ventilation system and fluorescent lighting. The cars were equipped with 100 h.p. traction motors and trucks that combined PCC truck features with New York's standard cast steel truck. One car was fitted with Budd's disk braking system.

Stainless steel construction, molded fiberglass ends, air conditioning, and a 70-mph maximum speed capability were features of a 162-car fleet built by St. Louis Car for Hudson & Manhattan successor Port Authority Trans-Hudson in 1962. Another 175 similar cars from St. Louis and builders in Canada and Japan followed over the next two decades. Led by one of the newest Kawasaki-built PA-4 cars, a Newark to World Trade Center train approached the Harrison station in Newark in May 1995. William D. Middleton.

(*Middle and bottom*) Montreal advanced the esthetics of metro car design with a fleet of 369 of these blue and white pneumatic-tired cars built by Canadian Vickers for the city's new Métro in 1966. Interior appointments included bright lighting and comfortable seating. Canadian Vickers Industries, Ltd., Author's Collection.

Pullman-Standard built 30 of these 70-foot, stainless steel "Airporter" cars for the extension of Cleveland's rapid transit line to the city's Hopkins Airport in 1968. Eastbound from the airport, a two-car train entered the downtown Cleveland Union Terminal in July 1969. Fred W. Schneider, III.

No. 5703, the first of a 100-car R12 order built by American Car & Foundry in 1948 for New York's IRT Division, was typical of the conventional, heavyweight steel cars built for New York's subways well into the post–World War II period. The exterior finish was a two-tone gray livery, with orange stripes. Sprague Library, Electric Railroader's Association.

A major variation from the normal course of New York subway car design was the 10-car R11 order built by the Budd Company in 1949. Intended as prototypes for the ill-fated Second Avenue subway, these handsome all-stainless steel cars incorporated a number of innovative features, including trucks with PCC features, and—on one car—a Budd disk braking system. Interiors featured fluorescent lighting, dust filters and germ-killing lamps in the ventilation system, and comfortable seating upholstered in a striped material. (both) New York City Transit Authority, from Fred W. Schneider, III.

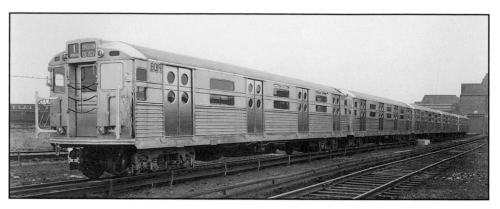

While other New York orders called for more conventional equipment, there was a steady stream of improvements to the basic design. Car bodies were built of welded low alloy, high-tensile steel to provide a smooth finish. Dynamic braking became the primary braking system, substantially reducing wheel and brake shoe wear, as well as permitting higher braking rates. Fluorescent lighting became standard. Some early postwar cars had such amenities as foam rubber seating with red leather upholstery, and tile floors, but the realities of New York's punishing service environment soon led to the use of fiberglass seats and plain floor covering.

The New York subway fleet was brightened in 1963 when an order went to Budd for 600 "Brightliner" stainless steel R32 cars that weighed a good five tons less than similar cars of high-tensile steel construction. In a major departure from standard New York practice, the last four cars delivered were fitted with Budd's lightweight Pioneer III trucks instead of New York's standard cast steel trucks. Otherwise, however, the R32's conformed to the basic New York design in their equipment and operating characteristics, and even the experimental Budd trucks were soon replaced with standard heavyweight trucks.

Two orders delivered by St. Louis Car in the late 1960s included some air-conditioned cars, and the second of these two orders—the R42 car—represented New York's first attempt to develop a stylized car. Designed by Raymond Loewy, the R42 featured dramatic sloping ends of molded fiberglass, with a large motorman's window on one side and an equally

After much experimentation with such amenities as foam rubber seating with leather or mohair upholstery, and a variety of configurations, the realities of New York's capacity needs and punishing service environment led to more austere solutions. This is the interior of a typical modern New York subway car, with longitudinal bench seats of durable fiberglass, plain vinyl tile floors, and plenty of stainless steel stanchions and grab handles for standing passengers. New York City Transit Authority, from Fred W. Schneider, III.

large fluorescent-lighted curtain route sign on the other. The slant nose design, however, reduced seating capacity and presented safety hazards for passengers moving between cars. The first 200 R42's were fitted with ungainly extension bars to eliminate the hazard, while the last 200 were completed with an entirely different fiberglass end design without the sloped nose. Another 400 R42 cars completed by St. Louis Car during 1968–69 featured similar molded fiberglass ends, stainless steel exteriors, and air conditioning. Even so, these handsome new cars retained the basic dimensions set by the Independent Subway's 1930 cars, and they were operationally compatible with earlier New York equipment.

New York finally broke with previous practice with an order for 300 R44 cars built by St. Louis during 1970–71. These were 75-foot cars, the longest ever built for the New York subways, and they were capable of speeds up to 80 mph, even though they would be limited to 50 mph until the elusive Second Avenue subway was completed. Another 52 R44's were ordered for Staten Island Rapid Transit in 1969, while Pullman-Standard built 754 R46 cars during 1974–78 that were nearly identical to the R44's except for New York's first use of an air suspension system. Between 1986 and 1989 Westinghouse-Amrail and Japan's Kawasaki delivered 425 similar R68 cars, while Kawasaki and Bombardier built a total of 1150 smaller R62 cars for the former IRT lines.

While older transit systems were constrained by existing conditions in the design of new rolling stock, the advent of "new generation" rail systems that began in the 1960s gave equipment designers a "clean slate" to develop new rolling stock that could effectively meet more demanding standards of performance and passenger appeal.

The first of these was the Port Authority Transit Corporation's new 14-mile high-speed line between Philadelphia and suburban Lindenwold, N.J., which opened in 1969. The Budd Company supplied an advanced fleet of 76 stainless steel cars that incorporated such amenities as comfortably upholstered seating, large tinted windows, and air conditioning to appeal to automobile oriented suburban commuters. The high performance cars were mounted on Budd's lightweight, air suspension Pioneer III trucks, and were equipped with four 160 h.p. traction motors that permitted high acceleration rates and a maximum operating speed of 75 mph.

The effort launched in the San Francisco Bay Area in 1962 to build a new kind of transit system—one that could successfully attract the freeway commuter away from his automobile—required an even more advanced rapid transit car. Clearly, the system's car design would have to reach far beyond normally accepted transit industry standards; to succeed, the BART car would have to provide a whole new level of performance, passenger comfort, and aesthetic appeal.

The development effort required to produce such a car was a long and costly one. BART's consulting engineers, Parsons, Brinckerhoff-Tudor-Bechtel, developed basic technical standards for the equipment during the mid-1960s. Testing of a wide variety of equipment components was a major part of the $11 million research and development program carried out on BART's 4.4-mile Mt. Diablo Test Track, which opened in 1965. Three laboratory cars were used in the extensive test program. Based upon overall size and performance standards set by the engineers, a detailed design for the configuration, interior arrangement, passenger amenities, and appearance of the car was developed under a contract awarded in 1964 to the Detroit industrial design firm of Sundberg-Ferar. A full-sized mockup of the final car design was completed by St. Louis Car in 1965 and widely displayed in the Bay Area.

An intensive development program produced a car design for BART that was unlike anything before it. No feature of the design was more visible than the futuristic molded fiberglass operator's pod for the "A" cars that operated at each end of a train. Ed Gregerman, BART superintendent of rolling stock, was in the cab in this August 1970 view of newly delivered car No. 101. Harre W. Demoro, from Fred W. Schneider, III.

A production contract for 250 cars—later expanded to 450 cars—was awarded to aerospace manufacturer Rohr Corporation in 1969. The fleet was divided between 274 mid-train B cars that were non-automatic control units 70 feet in length, while 176 A car control units were 5 feet longer through the addition of a molded fiberglass attendant's cab at one end. This sharply raked end cab with its single large, off center window was a highly distinctive design element that became a virtual signature feature of the BART system. Trains could be operated with any number of cars from two to ten, but an A car was required at each end of a train.

Although the basic arrangement and appearance of the car were fixed by the Sundberg-Ferar design, bids for car production were taken on what was largely a "performance specification" basis, which gave the successful builder wide latitude in the details of the car's design and construction. Rohr used this freedom to apply a variety of materials and production methods that, while common in the aerospace industry, were new to transit car building. Some of the builder's most important variations from conventional car building practice were in the design, fabrication and assembly of the BART car bodies. The Rohr design used monocoque construction, in which the entire car body is an integral, load carrying structure.

The sidewalls, which were fabricated as a single aluminum extrusion, acted as the car's principal load carrying members. These were riveted together with roof panels, floor beams, and floor panels to complete the car's integrated body structure. Roof and floor panels were fabricated of aluminum alloy sandwiched with foam. End panels and the attendant's cab on A cars were riveted to the roof panel and sidewalls. End panels were fitted with diaphragms and double sliding doors for easy passage between cars. Two 54-inch double sliding doors were provided on each side of both A and B cars.

Ecstatic models occupied "plush theater-type seats" in this mockup of the BART car interior put together by supplier American Seating Company. "Guaranteed seats" for all commuters was an early promise of BART designers that never quite came true, and standee handrails were later added to the low ceilings of the BART cars. Sprague Library, Electric Railroader's Association.

The contract for BART's initial car fleet went to Southern California aerospace supplier Rohr Industries. This was the BART assembly line at Rohr's Chula Vista (Calif.) plant, where aerospace fabrication methods were used to build the advanced metro cars. Bay Area Rapid Transit District.

Rohr's innovative approach to the structural design of the BART car was particularly notable for its exceptional success in weight reduction. Averaging about 800 pounds per seat, the BART car was the lightest high-speed transit car ever built, despite the weight penalties imposed by such features as air conditioning. The modern cars most nearly comparable to the BART car, PATCO's Budd-built Lindenwold Line cars, weighed 950 pounds per seat.

Because of the adoption of a broad track and lateral clearance gauge, as well as the use of a curved "fish belly" sidewall, the BART car design permitted the use of unusually wide and comfortable seating. Seats were foam padded and upholstered in fabric and vinyl. Each car seated 72 passengers, and had a maximum seated and standing capacity of about 210.

The interior finish of the cars made extensive use of such low maintenance materials as fiberglass ceiling panels and vinyl wall coverings. Windows were of green tinted safety glass, and fixed in place, since the cars were air-conditioned. Floors were carpeted throughout the car. This not only enhanced the car's passenger appeal, but also, together with such features as fixed windows, extensive car body insulation, and air suspension, contributed to an exceptionally low noise level.

The car's communications network included an intercom system that permitted communication between a passenger in any car of a train and the operator; a radiotelephone that linked the attendant with the control center, yard control stations, and mainline relay stations; and a train telephone PA system that permitted public address announcements to a train from the control center or a mainline relay station.

The truck developed for the car by LFM-Rockwell employed an articulated cast steel frame, with inside wheel bearings. Shock absorbers dampened both vertical and lateral motion. Wheels were of forged aluminum with steel tires, pressed onto hollow steel axles. An air suspension system controlled by car-leveling valves maintained the car floor at a 39-inch level above the rails in the longitudinal direction, and maintained the car floor level in the transverse direction regardless of the placement of the passenger load.

Each truck on the BART car was powered by two 150 h.p. traction motors, installed in a geared mounting parallel to the axles. This provided sufficient power for a 3 mph per second acceleration rate and a maximum speed of 80 mph. Power supply to the traction motors was regulated by a solid-state thyristor "chopper" control. A combination of dynamic braking with the traction motors and a hydraulic disc friction-braking system provided a normal braking rate of 3 mph per second, with an emergency rate of 4.5 mph per second.

Under normal conditions the BART car operated entirely under the control of the system's automatic train operation, or ATO, installation. Signals transmitted through track circuits were detected by the car's receiving antennas and converted to appropriate speed, braking, or door opening signals. Different coded sequences of frequencies provided eight possible speed commands up to 80 mph. The speed command was compared to the car's actual speed, and the car was automatically accelerated or braked to conform to the speed command. The ATO system also automatically brought a train to a halt at the proper position at station platforms. Signals were transmitted from the lead A car to the remainder of the train through train line circuits. In the event of an ATO failure a road manual control permitted a train's attendant to operate the train over the road in a non-ATO mode at speeds up to 25 mph, and there was a similar manual control for 10 mph yard operation.

The first years of operation were anything but smooth, as BART encountered a long string of performance and reliability problems with its sophisticated car. But in the end BART had what it wanted: a car that provided a level of performance and passenger appeal never before achieved on a rapid transit system. A new and demanding standard had been set for the industry.

Using the experience of the BART car as a starting point, the federal Urban Mass Transit Administration initiated an Urban Rapid Rail Vehicle and Systems Program intended to develop advanced rapid transit equipment. A first effort of the program was UMTA's State-of-the-Art Car, or SOAC, which was designed to demonstrate the application of the best current technology to a car that was compatible with existing rail systems. SOAC builder St.

In the 1970s the federal Urban Mass Transit Administration developed the State of the Art Car—SOAC for short—to demonstrate the application of new metro car technology to existing rail systems. In demonstration service on New York City Transit's D line, the two-car SOAC train stopped at Newkirk Avenue in Brooklyn in May 1974. For Brooklyn commuters expecting the arrival of their usual utilitarian subway train, the SOAC's futuristic molded fiberglass front end with its oversized windows must have come as quite a surprise. New York Transit Museum Archives, Brooklyn (Neg. ZCE35-14).

While the streamlined contours of such new generation rolling stock as the BART or SOAC cars were attractive to the general public and to the politicians and others promoting new rail systems, the everyday need for flexibility in assembling trains soon led to more practical designs. By the time Baltimore and Miami placed a joint order for the cars needed for their new metros in the early 1980s, metro car design had returned to the box-like configuration of earlier years. This was a Baltimore Metro train on an aerial section of the line near Reisterstown Plaza. Maryland Mass Transit Administration.

Louis Car constructed a pair of 75-foot stainless steel cars that incorporated such features as 175 h.p. traction motors, a new lightweight air-sprung truck, thyristor "chopper" control, and dynamic braking, augmented by pneumatic tread brakes, and were capable of 80 mph operation. Molded fiberglass ends featured a dramatic sloped front with oversized windows. Air suspension, sealed windows, insulation, and carpeted floors contributed to unusually quiet operation. Following their delivery late in 1972, the SOAC cars were tested at the Department of Transportation's High Speed Ground Test Center near Pueblo, Colo., and were then placed in test and revenue service at New York, Boston, Cleveland, Chicago, and Philadelphia during 1974–77. A second experimental train, the sloped nose, two-car Advanced Concept Train (ACT-1), was completed for UMTA by Garrett AiResearch of Torrance, Calif., in 1976, incorporating such innovative features as an energy storage flywheel propulsion system. Although tests were conducted with the ACT-1, a five-city demonstration was cancelled. Even though neither train was ever replicated for regular service, the effort helped to introduce and test a number of advanced ideas and components that found their way into other new rail equipment.

The car design developed for the Washington Area Metropolitan Transit Authority's new Metrorail system owed much to BART's extensive test program and early experience. WMATA staff and consultants Louis T. Klauder & Associates developed specifications for the car, while the aesthetic design was the work of Sundberg-Ferar, which had also designed the BART car. WMATA's initial order for 300 cars went to the Rohr Corporation, which had also built the BART car fleet. While there were many similarities between the two designs, particularly in their structural design and passenger amenities, there were important differences as well, and the WMATA car established an even higher level of automatic operation and sophistication.

The most visible difference was the end design. While the BART car had achieved a dramatic "space age" look with its raked end cabs, the design also made it more difficult to increase or decrease the size of trains, since one of the A cars had to be located at each end, and could be placed nowhere else in a train. The WMATA design allowed a much greater flexibility. The cars were arranged as married pairs, with some shared equipment, and an operating cab at each end of the pair. Unlike the BART A cars, a flat end and a train door at the operating end permitted coupling to another pair, thus allowing trains to be readily built up by coupling paired units. If not as dramatic as the BART design, the molded fiberglass Sundberg-Ferar end design was still an attractive one that conveyed a modern image unlike that of any conventional subway car.

While there were substantial differences in electrical and mechanical details, the Rockwell trucks and a propulsion package of four 192 h.p. Westinghouse traction motors provided an equivalent maximum operating speed of 80 mph and similar high performance acceleration and braking rates. Braking included both dynamic and hydraulic friction disk systems.

Significant advances over the BART car included an ability to remotely uncouple equipment anywhere in a train from the lead cab, the provision of a magnetic tape recorder similar to the "black box" used in aircraft to record significant operating information for later analysis in the event of an accident or other malfunction, and unprecedented provisions for the use of specialized test equipment for the car's many electrical, mechanical, pneumatic, and electronic devices. In one respect, however, the design reverted to an older technology, electing to use conventional cam controller hardware rather than the newer semiconductor chopper control employed by BART.

Rolling stock for still other new generation rapid transit systems followed closely in the path established by BART and WMATA, with the same sort of large, lightweight car body; passenger comfort and aesthetic features; and high performance characteristics. An initial 120 cars completed for the Metropolitan Atlanta Rapid Transit Authority by France's Franco Belge in 1978–82 were 75-foot, aluminum vehicles weighing only 38 tons each. Four 172 h.p. traction motors permitted a 3 mph per second acceleration rate and a 70 mph top speed. During 1982–84 the Budd Company built 208 75-foot stainless steel cars for new systems at Baltimore and Miami that virtually duplicated the performance characteristics of the earlier Washington and Atlanta car fleets.

By the beginning of the 1990s, further advances in electrical, electronic, and computer technology were bringing important improvements in rapid transit vehicle performance, efficiency, and reliability. Perhaps the most important of these was a shift to the use of A.C. traction motors, offering significant reductions in power consumption and maintenance expense, as well as much improved reliability. Still other advances in technology included microprocessor-based propulsion control, vehicle diagnostics, and fault monitoring systems that promised greatly improved overall vehicle reliability and availability.

Boston's MBTA became the first North American system to move into a large scale application of this new technology with a 1990 order for 86 new 70-foot stainless steel cars from Bombardier Transportation for the city's Red Line subway. An inverter group on each car converted 600-volt D.C. power to three-phase A.C. for the traction motors, and converted braking energy back into D.C. power for return to the third rail. Propulsion, braking, and car subsystem controls were linked with an on-board computer-controlled monitoring system, and the cars had an on-board diagnostic capability for their propulsion, braking, communications, and air conditioning systems. The Toronto Transit Commission was the next to adopt the new technology, with a late 1992 order for 216 new T-1 cars with similar equipment.

Meanwhile, New York City Transit was preparing for what would be the largest new technology fleet of all. Orders were placed in 1989 for two "New Technology Test Trains,"

Before ordering several thousand advanced design subway cars, New York City Transit thoroughly tested a pair of "new technology test trains" that entered test service in 1993. On the right is the ten-car Kawasaki-built R110A train designed for operation over the more restrictive clearances of the system's former IRT lines. Bombardier Transportation built the nine-car R110B train on the left to operate on the more generous clearances of former BMT and IND lines. The two trains were photographed at the Smith–9th Streets station in Brooklyn on the F Line against the background of a Manhattan skyline that was forever changed on September 11, 2001. Elijah Hilbert, Metropolitan Transportation Authority.

one designed for operation on the more restrictive clearances of the former IRT lines and the other for the former BMT and IND lines. Placed in test service in 1993, a ten-car R110A train supplied by Kawasaki was made up of 51-foot long, 8-foot 7-inch wide stainless steel cars that conformed to IRT dimensions, while a nine-car R110B train built by Bombardier was made up of 67-foot long, 9-foot 7-inch wide stainless steel cars for the BMT and IND lines. Both trains incorporated such advanced features as A.C. propulsion, regenerative braking, electronically controlled braking, air bag suspension, and on-board microcomputer diagnostic systems. Inboard bearing trucks fabricated from steel plate were 22 percent lighter than the standard New York truck. Performance objectives for the trains were to achieve twice the reliability of previous new equipment, and—through the use of A.C. propulsion and regenerative braking—to reduce energy use by 25 percent.

Interior design for the trains included such convenience features as electronic voice announcements, destination signs, and information displays; external speakers, allowing train crews to communicate with passengers on station platforms; and—on one train—an electronic strip map that displayed the train's location. Security features included a touch-strip activated silent alarm system, and a push-to-speak intercom for passenger to train crew communication.

Based upon several years of testing with the two "new technology" trains, New York City Transit formed specifications for what would be the largest order for new equipment in its history. By 1997 orders totaling $1.45 billion had been placed for 1080 new cars that incorporated advanced features similar to those of the test trains. Bombardier won an order for 680 R142 cars for the IRT lines, while Kawasaki was to build 400 R143 cars for the BMT and IND lines. First deliveries began in 2000. Early in 2001 NYCT added another 350 cars to Bombardier's R142 order, and planned still further orders for its new technology car fleet.

Light rail equipment went through a similar evolution over the last several decades of the century. By the 1950s virtually all of the surviving street railway lines with light rail characteristics had made a transition to the operation of the modern PCC streetcar, either as single units or in M.U. train operation. By the 1970s, however, these aging PCC fleets were ready for replacement, and the Urban Mass Transit Administration initiated an effort to develop a new U.S. Standard Light Rail Vehicle, or SLRV. An important feature of the SLRV design was the use of a two-section articulated car body. This gave the vehicle the flexibility to operate around the short radius curves often encountered on light rail lines while still providing a high capacity unit. The 71-foot SLRV provided space for a seated and standing capacity of well over 200 passengers. The cars were mounted on a monomotor power truck at each end equipped with a single 230 h.p. traction motor and an unpowered truck shared by the adjoining sections at the center, and were fitted with such features as resilient wheels, and rubber chevron and air spring suspension. Semiconductor chopper control, and a combination of dynamic, disc, and magnetic track brakes contributed to the car's high performance characteristics.

Aerospace manufacturer Boeing-Vertol landed a 1973 order for 275 of the SLRVs for the Boston and San Francisco light rail systems. Plagued by problems, the vehicles were years late in entering service, and never did reach their original performance and reliability goals. Boston's MBTA ultimately rejected a portion of its 175-car share of the order. Thirty of the rejected Boston cars eventually went to San Francisco, but there were no repeat orders for the SLRV.

A more successful effort to develop a new light rail vehicle was initiated by Canada's Urban Transit Development Corporation (UTDC) in the mid 1970s. This produced a 50-foot, double truck Canadian Light Rail Vehicle (CLRV) incorporating many of the advanced features specified for the SLRV. The Toronto Transit Commission acquired 196 of the CLRV's for its surface lines during 1979–82, and then followed up with an order for 52 76-foot articulated versions of the car. Another 50 86-foot versions of the UTDC articulated design were supplied during 1987–88 for Santa Clara County's Guadalupe Corridor light rail line in California.

Aerospace manufacturer Boeing-Vertol landed a contract to build a joint Boston-San Francisco order for 218 articulated Standard Light Rail Vehicles. While the design was plagued with maintenance and reliability problems, it did much to set the standard for configuration and passenger amenities for a new generation of modern light rail vehicles. This was a San Francisco Boeing SLRV in Taraval Street at Sunset Boulevard, inbound to downtown San Francisco on Line L, Taraval, in June 1984. William D. Middleton.

An articulated version of UTDC's single unit CLRV went to both the Toronto Transit Commission and California's Santa Clara County Transportation Agency. A southbound Guadalupe Corridor train of the big Santa Clara County cars entered the north end of San Jose's transit mall at First and Devine streets in April 1990. William D. Middleton.

Germany's Siemens Transportation was by far the most successful supplier of vehicles to North American light rail systems, with almost 600 of its standardized—or special—light rail vehicle designs in service or on order. The Siemens-Duewag U2 articulated design originally developed for Frankfurt, Germany, was one of the most popular. This was a U2a car built for the Sacramento Regional Transit District in 1986. William D. Middleton.

Aside from Toronto's single unit CLRV's, the only other new single unit designs included a fleet of 141 single unit cars built for Philadelphia's Southeastern Pennsylvania Transportation Authority by Japan's Kawasaki Heavy Industries during 1980–82, and 27 unusually large, 67-foot cars built for Buffalo's Niagara Frontier Transportation Authority by Japan's Tokyu Car Corporation in 1984. A much more popular choice for new light rail vehicle orders proved to be double-end, articulated cars similar in arrangement to the SLRV design of the 1970s, and ranging in size from an overall length of 71 feet to 92 feet.

The most popular articulated designs were those developed by Germany's Siemens-Duewag. New systems at Edmonton, Calgary, San Diego, and Sacramento ordered well over 200 of the Siemens-Duewag standard U2 design originally developed for Frankfurt, Germany. Almost as many more standard SD-100 and SD-400 cars were supplied to light rail systems at San Diego, St. Louis, Denver, and Salt Lake City, while special designs were developed for Los Angeles and Portland (Ore.). Bombardier's Concarril plant in Mexico supplied more than a hundred cars based upon Siemens designs for light rail lines in Mexico City, Guadalajara, and Monterrey.

In 1995 San Francisco's Municipal Railway began the replacement of its Boeing SLRV fleet with a second-generation modern light rail vehicle supplied by Italy's Breda Costruzione Ferroviarie. A train of the new cars arrived at Muni Metro's Fourth and King streets terminal at the Caltrain depot in October 1999. William D. Middleton.

A new approach of the '90s to light rail accessibility for the disabled was the development of partial low floor cars, which enabled wheelchair passengers to board from low platforms, usually with the aid of a bridging plate. This was a Massachusetts Bay Transportation Authority low floor vehicle on the Boston College line in June 2001. Italy's Breda supplied 100 of these Type 8 articulated cars. William D. Middleton.

Still other articulated designs were developed by European, Japanese, and Canadian builders. Italy's Breda Costruzioni Ferroviarie built articulated cars for Cleveland, San Francisco, and Boston, while Spain's Construcciones v Auxiliar de Ferrocarriles landed an order for new articulated cars for Sacramento in 1999. The European ABB Traction consortium built articulated cars for Baltimore that ranked as the largest in North America, with an overall length of 92 feet and seats for 85 passengers. Japan's Kinki Sharyo built special articulated designs for Boston and Dallas, and picked up a 1999 order for Santa Clara County (Calif.), while Sumitomo/Nippon Sharyo built a large fleet for Los Angeles. Canada's Bombardier built an initial articulated fleet for Portland (Ore.), and in 2001 was selected to build cars for the new Hiawatha Corridor light rail line at Minneapolis.

Advances in light rail vehicle technology in the 1990s paralleled those in metro equipment, including a shift to A.C. traction motors, and the addition of such technology as microprocessor-based propulsion control, vehicle diagnostics, and fault monitoring systems, with similar gains in energy efficiency, lower maintenance costs, and improved vehicle reliability and availability.

Another important advance in light rail vehicle design was the development of the low-floor car, which permitted wheelchair-bound passengers to board or alight from low-level platforms by means of an extended bridgeplate. These were partial low-floor, articulated vehicles with doors located in a depressed center section and steps leading to a section at each end at a normal floor level above the two power trucks. Instead of a conventional truck beneath the two adjoining sections, there was a short center section mounted on four wheels with stub axles, permitting the low floor to extend through the section. The first cars of this type were developed by Siemens for Portland's Tri-Met light rail system in 1995, while similar designs have since been developed by Breda for Boston, and by Kinki Sharyo for New Jersey Transit, with still another design under development by Bombardier for Minneapolis.

Now well into its second century, Chicago's elevated Loop remains today a vital element of the city's rapid transit network. A train of new stainless steel cars built by aerospace manufacturer Boeing-Vertol in the late 1970s headed a southbound train on the Loop at South Wabash and Madison in June 1987. William D. Middleton.

CHAPTER 8

A METROPOLITAN
RAILWAYS RENAISSANCE

The success of Tri-Met's light rail service, MAX, has been the subject of a lot of attention. What is generally not understood is that MAX is more than a transportation investment. MAX is part of a conscious strategy to shape regional growth by coordinating transportation investments with land use policies. MAX has been a vehicle to move people, to shape the region, defer highway investments, and to enhance our quality of life.

—G. B. Arrington, Jr., Director Strategic & Long Range Planning, Tri-County Metropolitan Transportation District of Oregon, in *Portland's Light Rail: A Shared Vision For Transportation & Land Use,* May 1992

THE LAST DECADES of the twentieth century were good ones for North America's metropolitan railways; for they saw a remarkable turnabout for this once-declining industry as aging rail lines were restored to sound condition and new ones began to carry growing numbers of urban passengers.

The key to rail transit's revival, of course, had been the growing recognition that urban public transportation—even if it was no longer viable as a for-profit private industry—repre-

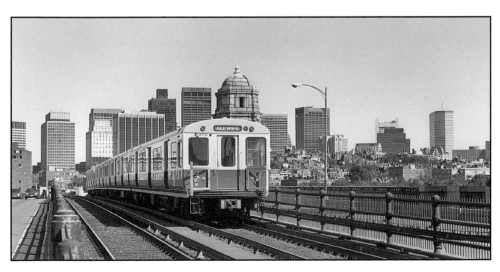

With city's downtown skyline on the horizon, an eastbound Red Line train crossed over the Charles River from Cambridge into Boston on the Longfellow Bridge in September 1991. Canada's Urban Transit Development Corporation built 58 of these handsome big red and white aluminum cars for the Massachusetts Bay Transportation Authority during 1985–88. Herbert H. Harwood, Jr.

The complexity of New York's rapid transit structures sometimes almost defies comprehension. One of these is this maze of elevated structure at Queensboro Plaza in Long Island City that funnels traffic between Manhattan and the Borough of Queens. A No. 7 line train approached the station on its way from Flushing to Times Square in 1996. Joe Greenstein.

The longest trip on the New York subways—31 miles on the A train—takes one all the way from 207th Street in upper Manhattan to the tranquil Atlantic shore at Far Rockaway. An A train crossed Broad Channel in 1999 on the long causeway that carries the trains across Jamaica Bay. Joe Greenstein.

sented a public service that was essential to any healthy metropolitan area. With this recognition came a consensus for public ownership and financial support for transit systems. In such major urban centers as New York, Boston, and Philadelphia some degree of public financing and ownership had been essential to the development of costly subway systems almost from the very beginning. As early as 1940, New York City had completed a transition to full public ownership and operation of its subway and elevated systems. Shortly after the end of World War II, new public authorities were formed to own and operate the Chicago and Boston transit systems. Other cities soon followed, and within several decades public ownership of transit systems had become very nearly universal.

While there had been some federal grants or loans through the Public Works Administration for depression-era subway construction at New York, Philadelphia, and Chicago, federal support did not begin on a broad, continuing basis until the 1960s. A major, if belated, shift in federal policy came with the Highway Act of 1962, which required for the first time a comprehensive and continuing planning process that at least considered other transportation alternatives. Federal capital funding for transit came first under the Housing and Urban Development Act of 1961, soon followed by the landmark Urban Mass Transportation Act of 1964, which then became the basis for continuing annual federal support for transit capital and operating costs.

This new federal support was complemented by strong matching support from state and local sources. While there seemed almost always to be a strong anti-transit element that had to be dealt with, more often than not voters went to the polls and approved the local sales or other taxes needed to support major transit system development. Over the next several decades, this support was translated into a massive reequipping and rehabilitation of America's existing rail systems, and a start to the construction of new rail lines and systems on a scale unlike anything seen for close to half a century. By 1980 U.S. subways and elevated railways were carrying more passengers than they had for almost 30 years. The number of light rail riders, which had reached a lowest-ever level of 124 million in 1975, had begun a steady increase.

The 1990s brought even greater federal support with the passage of the Intermodal Surface Transportation Efficiency Act of 1991—popularly known by its ISTEA acronym—which authorized an average of over $5 billion a year for transit over a six-year period. Reauthorization of transportation spending for a second six-year period produced the 1998 Transportation Equity Act for the Twenty-first Century—quickly dubbed TEA-21—which authorized a still higher level of transit funding at an annual average of almost $7 billion. Accompanied by equally strong public support for measures that would provide state and local shares of transit funding, U.S. rail transit entered an unprecedented period of growth. And while the financing process there was different, rail transit development was booming in major Canadian and Mexican cities, as well.

Something else was happening in most American cities, too, and it would significantly enhance the relevance of rail and other transit modes. This might best be termed the beginning of a reurbanization of America. Recovering from years of decay and decline, urban centers were being rebuilt and revived as centers of activity. After many decades of flight to suburban communities oriented largely to automobile transportation, growing numbers were rediscovering the convenience and attractiveness of urban life, and were becoming regular transit users as a result. City centers that had been losing population for decades began to grow again. Enlightened urban planning and land use policies that encouraged greater transit use were put in place. Higher density zoning was established around transit stations. Major activity centers were located for good transit access. Inner

Philadelphia upgraded its Broad Street subway in 1982 with 125 big stainless steel cars built by Japan's Kawasaki Heavy Industries, Ltd. A train of the big cars waited for a run at the Fern Rock shops in north Philadelphia in October 1987. Fred W. Schneider, III.

city neighborhoods were rebuilt into apartment and condominium developments. Planners and developers were beginning to organize entire residential and retail developments around transit in what was termed transit-oriented development, or sometimes "transit villages."

Successful examples were legion. Toronto was one of the best in North America, with coordinated land-use and transportation development policies that enabled transit to play a key role in urban growth. The combination of high-density land-use planning along transit routes with the accessibility provided by rapid transit helped to create real estate value, and Toronto's growth since its first subway opened in 1954 has been shaped in large part by the city's rapid transit system. Construction of Toronto's initial Yonge subway, for example, set in motion an extraordinary period of urban growth in the corridor. Total development between downtown Toronto and the subway's Eglinton terminal reached some $10 billion, and property values in the corridor increased by as much as ten times. Two-thirds of all this new construction was within walking distance of the Yonge subway.

By 1995 Portland (Ore.) had almost doubled its downtown employment base over a ten-year period through a strategy based upon improved transit service, including its new light rail line, coupled with reduced parking, and was expecting to add another 75,000 new jobs and 15,000 housing units to the central city by 2010. Higher density transit-oriented development around stations on the city's new West Side light rail corridor was expected to double the line's traffic over time.

At Washington, construction of the Metrorail subway system launched a sustained period of growth for the downtown area, largely centered on its rail stations. In suburban Virginia and Maryland, too, "smart growth" strategies centered on high-density development around rail stations produced extraordinary new residential and commercial concentrations. In the San Francisco Bay Area new "transit village" projects that concentrated high-density residential housing, retail shops, and commercial business around BART stations were springing up all over the regional rail system.

At Cleveland, a new Waterfront light rail line helped the city to transform a rundown area in the "Flats" along the Cuyahoga River and on the lakefront into a thriving entertainment area. Toronto's new Harbourfront rail line similarly helped the city convert its lake-front into a major residential and entertainment district. Major new arenas were placed at downtown locations served by rail lines at such diverse locations as Washington, St. Louis, and Portland (Ore.).

The combination of this new emphasis on an enhanced use of transit to help build more livable urban centers with an unprecedented level of public funding for new transit development produced an extraordinary renaissance of metropolitan railway systems in the last decades of the twentieth century.

Over the last 25 years of the century the number of subway and elevated metro systems in North American cities more than doubled, while the number of light rail systems almost tripled. In 2000, U.S. subway and elevated railway metros transported over 2.7 billion passengers, more than any other year since the end of World War II, while more than 307 million light rail passengers in 2000 represented an increase of some 131 percent from their all-time low in 1975.

As the new century began, this rail transit renaissance showed no sign of abating. Almost without exception, existing rail systems were building or planning new or extended routes, and entirely new rail systems were under construction or in planning in more than a dozen cities. According to the American Public Transportation Association, projects under construction, planned, or proposed could increase the total U.S. metro mileage by more than 20 percent, from 1270 miles to as many as 1560 miles, while light rail projects could increase total LRT mileage almost four-fold, from 439 miles to more than 1600 miles.

An interesting development that reflected the enormous modern growth in air travel was the growing number of direct rail transit links to airports. Cleveland built the first such connection in 1968. By 2001 nine U.S. airports had them, and there were more than a half dozen more under construction or planned.

Boston's Massachusetts Bay Transportation Authority was planning an innovative Urban Ring circumferential transit corridor that could include a substantial rail component, as well as a north shore extension of its Blue Line metro to Beverly. At New York, rail links from Kennedy Airport to the subways and the Long Island Rail Road were nearing completion, and a major subway extension to the La Guardia Airport in Queens was under study. It even appeared probable that Manhattan's long-delayed Second Avenue subway might soon be underway again.

Across the Hudson from New York, New Jersey Transit's new Hudson-Bergen light rail line was steadily being expanded over its planned full route, and a new Newark-Elizabeth light rail line was under construction. In southern New Jersey, NJ Transit's innovative Trenton-Camden diesel light rail line was slated to open in 2003, and the PATCO high-speed line between Philadelphia and Lindenwold was studying its first extension since the line opened in 1969. Philadelphia's Southeastern Pennsylvania Transportation Authority was developing plans for a new rail line in a long Cross County Corridor across the suburban counties north of Philadelphia. At Pittsburgh, planning was underway for a North Shore Connector that would link the existing "T" light rail system in downtown Pittsburgh with major development north of the Allegheny River.

Early in 2002 the Maryland Transit Administration completed a new Baltimore region light rail system plan that proposed the addition of some 50 miles of new metro and light rail lines over the next 20 to 40 years. A year earlier the Washington Metropolitan Area Transit Authority completed the full 103-mile rail system called for in its original plan adopted in 1969, and almost immediately began construction for the first of 19 new metro and light rail projects in a 25-year expansion plan that could add as many as 150 miles to the WMATA rail network. At Norfolk, Va., Hampton Roads Transit was completing studies for light rail lines that would form initial sections of what could become a regional rail system for Tidewater Virginia. In North Carolina, the Charlotte Transit System had begun planning for a South Corridor light rail line that would be financed, in part, from a sales tax measure approved by voters in 1998. At Atlanta, the Metropolitan Atlanta Rapid Tran-

The southern end of Baltimore's Central Light Rail Line was placed on the roadbed of a one-time interurban electric railway, the Baltimore & Annapolis, whose former station still stands at Linthicum, Md. A southbound train to Cromwell passed the old station in September 1993. William D. Middleton.

A Washington Metropolitan Area Transit Authority train made a stop at a typical suburban Metrorail station at Grosvenor, Md., in September 1987. The train was northbound over the Red Line into Montgomery County, Md. Fred W. Schneider, III.

The Metropolitan Atlanta Rapid Transit Authority's South Line station at Fort McPherson featured a massive pitched roof structure. A southbound train en route to Atlanta's Hartsfield International Airport made a station stop there in October 1990. William D. Middleton.

sit Authority was planning West and North line extensions to its steadily growing rail net-work. In Florida, the Jacksonville Transportation Authority had begun detailed studies for the first of several possible light rail transit corridors linked to the downtown Skyway Express automated monorail system. At Tampa, the Hillsborough Area Regional Transit Authority was planning a 20-mile light rail system that would link downtown Tampa with the University of South Florida and the Westshore business district.

At San Juan, Puerto Rico, construction was well advanced for the Tren Urbano metro that was expected to open in 2003, with studies already well along for the first of several projected extensions to the system.

In the Midwest, the Greater Cleveland Regional Transit Authority was planning extensions of its new Waterfront Line and the original Shaker Heights light rail line. Transit authorities serving Cincinnati and the northern Kentucky communities across the Ohio River were planning a light rail system that would link Cincinnati, Covington, Ky., and the Greater Cincinnati/Northern Kentucky International Airport. Another downtown-to-airport light rail line, as well as a northeast corridor line, was under study at Indianapolis, while the Transit Authority of River City at Louisville had begun preliminary studies of a South Central Corridor light rail line. At Chicago, extension of the Chicago Transit Authority's Kennedy Expressway line beyond O'Hare International Airport into the western suburbs was under consideration. Construction began early in 2001 for a 12-mile Hiawatha Avenue light rail line that will link downtown Minneapolis with the Twin Cities airport and the Mall of America. The line should open in 2004. At St. Louis, the Bi-State Development Agency opened a major extension of its MetroLink light rail line to Belleville, Ill., early in 2001. At the same time, construction began for a further extension that will reach Scott Air Force Base, while final design was in progress for a Cross-County line into the St. Louis suburbs.

At Memphis, an expanding downtown Main Street Trolley system operating with historic equipment was designed for later transition to a modern light rail system, and the Memphis Area Transit Authority had begun studies for an initial Southeast Corridor light rail route. Construction was in progress at New Orleans for a restoration of rail service to Canal Street, while studies were underway for a rail line in the Desire Street corridor. After

Not far north of the Chicago Loop, a northbound Ravenswood Line local train turned the sharp corner in the North Side "L" structure approaching the Sedgwick Avenue station in June 1987. Looming beyond are some of the high rent apartment blocks that line the Lake Michigan shore on the city's North Side. The train was made up of four of the stainless steel cars built for CTA under a 600-car order completed by the Budd company during 1981–87. William D. Middleton.

failed attempts to launch rail systems over several decades, construction finally began at Houston early in 2001 for a Main Street light rail line that should open in 2004. In August 2000 Dallas voters had approved a long-term financing measure to accelerate light rail construction, and Dallas Area Rapid Transit was completing new North Central and Northeast lines in stages over the 2001–03 period, while planning continued for additional routes in corridors extending northwest and southeast from downtown Dallas.

The Denver Regional Transit District, which had opened its Southwest light rail extension in July 2000, began construction of a Central Platte Valley Spur the following January, while preliminary work for a long Southeast Line started later in 2001. At least one more light rail corridor was under study. Late in 2001, in time for the 2002 Winter Olympics, the Utah Transit Authority rushed to completion an extension of its TRAX light rail system from downtown Salt Lake City to the University of Utah campus. Still other extensions toward a regional rail system were under study.

Following the March 2000 voter approval of a sales tax to finance a local share of the cost, Valley Metro at Phoenix began planning for a 20-mile light rail line that was expected to be under construction by 2003. At San Diego, the Metropolitan Transit Development Board continued steady expansion of the city's light rail system into a comprehensive regional rail network. Construction was in progress for a Mission Valley East extension that was expected to open in 2004, with a Mid-Coast extension north toward La Jolla scheduled to come next. In Los Angeles County, construction was in progress for a Los Angeles to Pasadena Blue Line light rail route that was scheduled to open in 2003, while a further extension east to Claremont was under study. Still other prospective Los Angeles rail extensions included a planned Blue Line extension from Union Station to East Los Angeles, and an Exposition Boulevard route from downtown west toward the beach communities. East of Los Angeles, the Orange County Transportation Authority was planning an ambitious CenterLine light rail system along the county's north-south spine.

Shared use of railroad rights-of-way has provided low cost routes for a number of modern light rail systems. This MetroLink light rail train westbound to the St. Louis airport is operating over a line shared with Norfolk Southern for nighttime freight operations after light rail service ends. The train was about to dive under Delmar Boulevard and the former Wabash Railroad Delmar station in April 1999. William D. Middleton.

Dallas Area Rapid Transit trains run right through Dallas Union Station, where they provide direct connections with both Amtrak intercity trains and the newly established Trinity Railway Express commuter service between Dallas and Fort Worth. A Blue Line train southbound to Ledbetter Drive met a TRE Budd Rail Diesel Car train at Union Station in the pre-dawn gloom of the early morning rush hour in August 1997. William D. Middleton.

San Diego's light rail system provides convenient connections with Amtrak services at the old Santa Fe depot in downtown San Diego. A San Diego Trolley train bound for the Bayside line that follows the San Diego waterfront curved past the station in January 1991. William D. Middleton.

Los Angeles County's east-west light rail Green Line between Norwalk and Hawthorne is entirely grade-separated, largely in the median of the new Century Freeway, and was designed for conversion to fully automatic operation, a change that has yet to come. An eastbound train arriving at the line's Norwalk terminal passed under the complex structures of a Century Freeway interchange in May 1997. William D. Middleton.

In northern California, the Santa Clara County Transportation Authority continued to expand its San Jose-centered light rail network. An initial Tasman East corridor extension was opened in 2001, with a second segment scheduled to open in 2004, while construction also began in 2001 for a north-south Capitol Corridor line east of San Jose. Next on the construction agenda was a major Vasona Corridor project that would link San Jose with Los Gatos. San Francisco's Municipal Railway began construction in 2002 for a Muni Metro light rail line in the Third Street Corridor south of downtown San Francisco that should open in 2005. A planned later extension would include a new downtown light rail subway. The Bay Area Rapid Transit District was expecting to complete its long-planned extension to San Francisco International Airport late in 2002. Likely to move ahead next was an East Bay extension that would take BART south from its present Fremont terminal to San Jose and Santa Clara. Still other prospective additions to the BART regional system included extensions to Livermore and Antioch. At Sacramento, the Regional Transit District had several major extensions under construction, with a new South Line, a Folsom extension, and a link to the downtown Sacramento rail station all scheduled to open during 2003–04.

At Portland (Ore.) the Tri-Metropolitan Transportation District of Oregon completed an extension of its MAX light rail system to the Portland International Airport in the fall of 2001, while construction was in progress for an Interstate MAX that was scheduled to add service in an Interstate Avenue corridor north from downtown Portland in 2004, and could eventually extend across the Columbia River to Vancouver, Wash. At Seattle, the Central Puget Sound Regional Transit Authority was nearing a construction start for an initial segment of a north-south Central Link light rail line that would operate between the Seattle-Tacoma International Airport and downtown Seattle, while a later extension would add service north to the University District.

A major extensions program begun in 1991 added 28 miles and nine stations to the Bay Area Rapid Transit system over the next decade. In April 1996 an eastbound train from San Francisco stopped at the North Concord/Martinez station on an extension of BART's Concord Line that had opened the previous December. The full extension to Pittsburg/Bay Point was completed by the end of 1996. William D. Middleton.

San Francisco's Muni Metro light rail riders get a splendid view of the city from Mission Dolores Park on the J-Church Line. One of the Muni's now-retired Boeing-built Standard Light Rail Vehicles made a passenger stop at the upper end of the park in May 1991. William D. Middleton.

Similar metropolitan railway growth was in store for major Canadian and Mexican cities as well. The Société de transport de la Communauté urbaine de Montréal began construction late in 2001 for an extension of the city's Metro system north to Laval, and was planning three additional Métro extensions, as well as three new surface light rail lines. The most recent addition to the Toronto Transit Commission's subway system, an initial segment of an east-west Shepard subway, was scheduled to open in mid-2002. In Alberta, both Calgary and Edmonton were moving ahead with still greater expansion of their light rail systems. In British Columbia, the Greater Vancouver Transportation Authority was opening its second automated SkyTrain line in several phases during 2001–02.

At Mexico City, expansion of the Sistema de Transporte Colectivo (STC) subway system had become virtually continuous as North America's largest city struggled to meet the transportation needs of its fast-growing population. A Metro and Light Rail Master Plan for the city contemplated more than doubling the size of the STC rail system to a 27-line, 300-mile network by 2020, and both Guadalajara and Monterrey had plans for expansion of their already extensive light rail systems into regional networks.

These were only some of the growth prospects for rail transit. Some cities—Hartford, Kansas City, Austin, and San Antonio among them—had turned down proposed rail projects, at least for now, while in still other cities a consensus was yet to be reached on what rail transit should be built, or how it should be paid for. But as urban populations continued to grow, and as growing numbers of cities discovered the extraordinary capacity of good rail systems—coupled with sound urban planning—to build more livable urban communities, it seemed all but certain that there was much more to come. Clearly, metropolitan railways promised to be even more a part of North American urban life in the twenty-first century than they had been in its nineteenth or twentieth.

The venerable double-deck Steel Bridge lift span over the Willamette River at Portland, Ore., carries railroad traffic on the lower level, and road and (since 1986) light rail traffic on the upper level. A Tri-Met Eastside MAX train for Gresham crossed the span on Armistice Day 1990. William D. Middleton.

A striking architectural feature of the Montreal Métro's Berri-UQAM station (formerly Berri-de Montigny) is the backlighted colored glass window that overlooks the Line 7 platforms. A westbound train loaded passengers there in September 1993. William D. Middleton.

Toronto transportation planners took inspiration from Chicago, and placed the new Spadina subway line in the median of the city's new Spadina Expressway. In this May 1988 view, an inbound train approaches the Eglinton West station. William D. Middleton.

The eastern terminus for Vancouver's automated SkyTrain metro at Surrey Central is a busy intermodal terminal that links the trains with connecting bus lines and park-and-ride facilities. An empty train pulled out of the station after unloading passengers from Vancouver in September 1995. William D. Middleton.

THE TECHNOLOGY OF RAIL TRANSIT

Elevated Railways

The early elevated railway structures were typically made up of relatively short, repetitive spans between supporting columns or frames, much like a long trestle. The earliest structures at New York and Brooklyn were of wrought iron construction, but steel had come into use in place of iron well before the end of the nineteenth century. Much of New York's first line, the New York Elevated Railway, was built with a "one-legged" structure, in which each track was carried by a single row of columns, usually placed at the curb line. A much more common arrangement, however, was a portal frame made up of two columns and a transverse girder that supported both tracks. In relatively narrow streets the columns were typically placed at the curb lines, while in wider streets they were placed within the street, where they represented a substantial impediment to street traffic. A variation from this usual arrangement was used for portions of the Frankford elevated at Philadelphia, in which the double-track structure was supported by T-shaped single columns placed in the center of the street.

The New York Elevated Railroad structure was typical of early elevated railway construction. Each track was supported by two latticed girders 33 inches deep and typically spanning 43 feet 4 inches between supporting columns. The structure provided a clearance of 14 feet 6 inches above the street. Author's Collection.

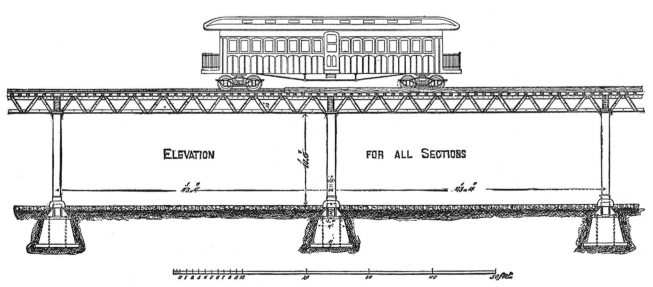

ELEVATION   FOR ALL SECTIONS

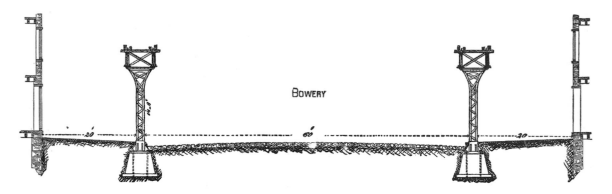

BOWERY

For much of its initial line, the New York Elevated used a "one-legged" structure, in which a separate line of columns supported each track. This is a section of the line in the Bowery, where the columns were placed on the curb line at each side of the 60-foot street. The columns were supported on foundations of brick and stone masonry that extended about 7 feet below the street level. Author's Collection.

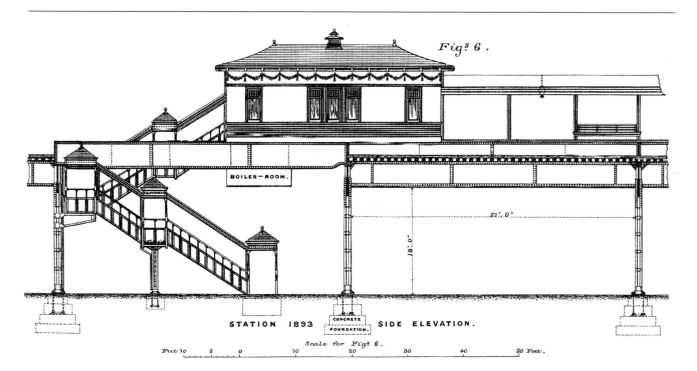

Fig. 6.

BOILER-ROOM.

STATION 1893   SIDE ELEVATION.

CONCRETE FOUNDATION.

Scale for Fig. 6.

This was a typical island platform station on the Brooklyn Elevated Railway. The illustrations are from a paper by civil engineer Othniel Foster Nichols published in the *Proceedings of the Institution of Civil Engineers*, 1896–97. (both) Philip E. Buchert Collection.

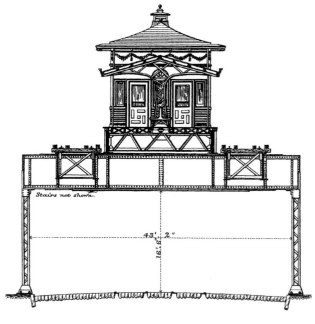

Stairs not shown.

43'. 2"

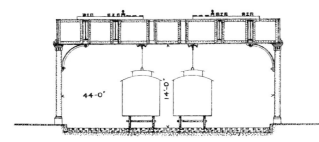

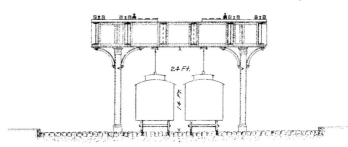

This 1897 proposal for the Boston Elevated Railway's planned El shows a typical arrangement of the structure, in which the transverse girders supporting the track structure span the width of the street between supporting columns. Author's Collection.

An alternate scheme for the Boston elevated shows the supporting structure arrangement planned for wide streets, which placed the supporting columns within the street. Author's Collection.

The supporting columns were supported by spread masonry or—later—concrete foundations typically carried to a depth of about 7 feet, but sometimes much deeper where required by special foundation conditions. Columns were typically built up of 15-inch rolled channel sections tied together with diagonal latticed bracing. In the one-legged structure they were flared out at the top to support the two longitudinal girders that carried the track. For the earliest New York lines the transverse girders between columns were latticed iron structures, while later lines most often used plate girders built up of riveted steel plates and angles. Each track was typically supported by two longitudinal girders spanning anywhere from about 34 to 45 feet between the transverse frames. These were usually of latticed construction on the earliest elevated roads, while plate girders were generally used for the later lines.

Fabrication and erection of the elevated railways was much like building a bridge, and their construction was typically taken on by bridge building firms. Construction began with the placement of column foundations, followed by raising of the columns and the erection of the superstructure. Usually this was accomplished by working from the completed structure with a traveler crane that erected the iron or steel framework ahead of itself as it went.

This view of Lake Street "L" erection at Chicago, dating to the early 1890s, shows a typical procedure for elevated railway construction. A steam-powered traveler crane operating along the top of the completed structure is lifting a girder into place between two supporting frames. Krambles-Peterson Archive.

The elevated structures were often marvels of intricate ironwork. This 1883 view of the Metropolitan Elevated Railway structure at a curve in uptown Manhattan shows a section of the line built by the Phoenix Bridge Company using its patented tubular wrought iron Phoenix column. By 1888 the Phoenix company was able to claim that it had built the structures for more than 30 miles of elevated track in New York. Library of Congress (Neg. LC-USZ62-063522).

However well they worked, the noisy and unattractive iron and steel structures of the early lines gave elevated railways a bad name. With the development of new metro systems in the last half of the twentieth century, the introduction of new materials and construction methods, most of them from modern highway construction practice, together with noise reduction measures and efforts to design a more attractive structure, made elevated railways a much more acceptable alternative.

Key to this new generation of elevated structures was the development of precast, prestressed concrete girders capable of spanning as much as 80 to 100 feet with a relatively shallow structure. Usually, these girders were cast and cured at a central yard and then hauled to the construction site for erection. In most modern aerial structures, the use of steel has been confined to unusually long spans, or to curved or other special structures where the greater flexibility available with steel fabrication is needed.

San Francisco's BART system, with some 23 miles of aerial structure, pioneered this new approach to elevated structures. A standardized elevated structure was made up of T-shaped

The San Francisco Bay Area's BART pioneered the use of precast, prestressed concrete girders for aerial rail lines. This shows the erection of a 75-foot girder for BART's Pittsburg/ Antioch extension in 1996. Bay Area Rapid Transit District.

Ground water conditions kept the Miami metro above ground on either an at-grade or elevated alignment. Aerial sections of the line were built with these innovative double-T precast, prestressed concrete girders. A crane lifted one into place in the structure near the Vizcaya station in March 1981. William D. Middleton.

Elevated sections of San Juan's Tren Urbano metro line were built with precast concrete segmental box girder sections that were erected into complete spans from launching girders and then post-tensioned in place. This one was erecting the structure near Deportiva in May 2000. William D. Middleton.

concrete piers supporting pairs of the precast, prestressed concrete box girders that carried the track. Engineers for Miami's Metrorail project pioneered the use of a double-T precast, prestressed concrete girder. At Atlanta, the contractor for more than a mile of elevated structure for the Metropolitan Atlanta Rapid Transit Authority introduced the use of precast segmental box girders. These were built with precast segments 10 feet long that formed a trapezoidal box girder. Two movable triangular steel trusses installed between supporting piers supported the precast segments until erection was complete and the span had been post-tensioned and become capable of supporting itself. Similar precast segmental box girder construction was used for rapid transit bridge construction at Edmonton, Alta., and Los Angeles, while more recently Puerto Rico's Highway and Transportation Authority employed segmental girder construction for elevated sections of San Juan's Tren Urbano metro.

Subways

The wide variety of geological conditions found below ground and a broad range of problems that can be encountered make subway construction in congested urban areas an inherently difficult process. Extensive utilities beneath the street must be temporarily supported and then relocated. Building foundations often require underpinning to prevent settlement or other damage.

"Cut-and-cover" construction has usually been the preferred method of tunneling for shallow depth subways, or for station construction. Typically, this is carried out by the placement of sheet piling or restraining steel and timber bulkheads on each side of the excavation area. Construction of a temporary deck permits the restoration of street traffic while excavation and construction continue. A modern alternative to sheet piling or bulkheads is the slurry wall technique. In this method, a reinforced concrete wall is constructed by excavating a trench anywhere from 1½ to 3 feet wide. This is kept filled with a heavy slurry—a thick soupy mixture—of water and bentonite clay to prevent collapse while the excavation is completed, steel reinforcing put in place, and the trench filled with concrete placed from the bottom up through a "tremie," displacing the slurry. Usually these concrete walls form part of the final subway or station structure as well as a temporary construction bulkhead.

Bored tunneling methods are used whenever deep tunneling is required, or sometimes to avoid the disruption of street traffic and the complexities of utilities relocation that typically accompany cut-and-cover construction. In hard material this has traditionally been done by drill-and-blast techniques using compressed air drills. In solid rock, tunnels were sometimes left unlined, but more often some form of masonry, concrete, or metal lining was installed. For soft ground tunneling, as well as underwater tunneling, some form of cylindrical shield was generally used. This shield is moved ahead by hydraulic jacks as the tunnel is excavated, and tunnel liners are placed behind the shield. Compressed air pressure was used to support the tunnel face against inflows of soil and water. The tunnel liners used in early shield tunneling were usually made up of segmental cast iron rings that were put in place immediately behind the shield as it advanced. More recently, segmental liners of steel and precast concrete have been used.

New tunneling methods and equipment have come into use for modern subway projects. Modern tunnel boring machines (TBM's) have proved to be much faster—and less costly—than traditional tunneling methods. Equipped with a variety of rolling disc cutters, cutterheads, or excavators, they can work in a wide range of ground conditions. As the TBM advances, a conveyor system carries the muck, or excavated material, to the rear for removal. Tunnel liners are placed behind the TBM as it advances. In some modern tunneling work, temporary precast concrete or steel liners are placed by the TBM, followed by later placement of a permanent cast-in-place concrete liner.

Two views of Broad Street subway construction at Philadelphia show typical cut-and-cover work. *(Right)* Portions of the subway were built through largely undeveloped areas, allowing easy cut-and-cover construction. This was a June 23, 1926, view of excavation south of Grange Avenue. *(Below)* In this March 2, 1926, view of the Broad Street work north from Fishers Avenue, the base slab and steel framework for the subway have been completed. Once the concrete walls and roof slab have been placed, the structure can be backfilled and the street restored. (both) City of Philadelphia, Fred W. Schneider, III Collection.

This March 1981 view of subway construction at Atlanta shows typical cut-and-cover work in a congested urban site. Steel H sections have been driven into the ground on each side of the tunnel and timber lagging installed to support the ground while the subway tube is built. Horizontal beams brace the sides and can be used to support utility lines or a temporary roadway if required. William D. Middleton.

When Chicago's first rapid transit subway finally got underway under State Street in 1939, much of the work was done by deep tunneling rather than cut-and-cover construction. Between Wacker Drive and 11th and State streets this massive 225-ton shield was driven through the clay by 24 hydraulic jacks at a rate of one foot an hour. In this view dating to December 12, 1939, the tunnel workers are removing clay forced through the doors in the front of the shield. Krambles-Peterson Archive.

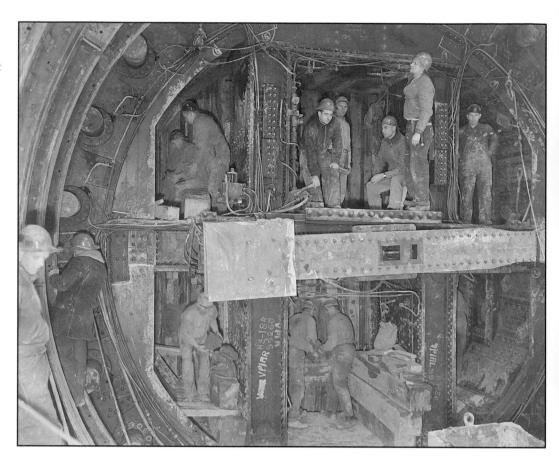

Early lined subway tunnels usually used a segmental cast iron lining. More recently, steel liners have been used. In this section of the Baltimore subway tunnel east of Lexington Market station built in 1980, the Maryland Mass Transit Administration experimented with the use of precast concrete tunnel liners. The test was a success, and the concrete liners have since been adopted for other subway tunneling. William D. Middleton.

In one recent example of TBM tunneling, the drilling of the Red Line subway at Los Angeles, the typical TBM used was a 200-ton, 185-foot-long machine with a 22-foot diameter shield. The shield was advanced by 16 100-ton hydraulic rams that were capable of exerting a force of 6 million pounds on the cutting edge of the shield. A back hoe excavator in the shield was capable of removing 850 cubic yards a day, allowing the machine to advance anywhere from 60 to 100 feet a day. Typical of modern tunneling practice, the machine used a laser guidance system. The 360-ton "Rail Blazer" TBM used to drill three miles of tunnel under the North Central Freeway for Dallas Area Rapid Transit's light rail system drilled an average 180 feet a day on its first pass to drill a southbound tube, and then did even better, with a record 326 feet in one day, on a second pass through the northbound tube.

Several recent North American tunnel projects have employed a new European tunneling technique known as the New Austrian Tunneling Method (NATM). In a conventional tunneling design for loose or unstable rock, excavation by drilling and blasting would have been followed by the installation of a permanent tunnel lining. In the NATM, rock removal is followed as quickly as possible by the placement of a sprayed concrete—called shotcrete—layer about 2 inches thick to stabilize and support the rock. This is then usually followed by the installation of rock bolts and wire mesh, and the placement of a second layer of shotcrete, about 4 inches thick, to complete the tunnel lining.

A fairly common alternative to shield tunneling for underwater tunnels is the trench-and-tube method, in which a trench is dredged in the bottom and prefabricated tunnel sections are lowered into position to form the tunnel. For the most notable recent example, BART's 19,000-foot Transbay Tube at San Francisco, 57 Tube sections, each 49 feet wide, 21½ feet deep, and anywhere from 330 to 350 feet long, were floated into position over a trench dredged in the bottom of the Bay, and lowered into place. Divers guided each section into position and it was then welded into place and the concrete lining completed.

This was the business end of "Bore-Regard," the 278-foot-long tunnel boring machine used to drill subway tunnels through the West Hills at Portland, Ore., for the Westside MAX light rail line during 1995–96. Tri-County Metropolitan Transportation District of Oregon.

At Chicago, the State Street subway crossing of the Chicago River was built by the sunken tube method. The twin tubes were built in a South Chicago dry dock, sealed, and towed up the lake front to the crossing site in the river, where they were sunk into a prepared bed in the river bottom and encased in concrete. Two tugs took the tubes up the river on October 16, 1939. Krambles-Peterson Archive.

This imaginative artist's view shows how each of the 57 sections of BART's Transbay Tube was lowered from the surface to its position in the tunnel bed dredged in the bottom of the Bay. Bay Area Rapid Transit District.

226

Track and Guideways

Track

Track for elevated railways and subways typically followed standard railroad practice. Almost all lines were built to the 4-foot 8½-inch standard gauge. A notable exception was Philadelphia's Market Street elevated line, which was built to a 5-foot 2¼-inch track gauge. More recently, the Bay Area Rapid Transit District, for reasons of greater stability and smoother operation at higher speeds, adopted a 5 foot 6 inch wide gauge.

The early elevated railroads typically employed a conventional track system carried on wood ties attached directly to the elevated structure, which contributed to their high noise level. A notable exception was Philadelphia's Market Street elevated, which was built with a concrete floor slab, allowing the use of crushed rock ballast. The early subways, too, typically used a conventional track system. The Interborough Rapid Transit, for example, was built with a concrete trough for each track, allowing the use of wood ties carried on crushed rock ballast.

More recent light rail and metro systems have adopted a variety of track systems. The use of continuous welded rail has become almost universal. For open track at surface level, some new lines have used wood ties on crushed rock ballast, but usually these new lines have used ballasted prestressed concrete ties with the clip fasteners required for welded trail. Baltimore's

This was typical subway track on Philadelphia's Broad Street subway at the newly completed Walnut-Locust station in downtown Philadelphia. The photograph dates to April 1930, just two weeks before a short extension south from City Hall was opened. City of Philadelphia, Fred W. Schneider, III Collection.

metro system adopted a twin-block concrete tie system for open track, while Boston's relocated Orange Line employed a direct fixation system to attach continuous welded rail directly to the bottom slab of open cut sections. For surface track located in urban streets, most new light rail systems have used a girder rail section which is rolled with an integral flangeway, while others have used standard rail and formed a flangeway in the concrete or asphalt paving between the rails.

For track on elevated structures or in tunnels, most modern metro systems have used some form of direct fixation fastener to attach the rails directly to either a continuous concrete ribbon or "plinth" cast-in-place on the aerial structure or tunnel invert slab. A common method of noise and vibration control in modern subways has been the use of what is called "floating slab" track construction. This employs precast concrete slab sections that are set in place on hard rubber "hockey puck" shock absorbers placed beneath and along the sides of each slab. Another recent system used for several North American elevated or subway installations is a variation of a French-developed STEDEF system. This uses precast, reinforced concrete rail support blocks together with both an elastic rail pad and a second elastic pad beneath the block. Each support block is encased in a rubber boot for sound and vibration insulation and embedded in a cast-in-place support slab.

Guideways

The pneumatic-tired metro system developed in France and adopted at Montreal and Mexico City employs both a standard track and separate runways and guide rails for the pneumatic-tired support and guidance system. Flanged steel wheels drop down onto standard gauge rails in the event of tire failure, and also guide a train through switches. Two continuous concrete runways attached to the subway invert support rubber-tired trucks, while guide rails for the horizontal guide wheels are mounted outside the runways.

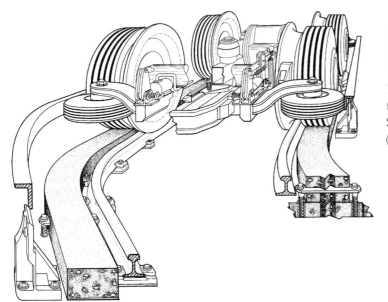

An isometric view shows how the French-originated pneumatic-tired system worked. Two continuous concrete runways carried the rubber-tired trucks, while guide rails were provided at each side for the horizontal guide wheels. Flanged wheels dropped down onto standard gauge rails in the event of tire failure, and guided a train through switches. Société de transport de la Communauté urbaine de Montréal (STCUM).

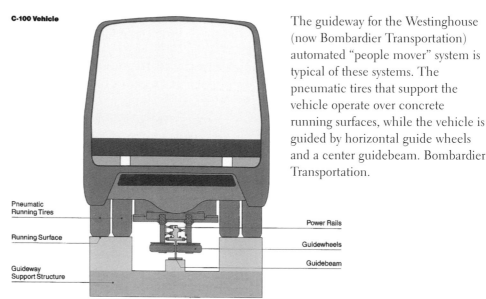

The guideway for the Westinghouse (now Bombardier Transportation) automated "people mover" system is typical of these systems. The pneumatic tires that support the vehicle operate over concrete running surfaces, while the vehicle is guided by horizontal guide wheels and a center guidebeam. Bombardier Transportation.

The various pneumatic-tired "people mover" transit systems typically operate over guideway systems that include continuous concrete runways for the pneumatic-tired vehicle, while the vehicle is guided by horizontal wheels bearing against a central guide beam.

Electrification and Current Collection

Power Supply

Almost all of the early rapid transit and light rail systems operate from a nominal 600-volt D.C. power supply. While some newer systems have maintained this 600-volt D.C. standard, most have gone to somewhat higher voltages. Most new metros have adopted power supply systems in the range of 700 to 750 volts D.C., a notable exception being San Francisco's BART, which adopted a 1000-volt D.C. supply. Most of the new light rail installations have adopted a 750-volt D.C. supply, with a major exception being the Metrorrey system at Monterrey, Nuevo Leon, which operates from a 1500-volt D.C. supply.

Present-day rapid transit systems all purchase electric power from public utility companies, but the heavy power demands of the early elevated railway and subway electrifications exceeded the capacity available from the public utilities, and the transit companies were obliged to build their own power generation plants. Three of the four Chicago elevated companies built their own power plants for electric operation, while the fourth, the Lake Street Elevated then under the control of traction magnate Charles Tyson Yerkes, purchased its power from three Yerkes-controlled street railway companies. The Brooklyn elevated lines built their own power plants, while the Boston Elevated Railway was able to power the Main Line elevated completed in 1901 from its already extensive system of street railway power plants. In order to electrify New York's elevated railways in 1901, the Manhattan Elevated Railway was obliged to construct an enormous generating plant along the East River. Rated at a maximum capacity of 100,000 h.p., it was said to be the largest generating plant in the world. The Manhattan's "world's largest power plant" title didn't last long. The even larger power station completed for the Interborough Rapid Transit only three years later was designed for an ultimate capacity of 132,000 h.p.

Power Distribution

Power was generated as alternating current for transmission to substations along the line. Power was sometimes transmitted at the generating voltage, but more often transformers were used to step up the voltage for greater transmission efficiency. At the substations or converter stations the transmission-line power was stepped down by transformers and then converted to the required current and voltage for train operation, almost always a nominal 600 volts D.C. Early substations accomplished this A.C. to D.C. conversion with some type of rotating conversion equipment. One type was a motor-generator set, which consisted of a synchronous or induction A.C. motor and a D.C. generator mounted on a common shaft. Another common type was the synchronous or rotary converter, which essentially incorporated the armatures of the motor and the generator into a single unit. The IRT's Manhattan power station and distribution system were fairly typical of early rapid transit power systems. Power was generated 11,000 volts, three-phase A.C. for transmission to substations, where transformers stepped down the power supply to 390-volt, three-phase A.C., which was then converted to 625-volt D.C. power for train operation by rotary converters.

In more recent installations mercury-arc or—most recently—solid state rectifiers have provided a more efficient means of converting A.C. to D.C.

Current Distribution

Third-rail distribution systems have almost universally been used for rapid transit installations. Typically this consists of a high conductivity steel rail mounted alongside the track and slightly higher than the running rails. Almost all rapid transit systems use an overrunning third rail in which the top of the rail is the contact surface. Less commonly used has been the underrunning type, in which the contact surface was at the bottom, affording considerably greater protection from sleeting or accidental contact. Third rail installation details and dimensions vary between systems, but a fairly typical example is the third rail system adopted as a New York City standard, which placed the inside face of the third rail 25½ inches from the inside face of the rail, and the top 3½ inches above the top of the running rails. The rail is supported by porcelain insulators that are attached to extra long ties spaced about every fourth or fifth tie. A bracket supports a protective wooden cover over the rail. Modern third rail installations sometimes employ an aluminum-clad rail, which provides much higher conductivity than a steel rail, while fiberglass covers are usually used in place of wood covers.

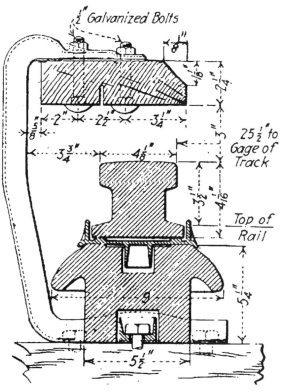

Typical of rapid transit third-rail installations was this standard design developed for New York City. The power rail was mounted on large porcelain insulators, while the wooden cover helped protect against sleeting or accidental contact. Author's Collection.

Because of the unsuitability of third rail for operation in city streets or in other non-reserved rights-of-way, North American light rail systems universally employ overhead trolley wire or catenary current distribution systems supported from poles. A few metro installations have used overhead systems as well. Some early conversions to electric operation of the steam-powered lines between Brooklyn and the seashore, for example, were initially equipped for an overhead trolley power supply because of extensive surface operation. Several outlying surface segments of the Chicago elevated system were originally operated with an overhead trolley system, and the Chicago Transit Authority still operates a portion of its Skokie Swift line from overhead catenary. Cleveland's Red Line metro uses an overhead catenary power supply, at least in part because portions of the line are shared with light rail trains. Because of the anticipated third rail problems during the winter from high winds and spray from the nearby ocean, surface portions of Boston's Blue Line to Revere Beach and Wonderland were built with overhead catenary.

Fare Collection

Fares for elevated lines and subways are almost always collected at stations. The early elevated roads and subways usually used tickets that were sold in the stations and collected as passengers entered the platforms. This later gave way to the use of turnstiles activated by coins or tokens. The modern availability of computers and electronics technology has permitted the development of much more sophisticated fare collection systems based upon the use of magnetically coded cards sold by ticket agents or—more often—from ticket machines. These typically are used to activate a turnstile to enter the platforms, with the correct fare for the trip being deducted from the total value of the card, usually when exiting from the platform at the end of a trip. Newer "smart cards" being used by some systems can be used to pay for parking and other purchases, as well as transit fares.

The traditional method of fare collection by the operator or a conductor once used by street railways has been almost entirely replaced in modern light rail systems by the "barrier free" or "proof-of-payment" fare system introduced from Europe. Passengers are required to have a valid pass or a ticket purchased from a ticket machine—and validated—before boarding a train through any door. Enforcement is provided through periodic ticket inspections by police or inspectors, with citations and fines for anyone traveling without a valid ticket or pass. Transit agencies have found that the system typically speeds operation by eliminating the delays experienced when the train operator must also collect fares, and most have found that the level of fare evasion actually goes down with the barrier-free system.

Rolling Stock[1]

Car Types

Passenger coaches for the first elevated railways were little more than slightly smaller versions of the equipment operated by steam railroads, the major difference being the absence of steps, which weren't needed for the high platform elevated stations. Passengers boarded and alighted from open platforms at each end of the car. This was not a very efficient arrangement for the frequent stops of elevated service, and a few lines introduced additional

---

1. A thorough discussion of the development of rapid transit car technology is included in *Chicago's Rapid Transit, Volume II: Rolling Stock/1947–1976*, edited by Norman Carlson and Walter R. Keevil and published as Bulletin 115 of the Central Electric Railfans' Association in 1976. While specifically concerned with the development of technology on the Chicago rapid transit system, it serves almost equally well as a summary of the evolution of rolling stock technology throughout the industry.

side doors at the center of each car, allowing passengers to enter or exit directly from the passenger compartment. The first IRT subway cars for New York continued to use the same arrangement as elevated cars, with entrance and exit through enclosed vestibules and doors at each end of the car. Tests with two different arrangements of additional side doors opening directly into the passenger compartment produced substantial savings in dwell time at stations, and all existing IRT cars were rebuilt to this arrangement, and it was specified for all new equipment.

The Boston Elevated Railway pioneered the next important step in rapid transit car design in 1912, when it acquired new cars for the Cambridge-Dorchester subway that provided three wide sliding doors on each side and omitted the end vestibules altogether. Brooklyn-Manhattan Transit introduced the idea of articulated cars in 1923 with its "Triplex," a 137-foot, three-unit car carried on four trucks, with adjoining sections sharing a common truck. This was followed during the 1930s with several designs for similarly arranged "multi-section" cars made up of five units. Both BMT and Chicago Rapid Transit acquired lightweight, three-section articulated cars that incorporated PCC car technology. The articulation principle was never widely adopted, however, and many rapid transit operators instead moved to the concept of "married pairs" of cars that shared auxiliary equipment and operated as a unit.

Special open cars were popular for summer travel on the New York elevated roads. These were covered cars, open at the sides, with seats extending across the full width of the car. Pull-down canvas curtains were provided in case of rain. Similar cars were built for the Columbian Intramural Railway that operated on the ground of the 1893 World's Columbian Exposition at Chicago. Most lines, however, were unwilling to invest in equipment that could be used only on a seasonal basis. Brooklyn Rapid Transit managed to provide open-air elevated travel in the summer without acquiring a duplicate car fleet through the use of what were called convertible cars. The BRT had 220 of these closed cars that could be converted to summertime open-sided cars by the use of removable side panels. Chicago's Northwestern Elevated also operated 40 semi-convertible cars fitted with windows that could be lowered into pockets in the sides below the window level.

Among the few special purpose cars acquired by elevated railways and subways were Chicago's funeral cars and the IRT's private car *Mineola*. For a few years the Hudson & Manhattan operated two special cars designed to accommodate standard station baggage carts that could be rolled onto the cars through open sides. These were operated between Newark and the Hudson Terminal in New York for the convenience of long distance passengers transferring between the Pennsylvania Railroad and H&M at Manhattan Transfer.

The earliest lines of the type now known as light rail typically operated with standard streetcar equipment, and most were later upgraded through the adoption of modern PCC streetcars. As further modernization of these lines began and as new light rail lines were developed in the 1970s, a few lines acquired new light rail vehicles of a conventional single-unit, double-truck arrangement. The most common choice, however, was a distinctive articulated car arrangement that was introduced in both equipment acquired from European manufacturers and new designs—such as the Standard Light Rail Vehicle—developed for North American systems. These were typically two-unit light rail vehicles carried on three trucks, with the two adjoining units sharing a common truck. A variation of this arrangement has been used for several low-floor vehicle designs. Instead of a truck at the center of the articulated vehicle, these typically employ a short low-floor center section fitted with four wheels on stub axles that supports the two adjacent units.

Trucks

The trucks employed for early elevated railway and subway equipment were typically slightly smaller versions of the equalized, four-wheel Master Car Builder (MCB) trucks used for most steam railroad passenger cars. Generally, the weight of the car body was

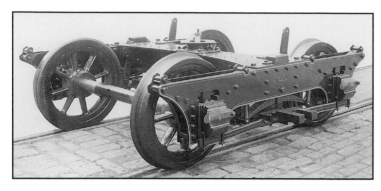

The first motor cars for Chicago's Metropolitan West Side Elevated in 1893 were equipped with this heavy, rigid truck from the Baldwin Locomotive Works. The motors and third-rail shoes had not yet been installed. H. L. Broadbelt Collection.

carried to each truck through a center bearing mounted on a transverse bolster beam. A king pin, or center pin, about which the truck rotated, connected the car body and the truck at the center bearing. Usually side bearing plates mounted on the car body and truck bolster prevented the car from rocking on the center bearing. In a typical MCB design, the truck used a floating bolster supported on elliptical leaf springs to carry the center bearing. These leaf springs usually rode on a spring plank supported by swing links from the truck frame. The frame in turn was carried on coil springs on the equalizer bars that spanned between the axles.

Generally, the wheelbase of these early rapid transit trucks ranged from about 5 feet to as much as 7 feet for motor trucks on some of the largest New York cars, while wheels ranged anywhere from 30 to 34 inches in diameter. Traction motors were mounted on motor trucks in what was termed an "inside hung" arrangement, in which the motors were suspended between the axles. These motor trucks could be extremely heavy, with some of the two-motor New York trucks weighing as much as 25,000 pounds.

More typical of MCB-type equalized rapid transit trucks was this 73-inch wheelbase Baldwin truck manufactured for Chicago's South Side Elevated in 1902. H. L. Broadbelt Collection.

The application of PCC technology that began in the 1930s brought much lighter car weights, and truck designs that were much smaller and lighter than the older MCB trucks, and much quieter in operation. The PCC-type trucks specified for Chicago Rapid Transit's experimental articulated trains of 1947–48, for example, incorporated such features as inboard bearings, smaller (28-inch diameter) resilient wheels, and much smaller and lighter motors mounted at right angles to the axles and driving them through automotive type drive shafts and gears. The result was a two-motor truck that weighed only 8600 pounds, less than half the

During the early 1960s the Chicago Transit Authority carried out an extensive test program with four PCC-type rapid transit cars that were equipped with experimental trucks and propulsion systems. This prototype CTA-1 truck, developed by CTA engineers from the test results, incorporated many of the advanced features that would appear in new generations of high-performance rapid transit trucks. C. E. Keevil, from Fred W. Schneider, III.

Whatever the virtues of the pneumatic-tired rapid transit system adopted for Montreal, truck simplicity was not among them. Each truck had four main rubber-tired wheels, four rubber-tired guidance wheels, and four flanged steel back-up wheels. Canadian Vickers Industries, Ltd., Author's Collection.

weight of a two-motor MCB truck. A whole new family of truck designs emerged from this application of PCC technology and an extensive Chicago Transit Authority test program with higher horsepower motors and a variety of experimental trucks that followed in the 1960s. At Chicago and elsewhere, these new truck designs incorporated such features as cast steel frames, inside bearings, hypoid gear drives, hollow axles, forged aluminum wheels, air suspension, and rubber noise and vibration dampers. The LFM-Rockwell HPD-3 truck developed for the BART system, just to cite one example, incorporated a 7-foot wheelbase and 30-inch diameter wheels, was powered by two 150 h.p. traction motors, and was capable of 70 mph maximum speeds. Yet it weighed just 10,400 pounds, less than half the weight of a comparable motor truck for a typical New York subway car.

Traction Motors

The most common type of motor for elevated railway and subway service was the series-wound D.C. motor, so called because its armature and field are wired in series. The performance characteristics of the series motor met the requirements of rapid transit service better than any other type of motor. These motors were typically designed for operation at 600 volts with horsepower ratings ranging anywhere from 50 to 200 h.p. The most common arrangement of motors on a car was to mount two motors on one truck, while the other truck was unpowered, with the required motor horsepower dependent upon a company's normal ratio of motor to trailer cars and its operating characteristics.

The customary method of traction motor installation employed the "wheelbarrow" mounting developed by Frank J. Sprague, which permitted the motor to be directly geared to the axle. One side of the motor frame contained bearings mounted on the axle. This permitted the motor to rotate slightly about the axle as a center, thus maintaining perfect alignment between the gearing on the axle and the armature shaft no matter how irregular the track or the motion of the axle. The other side of the motor was hung from the truck frame on a spring mounting.

Workmen in an Interborough Rapid Transit shop have lifted off the top of a D.C. series traction motor to reveal the armature. On the axle at the right, just inside the wheel, is the spur gear that was driven by the armature. New York Transit Museum Archives, Brooklyn (Neg. LSI-454).

Radical improvements in both traction motors and their mounting were introduced to rapid transit systems through the adoption of the technology developed during the 1930s for the PCC streetcar. Both General Electric and Westinghouse developed improved designs for lightweight, compact, high-speed 300-volt D.C. motors that were rated at 55 h.p. Weighing scarcely a third of the weight of a comparable standard traction motor, these new motors were a major contributor to the overall weight reduction achieved by the PCC technology. Unlike the traditional motor mounting developed by Frank J. Sprague, the PCC traction motors were mounted at right angles to the axles, and drove them through a hypoid gear connection. Continued development work has produced the much more powerful lightweight motors and drive systems that power the modern generation of high-speed, high performance metro equipment.

Modern designs for light rail vehicles introduced the idea of the monomotor truck, in which a single longitudinally mounted high-horsepower motor rated at anywhere from 200 to 400 h.p. powers both axles through flexible couplings.

The most significant recent development in traction motors has been the shift to A.C. propulsion in place of the traditional D.C. systems, which has reduced power consumption and maintenance expense and improved reliability. Key to the success of A.C. propulsion was the development of what were called gate turn off (GTO) thyristors, which in turn made possible the development of simple inverters for the conversion of D.C. to three-phase A.C. power. At the same time, the development of microprocessor technologies made possible the control systems needed for three-phase A.C. traction motors.

The three-phase, asynchronous motor used with A.C. propulsion systems is a much simpler and more rugged and reliable piece of equipment than the D.C. motor it replaced. Unlike the D.C. motor, it has no commutator, carbon brushes, or other components subject to wear, and it has the advantage of being fully sealed, preventing the intrusion of dirt and other contaminants. Savings of 50 percent or more in maintenance costs, twice the reliability, and energy savings of as much as 30 percent have been claimed for the new motors.

Control

In order to start or control the speed of a direct current motor the current and voltage must be controlled. This is usually done by introducing resistance in series with the motor, and by connecting two or more traction motors in different combinations of series and parallel. The resistance is gradually reduced as the motor speed increases until it can be eliminated altogether. The earliest Chicago elevated railway electrifications, in which a single car acted–in effect—as a locomotive, did this with a simple platform controller in which a drum rotated by the motorman made contact with various combinations of motor and resistance cables. A train was started with two motors in series in a circuit with maximum resistance. To accelerate the train the controller was rotated through a succession of points that gradually reduced the resistance in the circuit until the motors were operating in series without any resistance. Next, the motors were connected in parallel with the full resistance in the circuit. Further rotation of the controller gradually reduced the resistance until the two motors were operating in parallel at full line voltage.

This control system was quickly superseded by the multiple unit system developed by Frank Sprague during 1897–98, which enabled any number of motor cars in a train to be controlled from a single point. This was accomplished with a small pilot motor that operated a 600-volt controller on each motor car. This pilot motor was energized through a series of relays that were in turn energized through low voltage train line wires connected to a master controller operated by the motorman. Sprague sold his patents to General Electric, and both GE and Westinghouse subsequently introduced a variety of improved versions of multiple unit control that included such features as an automatic acceleration capability.

Improved PCC-type control systems provided both improved acceleration and braking performance and much smoother acceleration, and added a dynamic braking capability.

In dynamic braking, the traction motors act as generators to help brake a train, with the electrical energy being dissipated through resistance grids. The next major advance in control technology came with the development of what was called "chopper" control. This utilizes high-voltage, high-power semiconductors in place of resistances, eliminating both the inherent heat and energy loss. Chopper control also permitted the use of regenerative braking, in which the electrical energy generated by the traction motors in braking was returned to the power system. Still more advanced microprocessor based control systems have come into use with the shift to A.C. propulsion systems.

Current Collection

This is a typical modern current collector for third rail systems. The Ohio Brass Company.

Current collection from the third rail systems commonly used by rapid transit systems was accomplished with truck-mounted iron shoes, held against the top of the rail by their own weight. In protected third-rail installations with an inverted power rail, current collection was by means of an "underrunning" shoe held against the bottom side of the rail by spring pressure.

A few of the older light rail systems employ the traditional trolley pole method of current collection from overhead power systems, but most light rail systems, and the several metro systems that use overhead current collection, have adopted the use of pantographs. The pantograph supports a contact shoe held against the overhead contact wire by spring tension. In its traditional form the pantograph was a diamond-shaped frame that could adjust to variations in the height of the wire. More recently, several types of lightweight pantographs have come into use. The most common is the Faiveley pantograph, which has only a single arm instead of the usual diamond shape.

Brakes

Although several of the early elevated railways initially employed vacuum or straight air braking systems, the industry quickly standardized on the use of an automatic air braking system comparable to that used by North American steam railroads. This employed an air reservoir on each car that was kept charged from the brake pipe line to provide the brake cylinder pressure for braking. When it is in "release," the brake pipe line is at high

This is a modern Faiveley-type single-arm current collection pantograph. Faiveley s.a.

pressure and a triple valve charges the air reservoir while exhausting the brake cylinder, releasing the brakes. When the brake pipe pressure is reduced, the triple valve closes the brake cylinder exhaust and allows air to flow from the reservoir to the cylinder, applying the brakes. This system, with a number of improvements, remained the standard until the development of the PCC technology in the 1930s. PCC-type rapid transit cars utilized the traction motors for dynamic braking, with a spring applied, electrically released friction brake to complete the stop. Another widely used PCC feature was the magnetic track brake, which utilized electrical power from batteries to activate a spring-suspended electromagnetic brake that was attracted to the rail, providing a braking force from friction between the brake and the rail. Newer hydraulic friction disc braking systems have been developed to meet the braking needs of modern high-speed, high performance metro equipment, while the use of regenerative braking has become feasible with the development of solid state control and A.C. propulsion systems.

NORTH AMERICAN METRO AND LIGHT RAIL TRANSIT

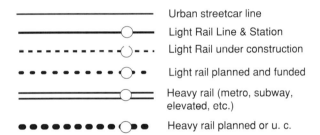

MASTER LEGEND

Urban streetcar line

Light Rail Line & Station

Light Rail under construction

Light rail planned and funded

Heavy rail (metro, subway, elevated, etc.)

Heavy rail planned or u. c.

Special legends appear on certain maps to cope with special modes or especially complex situations.

These profiles and maps provide a brief summary of the physical characteristics, scope, and traffic for all North American metro and light rail transit systems currently in operation or under construction. Excluded from this summary are all systems classified as commuter railroads or heritage streetcar lines. Unless otherwise indicated, track gauge is 4-feet 8½-inch standard gauge and traffic data is for 2001.

System maps are by G. Mac Sebree.

United States

New England States

BOSTON

Massachusetts Bay Transportation Authority (MBTA) operates both light rail and metro lines serving the Boston metropolitan area. The 28-mile MBTA light rail system originated with street railway lines opened in the late nineteenth century. Four Green Line light rail routes reach downtown Boston via the Tremont Street subway completed in 1897

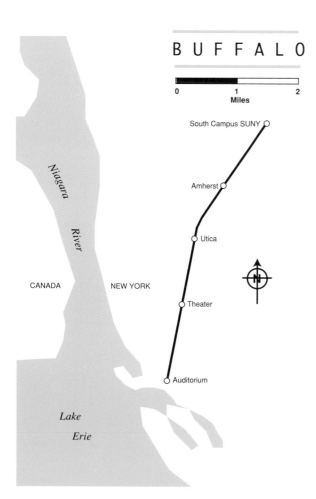

BOSTON

0 1 2
Miles

BUFFALO

0 1 2
Miles

that was North America's first subway, while a fifth route serves as an extension of the Red Line metro's Ashmont branch. The light rail system operates 219 modern articulated light rail vehicles and 12 PCC streetcars. Trains are powered from a 600-volt D.C. overhead trolley wire with pantograph or trolley pole (for PCC cars) current collection. The light rail system transports a weekday average of 230,000 passengers, and 67.4 million annual riders.

The Main Line Elevated, Boston's first metro, opened in 1901, and has since grown into a 37.5-mile system of three routes serving 51 stations with a fleet of 408 metro cars. Orange and Red lines are powered from a 600-volt D.C. third rail, while the Blue Line operates from third rail in subway and with pantograph current collection from an overhead catenary above ground. MBTA's three metro lines transport a weekday average of 465,000 riders, and an annual total of 136.4 million passengers. Current studies are considering the feasibility of a Blue Line extension north from Wonderland to Lynn or beyond, while a proposed Urban Ring project could include new light rail or metro between Dudley Square and Somerville.

Middle Atlantic States

BUFFALO

Niagara Frontier Transit Metro System, Inc. opened its 6.4-mile subway and surface light rail metro in 1985. The line serves seven surface and eight subway stations and operates 27 light rail vehicles. Power supply is from a 650-volt D.C. overhead catenary system with pantograph current collection. The line transports a weekday average of 25,000 trips and about 6.4 million annual riders. While the line was planned as the core of a regional rail system, funding has not been available for any extensions.

NEW YORK METROPOLITAN AREA

New York City Transit (NYCT), an agency of the Metropolitan Transportation Authority (MTA), operates the largest rapid transit system in the world. New York's first subway, the Interborough Rapid Transit, opened in 1904, and the system has grown almost continuously ever since. The 244-mile NYCT system, including the **Staten Island Railway**, includes 26 routes with a total of 685 main line track-miles, and serves a total of 490 stations with a fleet of 5875 metro cars. Trains are powered from a 625-volt D.C. third rail system. The system transports a weekday average of 4.3 million riders, and an annual total of 1.3 billion passengers. The most recent system expansion was the completion of the 63rd Street/ Queens Boulevard Line Connection in 2001, providing a connection with the East River tunnel at 63rd Street that expands capacity between Queens and Manhattan. Other major expansion currently in planning or under study includes a new Second Avenue subway on Manhattan, an extension to LaGuardia Airport in Queens, and an extension of the No. 7 line west from Times Square to a new West Side terminal.

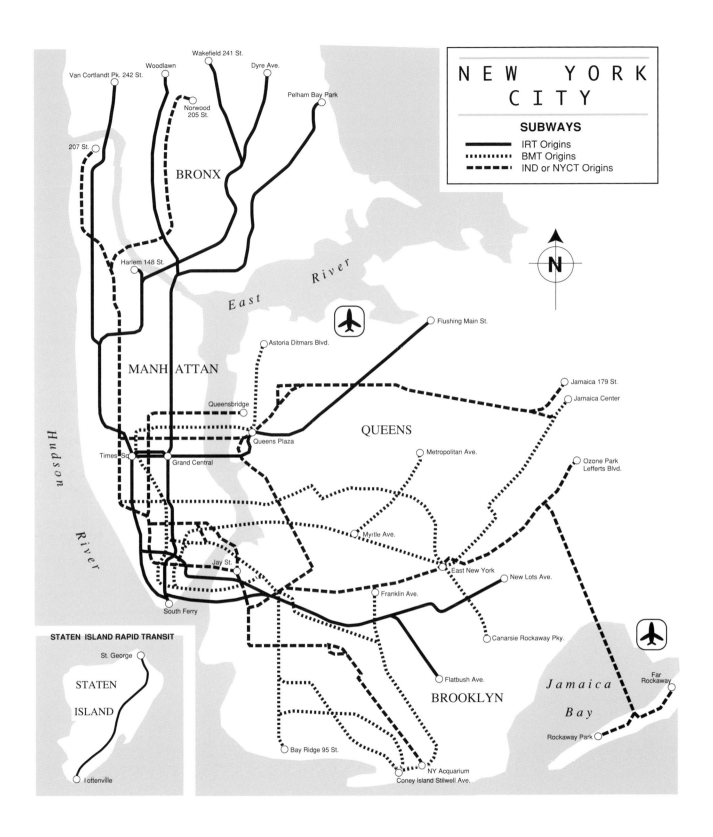

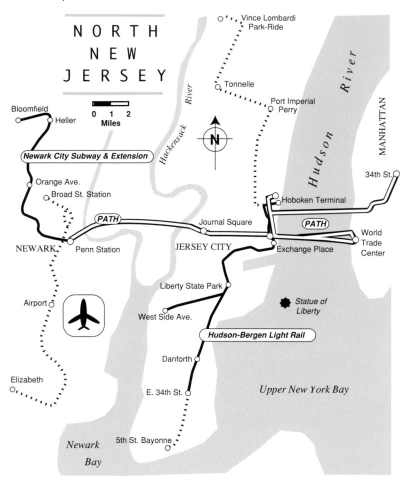

Port Authority Trans-Hudson Corporation (PATH) operates the former Hudson & Manhattan interstate metro service through the Hudson River tunnels between Manhattan and major New Jersey terminals at Hoboken, Jersey City, and Newark. The tunnels to mid-town Manhattan, under construction for more than 30 years, opened in 1908, while twin tunnels to lower Manhattan began operating the following year. The four-route, 13.8-mile system comprises 43.1 track-miles and serves 13 stations with 342 metro cars. Trains are powered from a 650-volt D.C. third rail. PATH transported a weekday average of 256,000 passengers, and an annual total of 74 million trips in 2000. Service through the tunnels to lower Manhattan has been suspended since the terminal facilities were extensively damaged in the September 11, 2001, terrorist attack on the World Trade Center. It is expected to resume to a temporary Manhattan terminal by 2004.

Port Authority of New York and New Jersey completed an extension of its Newark International Airport monorail system to a new Northeast Corridor rail station late in 2001. The 3 mile Bombardier (formerly AEG Monorail Systems) straddle-type monorail links three airport terminals with rental car areas, parking, and the new rail station.

At New York's John F. Kennedy International Airport the Port Authority is constructing an 8.1-mile fully automated Airtrain rail line that will link airport terminals with rental car areas, parking, the subway system, and the Long Island Rail Road. The system employs the Bombardier Advanced Rapid Transit linear motor technology and will operate with 32 ART vehicles. An initial section within the airport and linking it with the Howard Beach subway station opened in 2002, while a link to three subway lines and the LIRR at Jamaica is scheduled to open in 2003. The completed system is expected to transport 34,000 passengers daily.

New Jersey Transit operates two light rail lines in northern New Jersey. The Newark City Subway, built largely in the bed of the abandoned Morris & Essex Canal, opened in 1935. Following a modernization and extension completed in 2001, the 5.3-mile line serves 13 stations. NJ Transit opened the first 8.3 miles of a new Hudson-Bergen light rail line in 2000 that serves eight stations between Bayonne and Jersey City, while a further extension to Hoboken Terminal opened in 2002. The two lines are operated by a total of 45 low-floor articulated light rail vehicles powered from a 600-volt D.C. overhead catenary with pantograph current collection. The Newark City Subway transports a weekday average of almost 16,000 trips and an annual total of 4.7 million riders. The Hudson-Bergen line carried 2.1 million annual riders in 2001, and was transporting 15,000 daily trips by the end of the year. Additional Hudson-Bergen extensions in Bayonne and north to Bergen and a park-and-ride facility in Bergen County opening between 2003 and 2010 should complete the full planned 20.1-mile system. Construction began in 2002 for an initial mile-long section of a third NJ Transit light rail line, an 8.8-mile Newark-Elizabeth Rail Link that will be linked to the Newark City Subway. This first section should open by 2005. Planning was also in progress for a Union County segment of the line that would link Newark International Airport and mid-town Elizabeth.

Philadelphia Metropolitan Area

Southeastern Pennsylvania Transportation Authority (SEPTA) operates an extensive light rail and metro system serving the City of Philadelphia and its western suburbs.

The first of SEPTA's two metro routes opened along Market Street in 1907, and the system reached a total of 25 miles, serving 51 stations with the 1973 completion of the last extension to the Broad Street subway. Track gauge for the Market-Frankford line is 5-feet 2¼-inches, while the Broad Street route is standard gauge. The two routes are operated with 345 metro cars. Power is supplied from a 625-volt D.C. third rail system. SEPTA's metro lines board a weekday average of 282,000 riders and transport 86 million annual passengers.

The 68-mile SEPTA light rail system includes five former streetcar lines serving West Philadelphia that enter downtown Philadelphia via the Market Street subway, three suburban lines that radiate from the 69th Street western terminal of the Market-Frankford El-subway, and the rehabilitated Girard Avenue surface line in North Philadelphia, which is scheduled to resume operation in 2003. Track gauge is 5-feet 2¼-inches for the city lines, 5-feet 2½ inches for two former Red Arrow suburban lines, and standard gauge for the former Philadelphia & Western line to Norristown. Power is supplied from a 600-volt D.C. overhead trolley wire for all lines except the former P&W, which is powered from a 600-volt D.C. third rail system. A fleet of 185 light rail vehicles includes 141 single-unit light rail vehicles for the West Philadelphia and former Red Arrow routes, 26 high-speed cars for the Norristown line, and 18 rehabilitated PCC streetcars for the Girard Avenue surface line. The light rail system boards a weekday average of 83,300 passengers and transports 24.6 million annual riders.

Port Authority Transit (PATCO) operates a 14.5-mile high-speed metro between downtown Philadelphia and suburban Lindenwold, N.J. Opened in 1969, the line was the first of a new generation of highly automated metros. PATCO serves 13 stations with a fleet of 121 metro cars. The line is powered from a 685-volt D.C. third rail system. The high-speed trains boarded a weekday average of almost 38,000 passengers and 10.6 million annual riders in 2000. PATCO is studying the feasibility of extensions beyond Lindenwold into Gloucester and Cumberland counties.

New Jersey Transit is constructing a 34-mile, 20 station Southern New Jersey Light Rail Transit System that will operate over a former Conrail line between Trenton and Camden. The line will operate with 20 articulated, low-floor diesel-electric light rail vehicles. Service is expected to begin early in 2003.

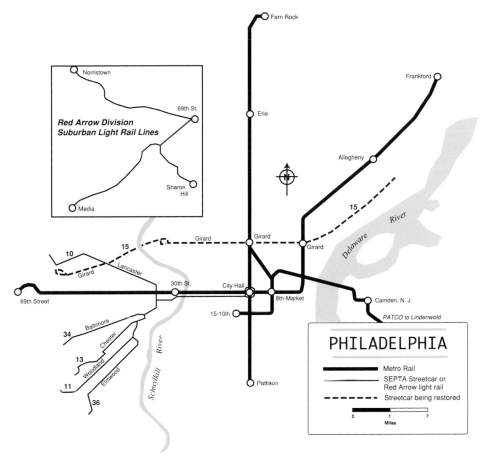

P I T T S B U R G H

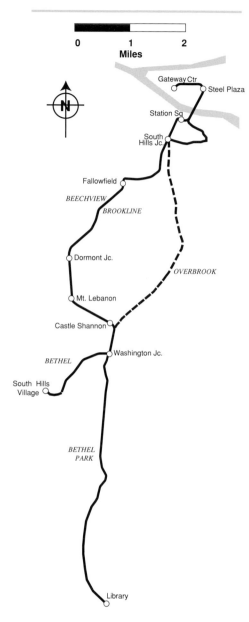

PITTSBURGH

Port Authority of Allegheny County completed rebuilding a first phase of its surviving South Hills trolley system into a modern subway and surface light rail system in 1987, and is now completing the conversion of the remainder of the system. The 25-mile "T" system will have a total of 45.8 main line track-miles when the next phase of work is complete in late 2003, and will serve a total of 23 stations. The system is operated with a fleet of 55 articulated light rail vehicles, with another 28 on order, and is powered by a 600-volt D.C. overhead catenary system with pantograph current collection. Track gauge is 5-feet 2½-inches. The system transports a weekday average of 26,000 trips and 7.4 million annual passengers. Engineering is in progress for a 1.6-mile North Shore Connector that will link the system's downtown subway with destinations on the north shore of the Allegheny River.

BALTIMORE

Maryland Transit Administration (MTA) operates both light rail and metro routes at Baltimore. The first section of the MTA's 15.5-mile metro opened in 1983 and its most recent extension to the Johns Hopkins Medical Center was completed in 1995. The system includes a total of 30.4 main line track-miles and 14 stations, and is operated with 100 metro cars. The system is powered from a 700-volt D.C. third rail system. Metro trains board a weekday average of 26,000 passengers and 13.6 million annual riders.

The first section of MTA's 30-mile Central Light Rail Line opened in 1992 and its most recent extensions to Baltimore's Pennsylvania Station and the Baltimore-Washington International Airport opened at the end of 1997. The line serves 32 stations and will have a total of 57 main line track-miles when current double-tracking projects are complete. Service is provided with 53 articulated light rail vehicles. Power is supplied at 750 volts D.C. from an overhead catenary system, with pantograph current collection. Light rail trains transport a weekday average of 54,000 passengers and 8.5 million annual riders.

WASHINGTON

Washington Metropolitan Area Transit Authority (WMATA) opened the first segment of its regional Metrorail system for the District of Columbia and adjacent areas in Virginia and Maryland in 1976, and completed the final section of a planned 103-route-mile system in January 2001. The double-track system includes five routes with a total of 83 stations. Metrorail operates a metro car fleet that will reach a total of 1006 when current orders are complete, and is powered from a 750-volt D.C. third rail system. The system transports a weekday average of 625,000 passengers. A 3-mile, two-station extension to Largo Town Center in Maryland is under construction, while projects in WMATA's 25-year expansion plan could add as many as 150 miles of new metro and light rail lines.

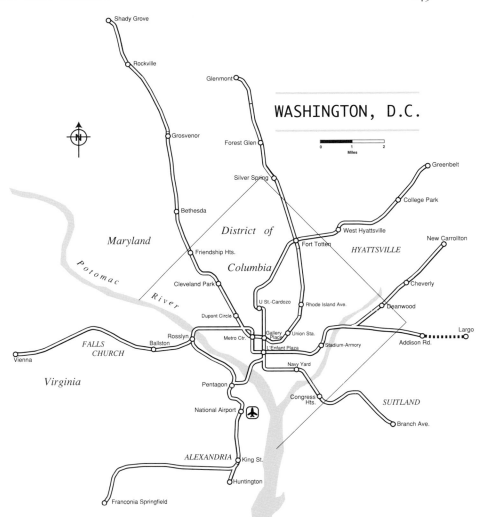

South Atlantic States

ATLANTA

Metropolitan Atlanta Rapid Transit Authority (MARTA) opened its first metro line in 1979. With the opening of a North Line extension to North Springs at the end of 2000, the rail system had grown to include three routes with a total of 47.6 miles, serving 38 stations. The system comprises a total of 95.2 main line track-miles and is operated with 340 metro cars. Power supply is at 750 volts D.C. from a third rail system. MARTA trains board a weekday average of 258,000 passengers and 25 million annual riders. Additional extensions are planned, with West Line and North Line extensions, and an East Line branch, the most likely expansion projects to move ahead next.

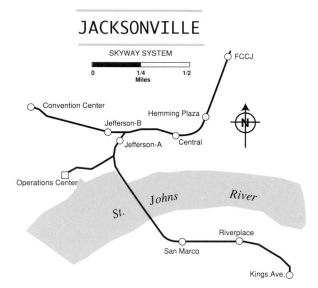

Jacksonville Transportation Authority (JTA) operates a fully automated Skyway Express monorail system that links the downtown Jacksonville area with bus routes and peripheral parking. An initial section of the system was completed in 1989 with the Matra VAL automated guideway technology, but in the build-out of the system this was replaced with the Bombardier UM III straddle-type monorail system operating over a single 32-inch-wide beam. The Skyway Express has 2.5 main line track-miles and 8 stations, and is operated with nine two-car trains. Trains are powered from a three-phase, 480-volt A.C. conductor rail. The system transports a weekday average of 2,500 riders, and 750,000 annual passengers. Studies are in progress for alignment alternatives for what could be light rail or dedicated busway routes that would be linked to the Skyway Express.

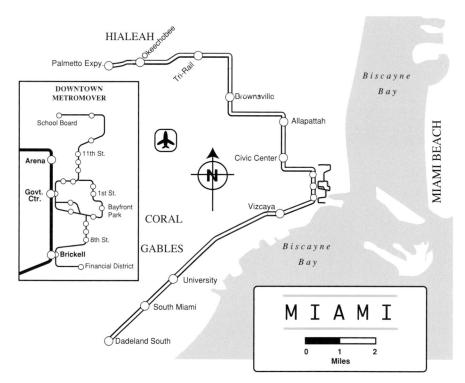

MIAMI

Miami-Dade Transit completed the first section of its single Metrorail route in 1984, and the most recent extension of the 22.5-mile metro opened in late 2002. Metrorail serves 22 stations and is operated with 136 metro cars. The line is powered from a 700-volt D.C. third rail system. Metrorail transports a weekday average of 48,000 passengers and 14 million annual riders. Planned major extensions have been stalled by the lack of local funding.

A Metromover people mover system acts as a downtown Miami distributor for Metrorail. An initial section of the line opened in 1986 and the full 4.4-mile route was completed in 1994. The fully automated system employs a pneumatic-tired guided vehicle system developed by Westinghouse (now Bombardier), and is powered by three-phase A.C. through three power rails. The line includes 10 main line guideway-miles and serves 21 stations with 29 AGT vehicles. Metromover carries a weekday average of 15,000 riders, and 4.2 million annual passengers.

SAN JUAN

Puerto Rico Highway and Transportation Authority is constructing a 10.6-mile Tren Urbano elevated, subway, and at-grade metro that will extend over an east-west route from Sagrada Corazón in San Juan to Guaynabo and Bayamon. The line will serve 16 stations with 82 metro cars. The line is expected to open in fall 2003. Planning is complete for a 1.2-mile extension from Sagrado Corazón to Minillas, in Santurce, while other projected extensions will expand Tren Urbano into a regional metro system.

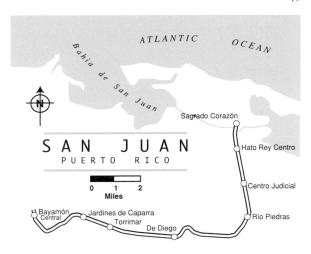

North Central States

CLEVELAND

Greater Cleveland Regional Transit Authority (RTA) operates three light rail and one metro route. The first section of RTA's 19.1-mile Red Line metro opened in 1955, and the line now serves 18 stations on a route extending from Cleveland's east side through downtown Cleveland to Hopkins International Airport. The Red Line operates over 36 main line track-miles with 60 metro cars. Power supply is from a 600-volt D.C. overhead catenary, with pantograph current collection. Metro trains transport a weekday average of 18,700 passengers and 5.4 million annual riders.

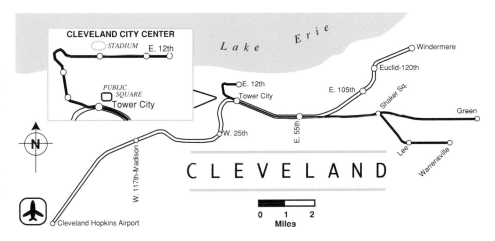

The 12.1-mile light rail system began operating in 1920 as the Cleveland Interurban Railway, while its most recent extension into downtown Cleveland's Waterfront area opened in 1996. Light rail and metro trains share trackage over a 2-mile section between E. 55th Street and the Tower City terminal in downtown Cleveland. The light rail system operates over a total of 30 main line track-miles and serves 34 stations with 48 articulated light rail vehicles. Power supply is from a 600-volt D.C. overhead catenary, with pantograph current collection. The three lines transport a weekday average of 13,700 passengers and an annual total of 4 million riders. RTA has been studying proposed extensions of the Waterfront light rail line and an eastward extension of the Van Aken Boulevard Blue Line.

DETROIT

Detroit Transportation Corporation operates a 2.9-mile downtown people mover system that opened in 1987. The single track, one-way elevated loop serves 13 stations with a fleet of 12 ART vehicles. The system utilizes Bombardier's fully-automated Advanced Rapid Transit (ART) linear motor technology. Power supply is 600-volt D.C. from dual power rails. The system transports a daily average of 6000 riders, and has carried as many as 54,000 in a single day during special events. Annual traffic is 2.2 million passengers.

Chicago

Chicago Transit Authority operates a 105-mile elevated and subway metro system made up of seven routes serving 143 stations. The oldest segment of the predominantly elevated CTA system opened in 1892 as the Chicago & South Side Rapid Transit Railway, while the newest line is the Southwest Line from the Chicago Loop to the city's Midway Airport, which opened in 1993. The system includes 222.6 miles of main line track and operates 1190 metro cars. Power is supplied from a 600-volt D.C. third rail system, with the exception of a segment of the Skokie Swift Yellow Line, which employs overhead catenary and pantograph current collection. CTA trains board a weekday average of more than 500,000 passengers, and an annual total of 147.2 million riders.

MINNEAPOLIS-ST. PAUL

Metro Transit, operated by the Metropolitan Council of Minneapolis and St. Paul, began construction early in 2001 for an 11.6-mile, 15-station Hiawatha Avenue light rail line that will connect downtown Minneapolis with the Minneapolis-St. Paul International Airport and the Mall of America at suburban Bloomington. Bombardier Transportation is building 18 low-floor articulated light rail vehicles for the line. An initial segment should open between downtown Minneapolis and Fort Snelling in 2003, with the entire line to be in operation in 2004. A 10-mile extension beyond Bloomington to Eagan and Apple Valley is under study.

ST. LOUIS

Bi-State Development Agency operates a 34.4-mile MetroLink light rail line that extends west from downtown St. Louis to the Lambert-St. Louis International Airport and east across the Mississippi River on the historic Eads Bridge to East St. Louis and suburban destinations in Illinois. The first Metrolink segment opened in 1993, and the line reached its present extent with the opening of an extension eastward from East St. Louis to Belleville, Ill., in 2001. The line serves 27 stations and is operated with 65 articulated light rail vehicles. The power supply is 750-volt D.C. from an overhead catenary system, with pantograph current collection. MetroLink trains board a daily average of almost 87,000 passengers, with an annual average of 14.3 million trips. An 8.8-mile extension eastward from Belleville to Scott Air Force Base and Mid-America Airport is planned, and construction began in 2001 for an initial segment from Belleville to Scott that should open in 2003. Construction began in 2002 for a 8-mile, nine-station Cross-County route that will extend from the Forest Park station on the present line to suburban Clayton and Shrewsbury. The line should open in 2005.

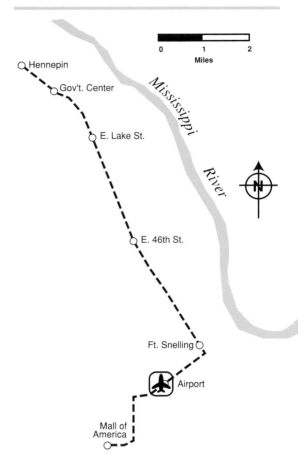

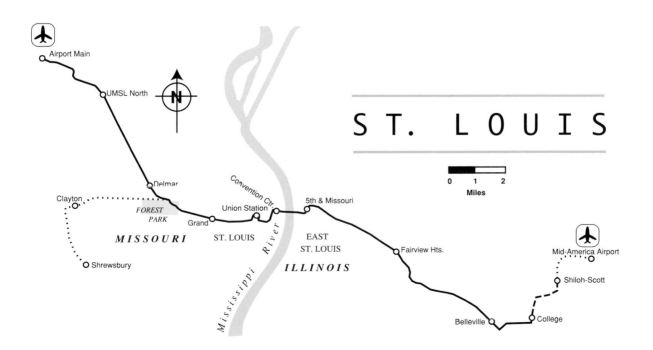

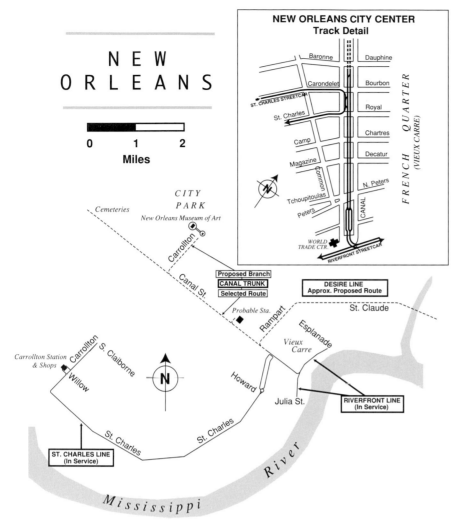

NEW ORLEANS

0 1 2
Miles

NEW ORLEANS CITY CENTER
Track Detail

South Central States

NEW ORLEANS

Regional Transit Authority (RTA) operates a unique 8.2-mile surface light rail system with rehabilitated vintage or replica streetcars. The RTA's St. Charles Avenue line began operation in 1835 with steam-powered equipment, while the Riverfront line dates to a 1988 conversion of railroad trackage along the riverfront. The system comprises a total of 16.4 main line track-miles. A fleet of 35 rehabilitated Perley A. Thomas streetcars built during 1923–24 operate the St. Charles line, while another seven replica cars operate the Riverfront line. Power is supplied at 600 volts D.C. from an overhead trolley wire, with trolley pole current collection. The two lines board a weekday average of 15,000 passengers, and transport an annual 4.5 million riders. Construction began in 2001 for a 4.1-mile line that will restore streetcar service in Canal Street from the Mississippi River to the Cemeteries. RTA shops are manufacturing 23 replica Perley Thomas streetcars for the new line, which should open in late 2003. Studies are also in progress for a proposed restoration of streetcar service in the Desire Avenue corridor.

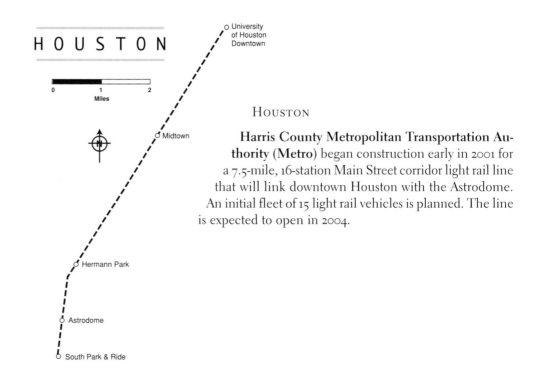

HOUSTON

0 1 2
Miles

HOUSTON

Harris County Metropolitan Transportation Authority (Metro) began construction early in 2001 for a 7.5-mile, 16-station Main Street corridor light rail line that will link downtown Houston with the Astrodome. An initial fleet of 15 light rail vehicles is planned. The line is expected to open in 2004.

DALLAS

Dallas Area Rapid Transit (DART) opened a 20-mile, two-route light rail "starter line"
system in 1996 that links downtown Dallas
with points north, south, and southwest of the
central business district. The opening of an
initial Northeast corridor line segment to
White Rock in September 2001 brought the
system to a total of 23 miles and 22 stations.
Additional Northeast line extensions to Garland and a North Central line to Plano opening in stages during 2002 and 2003 are
extending DART light rail to a total of 43.7
route-miles and will add another 12 stations to
the system. DART operates 95 articulated
light rail vehicles. Power is supplied from a
750-volt D.C. overhead catenary, with pantograph current collection. DART trains board
a weekday average of 40,000 passengers, and
transport 11.5 million annual riders. Studies
have been completed for northwest and
southeast corridor lines, as well as extensions
to the existing system.

Mountain States

DENVER

**Denver Regional Transportation District
(RTD)** opened a Central Corridor segment of
its light rail system through the downtown Denver area in 1994. With the addition of a Southwest Corridor line to Littleton and a Central
Platte Valley Spur, this initial line had been expanded to 15.8 miles by early 2002. The system
includes 24 stations and operates 31 articulated
light rail vehicles. Power is supplied from a 750-
volt D.C. overhead catenary, with pantograph
current collection. RTD trains board a weekday
average of 30,450 riders, and transport an annual
total of 8.9 million passengers. Construction began in 2001 for a 19.2-mile Southeast Corridor
line that is scheduled to begin operating in 2006
in the median of rebuilt and expanded freeways.
Still further extensions are planned.

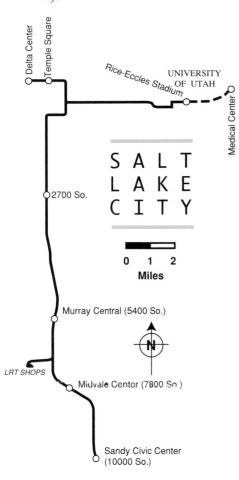

Salt Lake City

Utah Transit Authority (UTA) opened an initial north-south line of its 17.5-mile TRAX light rail system between downtown Salt Lake City and suburban Sandy in late 1999. With the completion of an extension from downtown to the University of Utah at the end of 2001, the system now comprises 34 track-miles and 20 stations. The line is operated with 33 light rail vehicles and is powered from a 750-volt D.C. overhead catenary system with pantograph current collection. TRAX transports a weekday average of 19,000 passengers and an annual total of 6.2 million riders. A further 1.5-mile extension to the University Medical Center is in design, while still other extensions are under study.

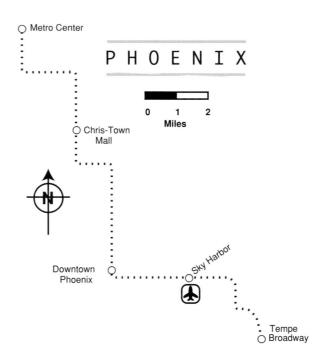

Phoenix

Valley Metro is planning a 20.3-mile Central Phoenix/East Valley light rail line that will extend south from the Chris-Town Mall to downtown Phoenix and then east to the Sky Harbor Airport, Tempe, and Mesa. Construction is scheduled to begin in 2003, with the line to open by the end of 2006. The line is envisioned as the core of an eventual valley-wide regional light rail system.

Pacific Coast States

San Diego

San Diego Trolley, Inc. operates a regional rail system that was the first modern U.S. light rail system when its first line opened between San Diego and San Ysidro, on the Mexican border, in 1981. The system has since been expanded with the addition of lines to the east and north, and the western end of a line through the Mission Valley, bringing the network to a total of 45.9 miles. The system now includes 92.1 main line track-miles and 47 stations, and is operated with a fleet of 123 articulated light rail vehicles. Power is supplied at 600 volts D.C. through overhead catenary or trolley wire, with pantograph current collection. Light rail trains board a weekday average of 83,300 passengers, and transport 28.9 million annual riders. A 5.9-mile Mission Valley East extension now under construction should open in 2004. A 3.4-mile section of a Mid-Coast line north from Old Town San Diego should be the next expansion project.

Los Angeles

Los Angeles County Metropolitan Transportation Authority (MTA), opened an initial north-south light rail line between downtown Los Angeles and Long Beach in 1990, while a second east-west line opened in the median of the new Century Freeway between Norwalk and Hawthorne in 1995. The 42-mile system now serves 36 stations with 82 light rail vehicles. Trains are powered from a 600-volt D.C. overhead catenary system through pantograph current collection. The two lines board a weekday average of 96,000 passengers and an annual total of 26.1 million riders. A 13.7-mile light rail line between Union Station and Pasadena is now under construction and should open in 2003, while a 24-mile second phase from Pasadena to Claremont is under study. Preliminary engineering is also in progress for a planned light rail route between Union Station and East Los Angeles.

The first segment of the MTA's Metro Red Line subway began operating early in 1993, and the full 11.1-mile line was completed between downtown Los Angeles and North Hollywood in the San Fernando Valley in June 2000. The subway serves 16 stations with 104 metro cars. Trains are powered from a 600-volt D.C. third rail system. A weekday average of 150,000 riders board the subway, while annual passengers total 33.8 million.

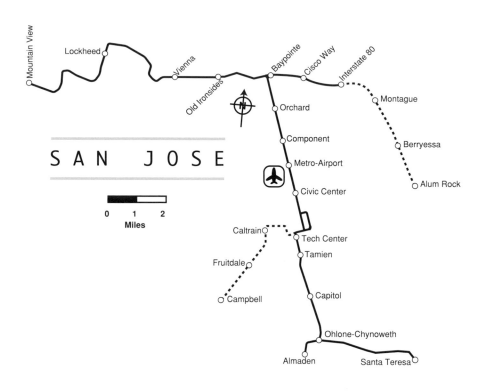

SAN JOSE

Santa Clara Valley Transportation Authority (VTA) operates a 30.3-mile light rail system that includes a Guadalupe Corridor route that extends north and south from San Jose, and lines branching east and west along Tasman Drive from the Guadalupe line north of downtown San Jose. The first segment of the system began operation in 1987, and it reached its present extent with the early 2001 opening of the Tasman East segment to Milpitas. The VTA rail system now includes 48 stations, and its initial fleet of 50 articulated light rail vehicles is currently being replaced by 100 low-floor articulated cars. Power supply is from a 750-volt D.C. overhead catenary system, with pantograph current collection. VTA trains boarded a weekday average of 25,700 passengers in 2000. Construction is in progress for a 2.9-mile second phase of the Tasman East Line that should open in 2004, and for a Capitol Corridor line that will extend service 3.5 miles southward from the east end of the Tasman line. Work is also underway for the first 5.3 miles of a Vasona Corridor rail line extending west from San Jose to Campbell that should open in 2004. A second phase of the project will extend the line to Los Gatos, while at least 12 more miles of new light rail for Santa Clara County have been approved for future development.

SAN FRANCISCO METROPOLITAN AREA

San Francisco Municipal Railway operates a 25.8-mile Muni Metro light rail system of five former streetcar routes which reach downtown San Francisco via a Market Street subway built as part of the BART rapid transit project. The most recent addition to the Muni Metro system was an extension to the Caltrain commuter rail station at 4th and King streets that opened in 1998. The system now includes 51.6 main line track-miles, 15 stations and nearly 200 stops, and is operated with 136 articulated light rail vehicles. Power supply is 600-volt D.C. from an overhead trolley wire, with pantograph current collection. In addition to Muni Metro, the Municipal Railway operates a 5-mile surface line on Market Street and the Embarcadero with 17 PCC and 10 Peter Witt-type streetcars. The line includes 10 main line track-miles, and is powered from a 600-volt D.C. overhead trolley wire, with trolley pole current collection. The combined Muni Metro routes and surface line board a weekday average of 164, 200 riders, and transport 49.7 million annual passengers. A 5.4-mile Muni Metro extension south in the 3rd Street corridor from 4th and King to Bayshore is under construction and should open in 2004. A planned 1.7-mile second phase of the project will include a new Central Subway that will extend across Market Street and under Geary and Stockton streets to Clay Street.

Bay Area Rapid Transit District (BART) operates a highly automated five-route, 104-mile regional metro system serving four Bay Area counties. The first line of BART's initial 71.5-mile system began operation in 1972, and with the completion of its most recent extension to the San Francisco International Airport at the end of 2002 BART had grown to a system of 224 main line track-miles serving 43 stations with a fleet of 669 metro cars. BART operates on a non-standard track gauge of 5 feet 6 inches. Power is supplied from a 1000-volt D.C. third rail system. The system boards a weekday average of 341,000

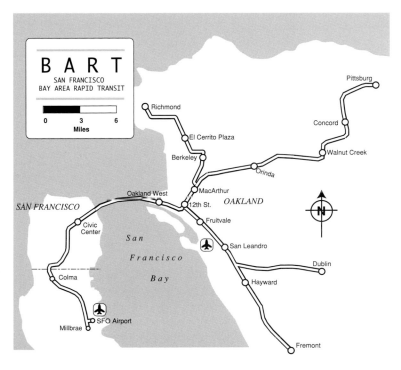

passengers and transports an annual total of 97.3 million trips. The next expansion projects likely to go ahead are a 5.6-mile East Bay extension from Fremont to Warm Springs, where it will be linked to a 16-mile Santa Clara County extension south to San Jose and Santa Clara. Studies have also been initiated for extensions from West Pittsburg to Antioch and from Dublin-Pleasanton to Livermore.

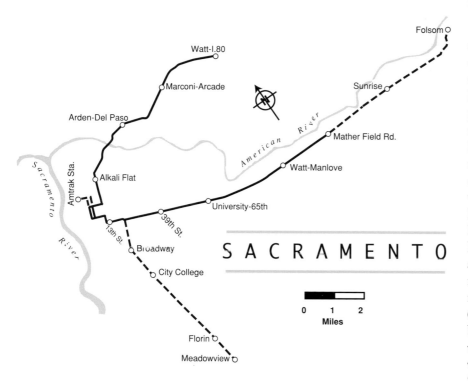

SACRAMENTO

Sacramento Regional Transit District (RT) operates a 20.6-mile light rail line that extends through downtown Sacramento from corridors to the east and northeast. The line began operation in 1987 and reached its present scope with the completion of a 2.3-mile Folsom line extension eastward to Mather Field Road in 1998, and the system now serves 31 stations. With the completion of a current 40-car order, the RT Metro fleet will total 76 articulated light rail vehicles. Power supply is from a 750-volt D.C. overhead catenary, with pantograph current collection. Light rail trains board a weekday average of 30,000 riders, and transport 8.6 million annual passengers. Additions to the rail system now under construction include a 6.3-mile South Line that should be complete by the end of 2003. A 10.9-mile extension eastward to Folsom should open in 2004. This will include a 0.7-mile connection from K Street to the historic SP depot in downtown Sacramento. Two additional high priority extensions now in the planning stages include a further 5-mile extension of the South Line and a 13-mile extension northward from downtown Sacramento to the airport.

PORTLAND

Tri-County Metropolitan Transportation District of Oregon (Tri-Met) operates a 38.5-mile MAX light rail system that includes routes extending east and west from downtown Portland, with a branch from the East Side line to the Portland International Airport. Tri-Met's initial Eastside MAX rail line opened in 1986, and the system reached its present scope with the opening of the airport line in September 2001. MAX now serves 54 stations with 78 articulated light rail vehicles. Power supply for the system is from a 750-volt D.C. overhead catenary, with pantograph current collection. Light rail trains board a weekday average of over 83,000 riders, and transport 22.3 million annual passengers. A 5.6-mile Interstate MAX line extending north along Interstate Avenue from northeast Portland to north Portland now under construction will open in 2004. Other potential light rail additions include an Interstate MAX extension across the Columbia River to Vancouver, Wash., and a route south from downtown Portland.

SEATTLE-TACOMA METROPOLITAN AREA

Central Puget Sound Regional Transit Authority (Sound Transit) is developing a Central Link light rail line as part of a regional transit system for the area. The planned 22-mile, north-south line will link the SeaTac International Airport with Seattle's University District through downtown Seattle. Work was to begin in late 2002 for a 14-mile initial section of the line between the SeaTac airport and downtown Seattle that will open in 2009. Sound Transit is also building a 1.6-mile Link surface light rail line that will link its Tacoma Dome commuter rail station with downtown Tacoma points. The line is expected to open in 2003.

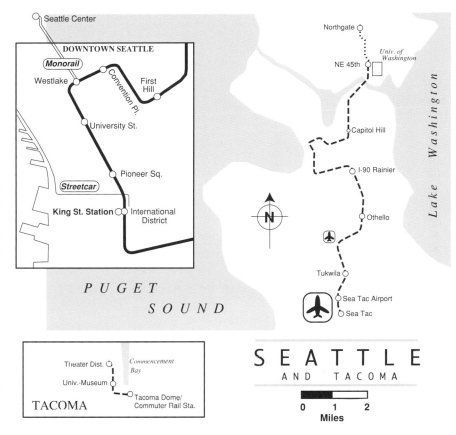

Canada

MONTREAL, QUEBEC

Société de transport de la Communauté urbaine de Montréal (STCUM) operates a 37.3 route-mile Métro subway system serving the City of Montreal and neighboring communities. The system's first two lines opened in 1966, and its most recent extension was completed in 1988. Four Métro routes include a total of 74.6 main line track-miles and 65 stations, and operate with 759 metro vehicles. Métro trains transport a weekday average of 760,000 passengers and 215 million annual riders. Métro employs a system of pneumatic-tired trucks operating on concrete running tracks developed in France, with flanged wheels and standard gauge running rails as a back-up system in case of tire failures. Power supply is from a 750-volt D.C. third rail. Construction began late in 2001 for a 3.2 route-mile, three-station extension of Métro Line 2 under the Riviere des Prairies to Laval that should open by the end of 2004. Planning studies were in

progress for projected Métro extensions and new light rail lines that could add more than 20 miles to the STCUM rail system, with an 8-mile light rail route from downtown Montreal to the south bank of the St. Lawrence likely to be the next to begin construction.

Ottawa, Ontario

OC Transpo opened North America's first diesel light rail transit line in October 2001, operating over a 5-mile route serving five stations. The service operates over a single-track Canadian Pacific line with a passing siding at mid-point. Three German-built Bombardier Talent articulated diesel trains operate the O-Train service.

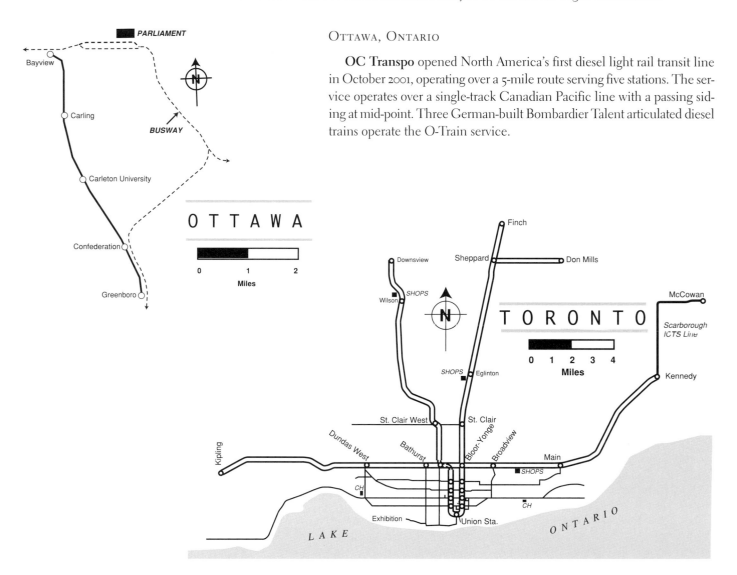

Toronto, Ontario

Toronto Transit Commission (TTC) operates a light rail and metro network serving the greater Toronto area. TTC's 97.7-mile light rail system is made up of modernized streetcar lines dating as far back as the late nineteenth century, with some new lines completed as recently as July 2000. Ten light rail routes comprise a total of 187.3 main line track-miles, and are operated with 248 light rail vehicles. The system operates from a 600-volt D.C. overhead trolley wire with trolley pole current collection. Track gauge is 4 feet 10⅞ inches. Light rail lines board a daily average of 271,000 passengers, and transport 66.5 million annual riders.

TTC opened its first subway metro line in 1954 and now operates a 39-mile system of three routes with a total of 71 stations, 78 main line track-miles, and 694 cars. Power supply is from a 720-volt D.C. third rail system. The subway system transports a weekday average of 822,000 passengers, and 258.6 million annual riders. The most recent metro extension, opened in September 2002, was an initial 4-mile, five-station segment of an east-west Shepard subway.

In 1985 TTC opened the first section of the highly automated, 4-mile Scarborough Rapid Transit line, utilizing the
UTDC-developed Advanced Rapid Transit (ART) linear motor technology. The system now comprises 8 main line track-
miles and serves six stations with 28 ART vehicles. Power supply
is 600-volt D.C. from dual power rails. The line transports a
weekday average of 42,300 riders, with an annual total of 9 million passengers.

EDMONTON, ALBERTA

Edmonton Transit System began operating the first new
light rail system in North America in 1978. The 7.8-mile line
reached its present scope with the 1992 completion of an extension across the North Saskatchewan River to the University of Saskatchewan. The line includes 15.6 main line
track-miles and serves 10 stations with 37 articulated light rail
vehicles. Power supply is 600-volt D.C. from an overhead
catenary system, with pantograph current collection. Light
rail trains board a weekday average of 38,000 riders, and transport 10 million annual passengers. Edmonton is now planning
a 6.2-mile, six-station southern extension from University to
Heritage Mall.

CALGARY, ALBERTA

Calgary Transit operates a 20.6-mile, two-route C-Train light rail
system that opened its first line in 1981. The system reached its present
form with the October 2001 completion of a southern extension, and
now serves 31 stations with 96 articulated light rail vehicles. The system operates on a wind-generated power supply at 600-volt D.C. from
an overhead catenary system, with pantograph current collection. C-
Train boards a weekday average of 187,000 riders, and transports 46
million annual passengers. Planned additions to the system include
1.9-mile southern and 1.9-mile northwest extensions now under construction that should open in 2003, while a 1.25-mile northeast extension is scheduled to open in 2006.

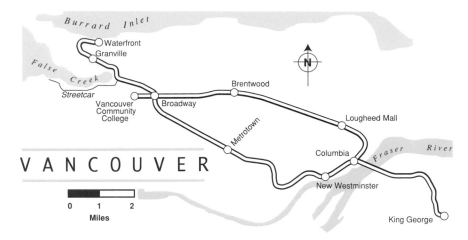

Vancouver, B.C.

Greater Vancouver Transportation Authority (TransLink) operates the fully automatic SkyTrain metro system. An initial 13.3-mile Expo Line began operating in 1986, and had been extended to a length of 18 miles, serving 20 stations, by 1994. The system uses Bombardier Transportation's Advanced Rapid Transit (ART) technology, which employs linear motor propulsion, steerable trucks, and the fully automatic SELTRAC train control system. A second, 13-mile Millennium Line now being completed between Vancouver Community College and New Westminster will extend SkyTrain to a total length of 31 route-miles by the end of 2002. The Expo Line's fleet of 150 Mark I cars has been supplemented by 20 larger Mark II cars, while another 40 Mark II's will operate the Millennium Line. Power supply is from a two-rail 600 V DC system mounted on vertical supports beside the track. SkyTrain transported a weekday average of 146,000 riders and 46.3 million annual passengers in 2000. Further SkyTrain extensions northeast from Lougheed Town Centre to Coquitlam Centre, west from Vancouver Community College, and south to Richmond and the Vancouver International Airport are under study.

Mexico

Mexico City, D. F.

Sistema de Transporte Colectivo (STC) operates the second busiest metro system in North America. STC opened its first metro route in 1969 and construction of new lines has continued almost without interruption ever since. With the completion of a final section of Line B to Ciudad Azteca late in 2000, the 11-line system reached a total of 125.3 miles, with 175 stations. Ten STC lines operate with the French-originated system of pneumatic-tired trucks operating on concrete running tracks, with flanged wheels and standard gauge running rails as a back-up system in case of tire failures. Power supply is from a 750-volt D.C. third rail. Line A employs a conventional steel wheel technology, with pantograph current collection from a 750-volt D.C. overhead catenary system. The ten pneumatic tired lines are operated with 2448 metro cars, while Line A operates an additional 208 cars. The system transports a weekday average of 4 million passengers. A 1996 update of the city's metro and light rail master plan calls for expansion of the STC network to a total of 27 lines and 300 miles by 2020. These will include 14 pneumatic-tired and three steel-wheeled metro lines, and ten light rail lines.

Servicio de Transportes Eléctricos (STE) operates a single 8-mile, 18-station light rail route between the outer terminal of the STC Metro Line 2 at Tasqueña and subur-

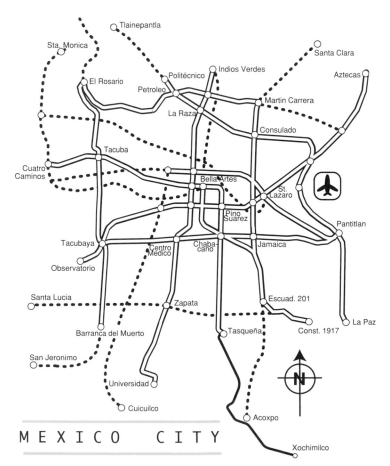

ban Xochimilco. STE completed modernization of the line from the last remaining section of Mexico City's once extensive street railway system in 1986. The line is powered from a 600-volt D.C. overhead catenary, with pantograph current collection. Service is provided by 12 articulated light rail vehicles. The line transported 18.2 million passengers in 2000.

GUADALAJARA, JALISCO

Sistema de Tren Electrico Urbano (SITEUR) serves Mexico's second largest city with a 14.9-mile, 29-station subway and surface light rail metro system. SITEUR's first line began operation in 1989. Service is operated with 48 articulated light rail vehicles. Power is supplied from a 750-volt D.C. overhead catenary, with pantograph current collection. The two lines transport a weekday average of 146,000 passengers and an annual total of 49 million riders. A rail transit master plan for Guadalajara calls for the eventual development of a seven-line, 80-mile system.

MONTERREY, NUEVO LEON

S. T. C. Metrorrey operates a 13.8-mile, 23-station light rail metro system in Mexico's third largest city. An initial elevated route opened in 1991, while a second route in subway was added in 1994. Service is provided with a fleet of 70 articulated light rail vehicles. Power is supplied from a 1500-volt D.C. overhead catenary with pantograph current collection. Metrorrey trains transported almost 44.3 million annual passengers in 2001. A long-range master plan for the system contemplates the development of a city-wide network of four principal lines, with several branches, totaling more than 48 miles.

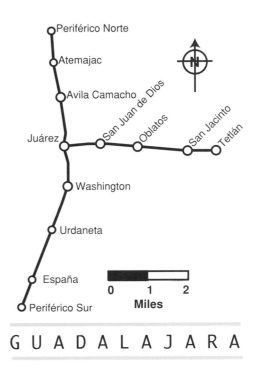

GUADALAJARA

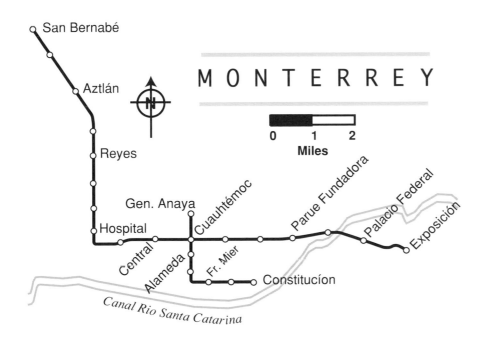

MONTERREY

BIBLIOGRAPHY

General Works

Books, Pamphlets and Periodicals

Bobrick, Benson. *Labyrinths of Iron: A History of the World's Subways.* New York: Newsweek Books, 1981.

————. *Parsons Brinckerhoff: The First 100 Years.* New York: Van Nostrand Reinhold Co., 1985.

Botzow, Hermann S. D., Jr. *Monorails.* New York: Simmons-Boardman Publishing Corp., 1960.

Holden, James W. "Subways and Els of the World," *Railroad Magazine*, Vol. 23, No. 3 (Feb. 1938): 4–25.

Hornung, Clarence P. *Wheels Across America.* New York: A. S. Barnes & Company, 1959.

Houser, Fred. "Boeing's State-of-the-Art Car: The big test begins in New York." *Railway Age*, Vol. 175, No. 11 (June 10, 1974): 26–28.

Middleton, William D. "California: Back on track." *Railway Age*, Vol. 188, No. 8 (Aug. 1987): 49–55.

————. "California in transit: Rail planners keep busy." *Railway Age*, Vol. 190, No. 11 (Nov. 1989): 51–55, 65.

————. *From Bullets to BART.* Chicago: Central Electric Railfans' Assn., Bulletin 127, 1989.

————. "ICTS: A tale of three cities." *Railway Age*, Vol. 185, No. 10 (Oct. 1984): 64–65, 67–69.

————. "Light rail lights up the west." *Railway Age*, Vol. 185, No. 9 (Sept. 1984): 114–117, 119.

————. "Light rail's star rises in the East." *Railway Age*, Vol. 187, No. 3 (Mar. 1986): 71–74.

————. "LRT: A continental guide." *Railway Age*, Vol. 191, No. 4 (Apr. 1990): 53–57, 64.

Miller, John Anderson. *Fares, Please!* New York: D. Appleton-Century Company, Inc., 1941.

Schneider, Fred W. III, and Stephen P. Carlson. *PCC: The Car That Fought Back.* Los Angeles: Interurban Press, Interurbans Special 64, 1980.

Sebree, Mac, Editor. 1994 *Light Rail Annual & User's Guide.* Pasadena, Calif.: Pentrex, 1994.

Shaw, Robert B. *A History of Railroad Accidents, Safety Precautions and Operating Practices.* Potsdam, N.Y.: Robert B. Shaw, 1978.

Smerk, George M. *The Federal Role in Urban Mass Transportation.* Bloomington and Indianapolis: Indiana University Press, 1991.

Wolinsky, Julian. "Light rail: One route to livable cities." *Railway Age*, Vol. 200, No. 7 (July 1999): 47–49.

————. "People-movers find their niche." *Railway Age*, Vol. 201, No. 12 (Dec. 2000): 55–56, 58.

Periodical Sources

The periodical coverage of rapid transit and light rail over the years is voluminous, and only very limited citations are included above or in the individual city listings below.

Electric Railway Journal provided the best overall coverage of all aspects of the construction, equipment, and operation of early rapid transit railways. This trade journal began publication in 1884 as *Street Railway Journal*, becoming *Electric Railway Journal* in 1908, and was then published as *Transit Journal* from 1932 until it ceased publication in 1942.

Headlights, a monthly publication of the Electric Railroaders' Association at New York, has provided detailed coverage of rail transit since it began publication in 1939. Its coverage of the renaissance of urban rail systems since the 1960s has been some of the most thorough anywhere.

Mass Transit is a current trade publication that provides coverage of all types of urban transit, including rail. It began publication in 1905 as the *Interurban Railway Journal*, changed in 1906 to *Electric Traction Weekly* and again in 1912 to just *Electric Traction*, before finally assuming its present title.

Railway Age, the leading trade journal of the railroad industry, has also covered the North American rail transit industry since 1963. Detailed annual surveys of rail transit developments by the author, with — since 1999 — Julian Wolinsky, have been published as "Light Rail Planner's Guide" or "Rail Transit Planner's Guide" special inserts to *Railway Age* February issues from 1988 to 1999, and as "Passenger Rail Planner's Guide" in March issues since 2000.

United States

Atlanta

Asher, Joe. "Atlanta Transit: MARTA gets moving at last." *Railway Age*, Vol. 176, No. 23 (Dec. 8, 1975): 20–22, 24.

Gorton, William S. "Atlanta: North-South Line Extensions Opened." Electric Railroaders' Assn., *Headlights*, Vol. 47, Nos. 10–12 (Oct.-Dec. 1985): 2–6.

———. "Underground Atlanta." Electric Railroaders' Assn., *Headlights*, Vol. 44, Nos. 11–12 (Nov.-Dec. 1982): 2–8.

Middleton, William D. "Atlanta's MARTA: Running well, still building." *Railway Age*, Vol. 182, No. 9 (May 11, 1981): 24–26, 29, 54.

Miklos, Frank S. "Rapid Transit Arrives in the Deep South." Electric Railroaders' Assn., *Headlights*, Vol. 42, Nos. 2–3 (Feb.-Mar. 1980): 2–10.

Schneider, Fred W., III. "MARTA's French Connection." Electric Railroaders' Assn., *Headlights*, Vol. 44, Nos. 11–12 (Nov.-Dec. 1982): 9–12.

Baltimore

"Baltimore: Metro Line Opens." Electric Railroaders' Assn., *Headlights*, Vol. 46, Nos. 7–8 (July-Aug. 1984): 2–6.

Middleton, William D. "Baltimore LRT: An intermodal, design-build triumph." Railway Age, Vol. 198, No. 10 (Oct. 1997): 73–76.

———. "Baltimore Metro: Ready to roll in '83." *Railway Age*, Vol. 183, No. 23 (Dec. 13/27, 1982): 51–53.

———. "Baltimore transit: Halfway there." *Railway Age*, Vol. 181, No. 3 (Feb. 11, 1980): 37–39, 44–45.

———. "Baltimore: Up and running." *Railway Age*, Vol. 193, No. 6 (June 1992): 50–51.

———. "LRT in '91 is Baltimore goal." *Railway Age*, Vol. 189, No. 5 (May 1988): 37–39.

Vantuono, William C. "New vitality for Baltimore." *Railway Age*, Vol. 196, No. 8 (Aug. 1995): 27–28, 31–32.

Boston

Brown, Burton G., Jr. "The Boston Subway: 1897, A Late Nineteenth Century Attack on the Emerging Mass Transit Problem," *The Bulletin*, National Railway Historical Society, Vol. 38, No. 3 (1973): 18–46.

Chiasson, George, Jr. *Boston's Main Line El: The Formative Years 1879–1908*. Electric Railroaders'
    Assn., *Headlights*, Vol. 49, 1987.
Clarke, Bradley H. and O. R. Cummings. *Tremont Street Subway: A Century of Public Service.*
    Boston: Bulletin No. 22, Boston Street Railway Assn., Inc., 1997.
Clarke, Bradley H. *The Boston Rapid Transit Album*. Boston: Bulletin No. 17, Boston Street Rail-
    way Assn., Inc., 1981.
————. *South Shore: Quincy-Boston*. Boston: Bulletin No. 10, Boston Street Railway Assn., Inc., 1972.
Cudahy, Brian J. *Change at Park Street Under: The Story of Boston's Subways*. Brattleboro, Vt.: The
    Stephen Greene Press, 1972.
Kimball, George A. "The Boston Elevated Railway," *The New England Magazine*, Vol. 24, No. 5
    (July 1901): 455–468.
Rapid Transit Lines in Boston. Boston: Boston Street Railway Assn., Inc., ca 1966.
"Your New Orange Line Extension is Ready!" Electric Railroaders' Assn., *Headlights*, Vol. 39, Nos.
    9–12 (Oct.-Dec. 1977): 2–8.

BUFFALO

Ellsworth, Kenneth. "Buffalo goes for LRRT—light rail rapid transit." *Railway Age*, Vol. 177, No.
    5 (Mar. 8, 1976): 36–37, 58.
Middleton, William D. "LRRT brightens Buffalo." *Railway Age*, Vol. 185, No. 12 (Dec. 1984): 74–75.

CHICAGO

Bullard, Thomas R. *Columbian Intramural Railway: A Pioneer Elevated Line*. Oak Park, Ill.: pub-
    lished by the author, 1987.
Chicago's Rapid Transit, Volume 1: Rolling Stock/1892–1947. Chicago: Central Electric Railfans'
    Assn., Bulletin 113, 1973.
Chicago's Rapid Transit, Volume 2: Rolling Stock/1947–1976. Chicago: Central Electric Railfans'
    Assn., Bulletin 115, 1976.
Krambles, George and Arthur H. Peterson. *CTA at 45*. Chicago: George Krambles Transit Schol-
    arship Fund, 1993.
Moffat, Bruce G. *The "L": The Development of Chicago's Rapid Transit System, 1888–1932*. Chicago:
    Central Electric Railfans' Assn., Bulletin 131, 1995.
Petzoid, Charles W. "Chicago: O'Hare Extension Completed." Electric Railroaders' Assn., *Head-
    lights*, Vol. 47, Nos. 4–5 (Apr.-May 1985): 2–8.
"Takeoff time for CTA's Midway Line." *Railway Age*, Vol. 194, No. 6 (June 1993): 42–44, 46.
Young, David M. *Chicago Transit: An Illustrated History*. DeKalb, Ill.: Northern Illinois University
    Press, 1998.

CLEVELAND

Electric Railways of Northeastern Ohio. Chicago: Central Electric Railfans' Assn., Bulletin 108, 1965.
Middleton, William D. "Cleveland: An end to Red Line blues?" *Railway Age*, Vol. 187, No. 5 (May
    1986): 57–59.

DALLAS

Middleton, William D. "For DART, a new timetable." *Railway Age*, Vol. 187, No. 5 (May 1986): 63–65.
————. "From turmoil, DART takes shape." *Railway Age*, Vol. 195, No. 9 (Sept. 1994): 67–71, 74, 76.

DENVER

Middleton, William D. "Denver welcomes light rail." *Railway Age*, Vol. 195, No. 10 (Oct. 1994): 61–
    62, 64, 66–68, 70–71.
Miller, Luther S. "Denver thinks big." *Railway Age*, Vol. 197, No. 12 (Dec. 1996): 45–46.

LOS ANGELES

Kizzia, Tom. "Los Angeles: Will tracks be back?" *Railway Age*, Vol. 175, No. 11 (June 10, 1974): 30–
    33, 37.

Middleton, William D. "Los Angeles: A green light for rapid transit." *Railway Age*, Vol. 181, No. 13 (July 14, 1980): 15.
———. "Los Angeles Metro gets a slow order." *Railway Age*, Vol. 185, No. 8 (Aug. 1984): 72–75.
———. "Los Angeles: Putting rail transit back on the map." *Railway Age*, Vol. 183, No. 17 (Sep. 13, 1982): 72–74.
———. "Los Angeles transit: Once more a grand plan." *Railway Age*, Vol. 177, No. 9 (May 10, 1976): 36–37, 54.
———. "Moving people: Los Angeles' hopes are high." *Railway Age*, Vol. 176, No. 19 (Oct. 13, 1975): 26, 28–29.
———. "Rapid transit for Los Angeles: An impossible dream?" *Railway Age*, Vol. 175, No. 23 (Dec. 9, 1974):

MIAMI

"Miami Metro." Electric Railroaders' Assn., *Headlights*, Vol. 53, No. 12 (Dec. 1991): 2–6.
Middleton, William D. "Miami transit: On schedule, on budget." *Railway Age*, Vol. 182, No. 11 (June 8, 1981): 18–23.

NEW ORLEANS

Middleton, William D. "More rail for New Orleans?" *Railway Age*, Vol. 192, No. 12 (Dec. 1991): 49–50, 52.
———. "New life for a landmark line." *Railway Age*, Vol. 188, No. 3 (Mar. 1987): 64–65.

NEW YORK METROPOLITAN AREA

Carleton, Paul. *The Hudson & Manhattan Railroad Revisited*. Dunnelon, Fla.: D. Carleton Railbooks, 1990.
Cohen, Paul L. "The Making of a Standard: Development of the BMT's Standard Subway Car." *Electric Lines*, Vol. 3, No. 4 (July-Aug. 1990): 20–28.
Cudahy, Brian J. *The Malbone Street Wreck*. New York: Fordham University Press, 1999.
———. *Rails Under the Mighty Hudson*. Brattleboro, Vt.: The Stephen Greene Press, 1975.
———. *Under the Sidewalks of New York: The Story of the Greatest Subway System in the World*. Brattleboro, Vt.: The Stephen Greene Press, 1979.
Cunningham, Joe. *Interborough Fleet*. Belleville, N.J.: Xplorer press, 1997.
Cunningham, Joseph and Leonard DeHart. *A History of the New York City Subway System: Part II, Rapid Transit in Brooklyn*. New York: published by the authors, 1977.
Derrick, Peter. *Tunneling to the Future: The Story of the Great Subway Expansion That Saved New York*. New York: New York University Press, 2001.
Fischler, Stan. *Uptown, Downtown: A Trip Through Time on New York's Subways*. New York: Hawthorn Books, Inc., 1976.
Fitzherbert, Anthony. "'The Public be Pleased': William G. McAdoo and the Hudson Tubes." Electric Railroaders' Assn., Supplement to *Headlights*, Vol. 26, No. 6 (June 1964).
Gibbs, George. "Origins of the Steel Passenger Car," *Railroad History*, No. 138 (Spring 1978): 71–73.
Goldsmith, Francis, J. "Red Mike & the Subways." Electric Railroaders' Assn., *Headlights*, Vol. 50, Nos. 5–6 (May-June 1988): 3–10.
Greller, James C. and Edward B. Watson. *The Brooklyn Elevated*. Hicksville, N.Y.: N.J. International, Inc., 1988.
Greller, James Clifford, *New York City Subway Cars*. Belleville, N.J.: Xplorer press, 1996.
———. *Subway Cars of the BMT*. Belleville, N.J.: Xplorer press, 1996.
Groh, Karl. "Above the Streets of Brooklyn." Electric Railroaders' Assn., *Headlights*, Vol. 37, Nos. 9–11 (Sept.-Nov. 1975): 2–20.
Hood, Clifton. *722 Miles: The Building of the Subways and How They Transformed New York*. New York: Simon & Schuster, 1993.
"Hudson and Manhattan Railroad," *Electric Railroads No. 27*, Electric Railroaders' Assn., Inc. (Aug. 1959).
Kashin, Seymour. "The BMT Dabbles With Light Weight Cars," *Electric Lines*, Part I, Vol. 1, No. 1 (Nov.-Dec. 1987): 20–22; Part II, Vol. 1, No. 5 (July-Aug. 1988): 14–17, 37–38; Part III, Vol. 2, No. 16 (Nov.-Dec. 1989): 4–5, 20–26.
Kramer, Frederick A. *Building the Independent Subway*. New York: Quadrant Press, 1990.

Lavis, Fred. *Building the New Rapid Transit System of New York.* Reprinted from *Engineering News*, 1915. Reproduced by Xplorer Press, Belleville, N.J., 1996.

McAdoo, William Gibbs. *Crowded Years: The Reminiscences of William G. McAdoo.* New York: Houghton Mifflin Company, 1931.

Miller, Luther S. "NYCTA invests for growth." *Railway Age*, Vol. 194, No. 9 (Sept. 1993): 83–84, 86, 88.

Miller, Luther S. "PATH: 25 going on 80." *Railway Age*, Vol. 188, No. 9 (Sept. 1987): 71–72, 107.

"New York's El Lines," *Electric Railroads No. 25*, Electric Railroaders' Assn., Inc. (Dec. 1956).

Quinby, E. J., and Freeman Hubbard. "Third Avenue El," *Railroad Magazine*, Vol. 67, No. 4 (June 1956): 12–29.

Rapid Transit in New York City and in Other Great Cities. New York: Chamber of Commerce of the State of New York, 1905.

Reed, Robert C. *The New York Elevated.* South Brunswick and New York: A. S. Barnes & Company, 1978.

Reich, Sy. "A Robot Named SAM." Electric Railroaders' Assn., *Headlights*, Vol. 36, No. 9 (Sept. 1974): 2–5.

Rinke, Herman. "New York Subways: Fifty Years of Millions," *Electric Railroads No. 23*, Electric Railroaders' Assn., Inc. (Oct. 1954).

Vantuono, William C. "A high-tech ride into the 21st Century." *Railway Age*, Vol. 198, No. 6 (June 1997): 75–76, 78.

———. "Inside New York's new subway cars." *Railway Age*, Vol. 200, No. 8 (Aug, 1999): 73–74, 76.

White, John H., Jr. "Spunky Little Devils: Locomotives of the New York Elevated," *Railroad History No. 162*, Railway & Locomotive Historical Society (1990): 20–79.

Ytuarte, Christopher. "Track to the future." *Railway Age*, Vol. 202, No. 7 (July 2001): 33–37, 50.

PHILADELPHIA METROPOLITAN AREA

Cox, Harold E. *The Road from Upper Darby: The Story of the Market Street Subway-Elevated.* New York: Electric Railroaders' Assn., Inc., 1967.

Fitzherbert, Tony. "50 Years of the Broad Street Subway." Electric Railroaders' Assn., *Headlights*, Vol. 41, Nos. 1–3 (Jan.-Mar. 1979): 2–14.

Vigrass, J. William. *The Lindenwold Line: The First Twenty Years of the Port Authority Transit Corporation.* Palmyra, N.J.: West Jersey Chapter, National Railway Historical Society, 1990.

PITTSBURGH

Lewis, Robert G. "Pittsburgh: More light rail?" *Railway Age*, Vol. 189, No. 12 (Dec. 1988): 37–39.

Middleton, William D. "Pittsburgh awaits 'T'-Day." *Railway Age*, Vol. 188, No. 5 (May 1987): 43–44, 47–48.

PORTLAND, ORE.

Middleton, William D. "Portland light rail: Ready to start building." *Railway Age*, Vol. 182, No. 15 (Aug. 10, 1981): 32–36.

———. "The MAX makes its debut." *Railway Age*, Vol. 187, No. 9 (Sept. 1986): 72–73, 75, 77, 79.

Vantuono, William C. "Tri-Met goes low-floor." *Railway Age*, Vol. 194, No. 7 (July 1993):49–51.

ST. LOUIS

Kramer, Jerome V. "Metro Link: Transportation plus." *Railway Age*, Vol. 194, No. 8 (Aug. 1993): 107–109.

Middleton, William D. "Will St. Louis be next in the light rail parade?" *Railway Age*, Vol. 188, No. 7 (July 1987): 58–60.

Tuzik, Robert E. "What's different about St. Louis light rail." *Railway Age*, Vol. 191, No. 8 (Aug. 1990): 50–52.

SALT LAKE CITY

Miller, Luther S. "Utah Transit's game plan." *Railway Age*, Vol. 202, no. 10 (Oct. 2001): 41, 45, 47.

San Diego

Middleton, William D. "San Diego's trolleys are ready to roll." *Railway Age*, Vol. 182, No. 13 (July 13, 1981): 42–45.

San Francisco Metropolitan Area

"BART Opens Under San Francisco Bay," and other articles. Electric Railroaders' Assn., *Headlights*, Vol. 36, Nos. 10–12 (Oct.-Dec. 1974): 2–27.

Friedlander, Gordon D. "BART's hardware—from bolts to computers," *IEEE Spectrum*, Vol. 9, No. 10 (Oct. 1972): 60–72.

———. "More BART hardware," *IEEE Spectrum*, Vol. 9, No. 11 (Nov. 1972): 41–54.

———. "The grand scheme," *IEEE Spectrum*, Vol. 9, No. 9 (Sept. 1972): 35–43.

Harsch, Albert F. "'Dry runs' by computer," *IEEE Spectrum*, Vol. 9, No. 9 (Sept. 1972): 43–46.

Middleton, William D. "A slow order for BART." *Railway Age*, Vol. 176, No. 9 (May 12, 1975): 18–20, 42.

———. "BART girds for growth." *Railway Age*, Vol. 182, No. 21 (Nov. 9, 1981): 22–25, 43.

———. "BART heads for the airport." *Railway Age*, Vol. 197, No. 8 (Aug. 1996): 52–54.

———. "Let's Take a Last Look Down Market Street." Electric Railroaders' Assn., *Headlights*, Vol. 37, Nos. 7–8 (July-Aug. 1975): 2–7.

———. "San Francisco: Getting ready for the Muni Metro." *Railway Age*, Vol. 176, No. 11 (June 9, 1975): 26–27, 32.

———. "Thousands switch from bus to rail as BART closes the transbay gap." *Railway Age*, Vol. 175, No. 19 (Oct. 14, 1974): 20–22, 26–27.

———. "Trouble-plagued BART brings in a new team of problem-solvers." *Railway Age*, Vol. 177, No. 7 (Apr. 12, 1976): 24–27, 52.

San Jose, Calif.

Middleton, William D. "San Jose goes all the way." *Railway Age*, Vol. 192, No. 8 (Aug. 1991): 63–64, 66, 68A.

San Juan, Puerto Rico

Middleton, William D. "Tren Urbano: San Juan's world-class metro." *Railway Age*, Vol. 201, No. 8 (Aug. 2000): 81–84.

Seattle

Asher, Joseph. "Seattle spells relief r-a-i-l." *Railway Age*, Vol. 200, No. 9 (Sept. 1999): 67–68, 72–73, 75.

Washington, D.C.

Ellsworth, Kenneth G., "Washington: Metrorail heads for pre-Bicentennial opening." *Railway Age*, Vol. 176, No. 7 (Apr. 14, 1975): 30–32, 34–35.

"Metro Here and Now," and other articles. Electric Railroaders' Assn., *Headlights*, Vol. 38, Nos. 4–6 (Apr.-June 1976): 2–23.

Middleton, William D. "Washington's magnificent Metro." *Railway Age*, Vol. 202, No. 9 (Sept. 2001): 67–68, 70, 72, 74.

"Moving People: Day 1 on the Washington Metro." *Railway Age*, Vol. 177, No. 7 (Apr. 12, 1976): 20–23.

Canada

Calgary

Bain, D. M. *Calgary Transit Then & Now*. Calgary: Kishorn Publications, 1994.

EDMONTON

Kizzia, Tom. "Edmonton: Light rail, all the way." *Railway Age*, Vol. 177, No. 22 (Dec. 13, 1976): 24–25, 28.

Miklos, Frank S. "Edmonton: A Case for Light Rail." Electric Railroaders' Assn., *Headlights*, Vol. 40, Nos. 9–12 (Oct.-Dec. 1978): 2–7.

Thompson, John D. "Edmonton: Building for the Future." Electric Railroaders' Assn., *Headlights*, Vol. 39, Nos. 2–3 (Feb.-Mar. 1977): 8–12.

MONTREAL

Ichniowski, Tom. "Montreal Metro: Improving the quality of life." *Railway Age*, Vol. 177, No. 22 (Dec. 13, 1976): 22–23.

"Montreal Metro Opens." Electric Railroaders' Assn., *Headlights*, Vol. 29, No. 1 (Jan. 1967): 2–13.

Montréal Metro, The. Montreal: Communauté urbaine de Montréal, 1983.

Swindler, John C. "Montreal: Rapid Transit for the Olympics." Electric Railroaders' Assn., *Headlights*, Vol. 39, Nos. 2–3 (Feb.-Mar. 1977): 2–7.

OTTAWA

Middleton, William D. "What's happened to the diesel rail car revival?" *Railway Age*, Vol. 201, No. 7 (July 2000): 54–55, 56.

TORONTO

Bromley, John F. and Jack May. *Fifty Years of Progressive Transit: A History of the Toronto Transit Commission*. New York: Electric Railroaders' Assn., Inc., 1973.

Pursley, Louis H. *The Toronto Trolley Car Story, 1921–1961*. Interurbans Special 29, Los Angeles, 1961.

"Toronto: Bloor-Danforth Subway Opens." Electric Railroaders' Assn., *Headlights*, Vol. 28, No. 4 (Apr. 1966): 2–8.

VANCOUVER

Middleton, William D. "ICTS: A tale of three cities." *Railway Age*, Vol. 185, No. 10 (Oct. 1984): 64–65, 67–69.

Mexico

GUADALAJARA, MEXICO CITY, AND MONTERREY

Bottoms, Glen D. and Luis Léon Torrealba, "Metro de la Ciudad de México." Electric Railroaders' Assn., *Headlights*, Vol. 36, No. 7 (July 1974): 8–10.

Middleton, William D. "Moving Mexico City's millions: The rail solution." *Railway Age*, Vol. 177, No. 19 (Oct. 11, 1976): 36–37.

———. "Moving Mexico's millions, by rail." *Railway Age*, Vol. 195, No. 12 (Dec. 1994): 58–61.

Miller, Luther S. "Mexico in transit." *Railway Age*, Vol. 201, No. 10 (Oct. 2000): 37–38.

INDEX

William D. Middleton, a transportation historian and journalist, is the author of eighteen books, including *The Time of the Trolley*, *The Interurban Era*, and *When the Steam Railroads Electrified*, which together with *Metropolitan Railways* form a comprehensive illustrated history of electric railway transportation in North America. Middleton's professional career included 29 years in the U.S. Navy's Civil Engineer Corps, and another 14 years as chief facilities officer for the University of Virginia.